THE PURPOSE
OF PHYSICAL
REALITY

THE PURPOSE OF PHYSICAL REALITY

John S. Hatcher

Bahá'í
PUBLISHING
Wilmette, Illinois 60091

Bahá'í Publishing, Wilmette, Illinois 60091-2844

Copyright © 1987, 2005 by John S. Hatcher. All rights reserved
New edition published 2005
Printed in the United States of America on acid-free paper ∞
07 06 05   3 2 1

Library of Congress Cataloging-in-Publication Data

Hatcher, John, Dr.
   The purpose of physical reality / John S. Hatcher.— New ed.
      p. cm.
   ISBN 1-931847-23-1
      1. Bahai Faith—Doctrines. 2. Theodicy. 3. Spirituality. 4. Cosmology.
   I. Title.

BP370.H38 2005
297.9'32—dc22

                                                           2005048279

Cover design by Robert A. Reddy
Book design by Suni Hannan

In Loving Memory
of
Helen Hardman Hatcher
and
Albert Spottswood Hatcher

CONTENTS

ACKNOWLEDGMENTS

I wish to express my profound appreciation first of all to the Association for Bahá'í Studies for publishing this work in its initial form as *The Metaphorical Nature of Physical Reality* in 1977. I also thank the Bahá'í Publishing Trust for encouraging me to fashion that monograph into *The Purpose of Physical Reality: The Kingdom of Names*, which was published in 1987. Finally, I want to thank Lee Minnerly, general manager of the U.S. Bahá'í Publishing Trust, and Terry Cassiday, senior editor and director of acquisitions, for encouraging me to rewrite this work in its present form.

Preface:
Suddenly, Thirty Years Later . . .

When I first became interested in the Bahá'í Faith, my initial attraction was to the principle that belief results not from blind acceptance of dogma but from independent investigation of truth. Bahá'u'lláh, the Prophet and Founder of the Bahá'í Faith, repeatedly asserts that the study of religion should not be the exclusive province of academics or theologians. He states that all of us are required to immerse ourselves in the ocean of holy scripture that we "may unravel its secrets, and discover all the pearls of wisdom that lie hid in its depths" (Kitáb-i-Aqdas, ¶182).

As an educator, I sensed in this exhortation an underlying wisdom about authentic learning—that the process of studying the holy texts requires the same rigor and systematic methodology with which I had approached my study of all other literature. Related to this realization was my increasing appreciation as a professor that education is not merely the acquisition of information. Authentic education is a process of helping others acquire tools for individual study.

In a similar vein, during my forty-three years of university teaching, I have come to appreciate how important it is to convey to my students the distinction between this idea of true learning and the commonly held notion that education is little more than the capacity to parrot information that someone else has discovered. The retention of the intellectual history of human thought has value, certainly, but it is the story of how someone else learned—it is not a substitute for our own ventures into the realm of creative thought, however much these stories can inspire us to attempt the same sort of quest.

In 1973, having been a Bahá'í for thirteen years and a college professor for ten, I sensed one evening as I perused some of the words revealed by Bahá'u'lláh that a very personal challenge lay at the heart of His exhortation that all become independent seekers after truth. I felt I was being called as an aspiring scholar and teacher to employ in my study of the Bahá'í Faith and its texts the same critical principles and methodological tools I had found so valuable in learning to study and explicate Chaucer, Shakespeare, Milton, and Eliot. I further realized that without this same quality of study, my understanding of the Bahá'í texts would, for me, feel limited. Even though I might be able to intuit some spiritual wisdom and insights as I became inspired by various passages in the vast corpus of Bahá'í texts—much as I had during childhood when I was leafing through the Bible as a believing Christian—I would fail to apprehend the unifying themes and subtle layers of meaning that dwell beneath the surface of scripture. To fully grasp their implications, I would need to approach these texts as systematically and seriously as I had my other literary scholarship.

The idea was hardly profound, and yet it had taken ten years for it to penetrate my consciousness, for me to realize that a casual, periodic, and unsystematic approach to literature, which was at the very heart of my beliefs about reality, was no longer sufficient for me. My sincere belief that there is an underlying logic in the sometimes veiled, concealed, metaphorical, and symbolic language of the Prophets further encouraged and excited me to pursue a study of scripture as literature.

On that same evening as I thumbed through the pages of Bahá'u'lláh's Book of Certitude, something else occurred to me—something so obvious that I was stunned I had never considered the proposition so clearly before: If what I professed to believe was that this text and these words were from a divine intermediary, a Manifestation of God (Bahá'u'lláh), I could dare pose whatever question I desired, and, with sufficient study and effort, I could be assured that the answer would be there if I had the sufficient patience, perseverance, and adequate wit to recognize the answer when it appeared before me. Indeed, I realized that this was precisely the process these same verses were exhorting me to do!

Tantalized by these realizations, I began that same night a project that so far has lasted over thirty years, a quest to discover an answer to what would be for me the most fascinating and enigmatic question I could conceive: If God is omnipotent and could have created us in whatever way He desired, why did He determine that it would be a good idea for essentially spiritual beings (human souls) to begin an eternal existence in an associative relationship with a physical body that operates in a physical reality?

After all, according to the Bahá'í statement of human purpose—and according to human purpose as described by most revealed religions—our goal is to become spiritual. Why, then, did this omnipotent Being not create us already the way He wanted us? Or even more to the point, if He wants us to take part in this process of becoming spiritual, why did He fashion us in such a way that we begin in an environment more suitable for that purpose instead of a reality that seems virtually calculated to deter or distract us from our inherent purpose?

The first result of that quest was an essay entitled "The Metaphorical Nature of Physical Reality," which I delivered in 1977 at the annual meeting of the only Bahá'í academic society that existed at the time, the Canadian Association for the Studies of the Bahá'í Faith. The next year the editorial board of that body published the paper as a monograph—volume 3 of *Bahá'í Studies*, published in November 1977.

The article enjoyed some success in Bahá'í circles and was republished in the summer of 1978 in an issue of *World Order* magazine under the same title. A condensed version of the article entitled "Life as Metaphor" was also published in 1983 in *The Bahá'í World*, volume 18.

Over the next several years, I continued writing about other equally subtle questions related to this question of theodicy (God's justice). The fact is, I took great delight in thinking myself into corners, I suppose because I knew that with diligence and help from the vast ocean of Bahá'u'lláh's writings, I could think my way out again. I studied and wrote about such subjects as the Bahá'í concept of justice and the Bahá'í concept of the afterlife. And in 1986, at the request of the Bahá'í Publishing Trust of the United States, I wrote *The Purpose of Physical Reality: The Kingdom of Names*, which was published in 1987.

This book went through three printings and was then reprinted with a few minor changes in 1996. In the meantime, in 1994, George Ronald Publishers of Oxford, England, had brought out my sequel to this book entitled *The Arc of Ascent: The Purpose of Physical Reality II* (which I sometimes refer to as "Son of Physical Reality"). Where the first book had focused on the problem of God's purpose and justice in relation to the individual attempt at spiritual development, this second book revealed that any attempt at individual spiritual ascent necessarily involves us in social exercises and relationships because we are inherently social beings.

In spring of 2005 Bahá'í Publishing brought out *Close Connections: The Bridge between Spiritual and Physical Reality*, the third book in my attempt to deal with the theme of the Bahá'í paradigm of God's justice. This work compares how God runs the physical universe with how our souls run our physical bodies and administer our individual physical experiences.

Now, having found some satisfying answers to the questions I began to ponder over thirty years ago, I once again reassess this initial foray into the plan of God to discover as best I can His reasoning for creating physical reality so that I myself might become a creator of sorts—as writer, teacher, as a Bahá'í. For however often I reflect on the question that was bequeathed to me that night, I always find myself revising, revisiting, and re-envisioning my thoughts about this strange classroom we share while we attempt to discover the rightful place of things physical in our lives and our rightful place in the eternal plan of God as He has revealed that plan through the successive Manifestations He has sent to educate us down through the ages—those concealed souls Who have sacrificed themselves that we might become increasingly human and humane.

—John S. Hatcher, 2005

THEODICY AND YOU:
THE SEARCH FOR METAPHYSICAL
JUSTICE IN A PHYSICAL WORLD

The essence of all that We have revealed for thee is Justice, is for man to free himself from idle fancy and imitation, discern with the eye of oneness His glorious handiwork, and look into all things with a searching eye.

—Bahá'u'lláh

In contrast to most institutionalized religions, the Bahá'í Faith teaches that theology is logical and that we should examine our religious beliefs with the same rational faculties and rigorous standards with which we probe the phenomenal world. From such a view questioning is not deemed heretical but as an essential tool for acquiring belief.

One indication of the respect the Bahá'í Faith holds for such independent investigation of truth as an aid to understanding spiritual reality is the fact that the major works of Bahá'u'lláh, the Prophet and Founder of the Bahá'í Faith, are derived from His responses to questions, whether from believers or nonbelievers. For example, the Kitáb-i-Íqán (Book of Certitude), the central repository of Bahá'í doctrine, is Bahá'u'lláh's response to "questions addressed to Bahá'-u'lláh by the as yet unconverted maternal uncle of the Báb," Prophet and Founder of the Bábí religion and Herald of Bahá'u'lláh.[1] Like-wise, one of the greatest compendiums of succinct statements of Bahá'í beliefs about foundational theological and philosophical matters is *Some Answered Questions*, which contains the responses of 'Abdu'l-Bahá—Bahá'u'lláh's eldest son and successor—to many questions posed to him by Laura Clifford Barney, an early Ameri-can Bahá'í. Similarly, a great deal of the valuable guidance available to individuals and to Bahá'í communities and administrative bod-ies are answers to questions sent to Shoghi Effendi Rabbání, the designated Guardian of the Bahá'í Faith. The major compilations of his letters are his studied responses to the volumes of mail he received daily from the worldwide Bahá'í community. Likewise, the supreme governing and legislative body of the Bahá'í Faith, the Universal House of Justice, regularly publishes collections of its answers to questions raised by individuals and Bahá'í administra-tive institutions.

In short, one major method by which Bahá'ís are urged to attain conviction or "enter the City of Certitude" is to consider thought-fully the logical basis for accepting the teachings of the Bahá'í Faith. For only through study and reflection—a process which necessar-ily results in thoughtful questions—can religious belief or any other sort of knowledge become a reliable basis for understanding reality and our relation to it. Therefore, where some religions have estab-lished a body of learned clerics or scholars who interpret religious scripture and teachings for the laity, Bahá'u'lláh abolished the clergy and commanded that each individual investigate truth indepen-dently: "Immerse yourselves in the ocean of My words, that ye may unravel its secrets, and discover all the pearls of wisdom that lie hid in its depths."[2]

Yet in spite of all this encouragement that Bahá'ís consider the rational basis for belief, one essential question rarely gets asked, not because it is forbidden, not because the answer is unavailable in the Bahá'í writings, but probably because most people do not think to ask it. The question concerns physical reality—why it exists and how it works in a universe created, so Bahá'í scriptures affirm, by a loving and caring Deity whose sole objective as Creator is to devise a means by which human beings can come to know and worship Him and benefit therefrom.

This critical question is sometimes dismissed with a self-evident but inwardly unsatisfying response: Since God fashioned physical reality and since it is His intention that we develop spiritually, then physical reality must be a benevolent creation that somehow facilitates spiritual development. Another frequent but no less inadequate response to the purpose of physical reality is that our physical experience is a period of testing wherein we acquire spiritual attributes by means of dealing with difficulties and suffering and, ultimately, with the deterioration of our own physical bodies.

These answers may be true. On some level they may be initially comforting, but they do not penetrate to the heart where the question is conceived in the first place. They do not really satisfy us by responding to the paradox of why, if we are essentially spiritual beings, we are ordained to take our beginning in a physical environment that most of the time seems antithetical to all we proclaim the Creator to be and to all we proclaim the Creator would have us become.

To some, the Bahá'í writings themselves may appear enigmatic and even contradictory concerning what should be our attitude about physical reality. For example, in one passage Bahá'u'lláh seems to admonish us to become detached from physical things: "Abandon not the everlasting beauty for a beauty that must die, and set not your affections on this mortal world of dust." But in another passage He commands us to become thoroughly involved in the physical world, even to the point of suggesting that mundane physical actions are the most important gauge of spiritual achievement: "The best of men are they that earn a livelihood by their calling and spend upon themselves and upon their kindred for the love of God, the Lord of all worlds."[3]

Clearly these statements regarding physical reality are not necessarily contradictory. The first passage cautions us not to allow attachment to physical reality to distract us from our primary goal in life—to become ever more refined as human beings. Furthermore, Bahá'u'lláh has provided humankind with those laws and institutions essential to guiding us in establishing the appropriate relationship with and utilization of physical reality in the various aspects of our daily life. Therefore, the question of why there is a physical reality might seem somewhat unnecessary or superfluous. Indeed, it could be that the very comfort that these guidelines and boundaries offer us helps explain why the question about the purpose of physical reality rarely gets asked.

But the question does not go away. Whether articulated or not, the question resides within us, either as some constant background noise, like static on a radio, or as some discomfiting pain that we can, for the most part, largely ignore most of the time. But whether or not we have become acclimatized or accustomed to this lingering question, we will confront it face to face if we live long enough. The gradual decline of our physical bodies will ensure that we do. And if we have neglected to consider the question, let alone arrive at some relatively satisfying answers, we might find ourselves a bit devastated.

Our certitude and conviction may be shaken by the repeated images of blatant injustice rampant in a supposedly just creation. Our faith may falter in the maelstrom of our own personal encounters with events that often seem to deny the existence of any God, let alone a beneficent Creator. Or else we may find ourselves gradually ever more fragmented as we attempt to segregate our lives by trying to choose between the worthy goal of devoting ourselves to professional achievement and the more explicitly spiritual objectives of assisting a suffering humanity.

The end result of this internal dichotomy may well be that we come to accept a vision of ourselves as precariously tottering between two worlds, the end result being that we approach physical things with a persistent and haunting sense of guilt or anxiety. In the Bahá'í texts there is no such puritanical approach to physical experience: We are encouraged to enjoy the material bounties of this life so long as these interests do not deter us from our ultimate objective of spiritual development: "Should a man wish to adorn himself with the ornaments of the earth, to wear its apparels, or partake of the benefits it can bestow, no harm can befall him, if he alloweth nothing whatever to intervene between him and God. . . ."[4]

The problem with this advice is trying to determine at what point material involvement begins to "intervene" between ourselves and our efforts to be spiritual beings. How do we live simultaneously in two disparate realities? Furthermore, this dilemma is compounded by our daily experience—we sense within us two natures, one spiritual, rational, and transcendent, the other appetitive, acquisitive, and mundane. What is worse, more often than not the fulfillment of one aspect of our nature seems to deny fulfillment of the other.

Certainly the solution to the conflict we encounter as spiritual beings associating with a physical environment is beyond our complete comprehension. Nevertheless, this fundamental fragmentation of our daily existence cannot long remain unresolved without eroding to some degree our personal conviction and our effort to live an integrated life. Indeed, were we to discover even a portion of the answer to this paradox, we could be greatly strengthened in our resolve to take full advantage of the unique opportunities afforded by the brief physical experience that constitutes earthly life. For if God is a wise and loving educator and could have created whatever environment for us that He wished, there must have been a very special reason He chose to have us begin an eternal spiritual journey in an environment so bewildering to our lofty purposes, especially our desire to maintain belief in a just and loving God.

The quest for such an answer or answers must begin by dividing this overwhelmingly huge question into manageable parts. For example, we can benefit from examining some of the classic attempts to respond to the question of "theodicy"—attempting to discover Divine Justice in an ostensibly unjust creation. Second, we can compare the classical and contemporary responses to the perspective offered in the authoritative Bahá'í texts since, according to Bahá'í belief, these teachings are designed to respond to all philosophical and theological questions relevant to the contemporary human condition.

After establishing the fundamental problems that relate to the question of physical reality, we can then delineate a more exacting and encompassing vision of the Bahá'í model of physical creation as a sane and just environment for our instruction. In particular, we can explore the essentially metaphorical nature of physical reality and our dramatic participation in it.

The conclusion of our study will be the most exciting and the most important part of all—after we attempt to figure out how physical life can teach us spiritual lessons, we will examine the relationship between how we perform here in the physical realm and what we will experience in the life hereafter once our soul dissociates from the physical or metaphorical self that is our body.

2

JUSTIFYING GOD: SOME CLASSIC APPROACHES TO THE PROBLEM OF THEODICY

Theodicy is a theological problem that arises for any philosophical or religious view that affirms the following three propositions: (1) God is almighty, (2) God is perfectly good, and (3) evil exists. If evil exists, it seems either that God wants to obliterate evil and is not able to—and thus his almightiness is denied—or that God is able to obliterate evil but does not want to—and thus his goodness is denied.

—Encyclopaedia Britannica

If God is good, how can there be evil in His creation? If we do not believe in God, we need not trouble ourselves by searching for justice in physical reality. We may try to analyze the physical laws of the universe, to impose order in our society, or to be fair in our relationships with others if we think it expedient to do so. But if we do not believe in a Divine Creator, we need not trouble ourselves looking for or expecting justice in creation as a whole.

Natural laws of cause and effect can adequately describe the cosmos and our relationship to it, and we can still manage to get along with our neighbors. Besides, such a view need not be dreary or fatalistic, but it must, by definition, accept the "purpose" of physical reality as solely that meaning which we invent or attribute to a reality that has no inherent purposes or values of its own.

But if we wish to ascribe to physical reality or to discern in creation and our participation in it a divine foundation or a morally based rationale, we must assume that there is purpose latent within the system, however veiled or concealed it might be. Indeed, we must presume that a divinely created reality is endowed with justice permeating everything that happens in physical reality, whether events be the most trivial aspects of our daily lives or the most encompassing laws that govern the structure and organization of the universe as a whole.

It is from those thinkers and writers who have affirmed a belief in a divine Creator that have derived the most powerful attempts to discover and describe the nature of justice in a world created by God. Consequently, if we ourselves wish to consider the possibility that creation is divine in origin, we would do well to review some of the milestones in the attempts to vindicate God's creation by explaining the appearance of evil and dysfunction within His creation.

PLATO'S *THE REPUBLIC* (CA. 378 B.C.)

Though one of the earliest recorded attempts to discover justice in the physical world, Plato's dialogue *The Republic* has endured as one of the most influential and penetrating discussions of the subject. Basing his artful dialogue on the ideas of his teacher Socrates, Plato avoids much direct discussion of theology per se, though the character of Socrates in the dialogues does attribute the infusion of spiritual qualities into physical creation as the emanation of a single divine source, the Good. It is worth noting in this regard that, according to 'Abdu'l-Bahá, one source of Socrates' monotheistic beliefs—for which Socrates was later executed—was his association with Jewish scholars:

> He visited the Holy Land and studied with the prophets of Israel, acquiring principles of their philosophical teaching and a knowledge of their advanced arts and sciences. After his return to Greece he founded the system known as the unity of God.[1]

In another passage 'Abdu'l-Bahá states that the basic evidence of the Judaic influence is found in Socrates' concept of the unity of God and in his teaching about the immortality of the soul:

> It is recorded in eastern histories that Socrates journeyed to Palestine and Syria and there, from men learned in the things of God, acquired certain spiritual truths; that when he returned to Greece, he promulgated two beliefs: one, the unity of God, and the other, the immortality of the soul after its separation from the body. . . .[2]

Bahá'u'lláh also praises the thinking and influence of Socrates, particularly his theory of "forms"—sometimes called the theory of "ideas"—the assertion that physical reality is but a reflection or expression of a metaphysical or spiritual reality:

> He it is who perceived a unique, a tempered, and a pervasion
> nature in things, bearing the closest likeness to the human spirit,
> and he discovered this nature to be distinct from the substance
> of things in their refined form. He hath a special pronounce-
> ment on this weighty theme.[3]

While Bahá'u'lláh may have been alluding to any number of
Plato's dialogues that discuss the theory of ideas, it is likely that He
was referring to *The Republic*, the avowed objective of which is to
define justice. In the course of Socrates' discussion of the nature of
justice in the individual, the discussion rapidly becomes an explicit
analysis of how we can employ physical experience to learn spiritual lessons.

The work begins with participants in a discussion about the merits of some traditional views of justice. The character Socrates then
suggests that the best method for understanding justice in an individual might be first to determine how justice might work in "larger
proportions," in a just society or state.[4] Thus it is that the participants in the dialogue begin devising a just government, a republic.

The resulting discussion provides a fruitful series of analogies—
the individual compared to a state and, by implication, the state
compared to physical reality itself. In effect, the search for justice
goes far beyond any explicit political doctrine and tackles the essential issue of how physical reality can be perceived as having spiritual significance.

After lengthy debate and consideration of what creates justice in
a political structure, the participants in the dialogue conclude that
the guiding principle of a just state is the principle of propriety—
each thing doing that for which it is especially well suited or created. Having determined the various components of this structure
and what function each person should perform in the operation of

the community, the participants conclude that everyone in this republic should work in harmony for the mutual benefit of the whole.

The rulers in the republic should naturally be the wisest and most magnanimous of the citizenry, altruistic "philosopher-kings" who will make the major governmental decisions. The military, the most physically able, should function to protect the state. The poets should devise allegorized myths and parables to explain abstract principles of virtue to the unlearned masses. The craftsmen and artisans should employ their tools to fashion buildings, furniture, and so on. The farmers should produce and supply the food, and the shopkeepers should distribute the goods.

The careful detail with which Plato's Socrates builds this state, this republic, or aristocracy (literally a rule by the "best"), has led many to conclude that *The Republic* is primarily a political treatise. Plato has even been vehemently censured by some critics for the rigidity and, as they perceive it, the totalitarian implications of his political exercise.* These interpretations mistakenly take the work at face value and totally miss its allegorical intent, which is to define justice in the individual.

As with the state, for example, the overriding principle of justice in the individual is the harmony produced when one abides by the rule of propriety, each constituent faculty of the individual doing that for which it is best suited, with the whole organism striving harmoniously toward a unified objective. By analogy, the rational mind, like the rulers or guardians of the state, makes major decisions about personal goals and the proper course of action for fulfilling those aspirations. The body, like the military in the state, defends the physical edifice, and so on:

---

* The process of ascent from physical attraction to an appreciation of spiritual attributes Plato sets forth explicitly in the dialogue *Symposium*.

Only when he has linked these parts together in well-tempered harmony and has made himself one man instead of many, will he be ready to go about whatever he may have to do, whether it be making money and satisfying bodily wants, or business transactions, or the affairs of state. . . . Any action which tends to break down this habit will be for him unjust. . . .[5]

In the context of this analogy, injustice is defined by a lack of due respect of each part for the others or the violation of the law of propriety so that there is disharmony among our human faculties. Such disharmony might occur, for example, if we allow lesser powers, such as our passions, to usurp the governing authority of the mind. Likewise, such discord and "injustice" occurs when we allow ourselves to become fragmented in such a way that we are in a condition of internal warfare or turmoil. Injustice is thus a violation of internal propriety and harmony.

For Plato the logical result of maintaining harmony and propriety is progressive enlightenment. Even as the political state cannot remain static, neither can the individual. Likewise, what keeps the state in forward motion is the guidance of the whole toward the objectives that the guardians (or philosopher-kings) have perceived as a result of their enlightenment. In the individual the mind must gain insight and then discover the best means of translating insight into beneficial action.

To demonstrate how human spiritual progress takes place, Socrates, in Book VII of *The Republic*, uses an analogy that explains his theory of "forms" in his famous allegory of the cave. In this analogy Socrates portrays men bound to chairs in a cave and facing a wall. Behind and above them is the mouth of the cave, in front of which people pass by. The analogy gets more complicated than that, but let us simplify the process a bit. A fire outside the cave causes the passing figures to cast shadows on the wall of the cave so that the bound prisoners, who cannot turn to see the source of the shadows, naturally conclude that what they see is reality.

Among the prisoners in the cave is one who is dissatisfied with his constraints, who so yearns for knowledge and enlightenment that he breaks free from his bonds and turns to see the source of the images. Through great effort he scales the rough walls of the cave and discerns the source of the shadows, the figures themselves. Then he sees that it is the fire behind them that casts the shadows on the walls.

Not satisfied that he has discovered the ultimate expression of reality, he ventures forth from the cave into the sunlight, but the brightness of the sun forces him to look at the ground and shade his eyes. There he notices the shadows of trees and other objects, which he now perceives to be reality. But as his eyes become accustomed to the light, he is able to look up and see the objects themselves and realize that they are a higher expression of reality than the mere shadows they cast upon the ground.

Ultimately this determined one lifts his eyes to the heavens and beholds, above and beyond all objects, the sun itself, the source of all reality:

> He would need, then, to grow accustomed before he could see things in that upper world. At first it would be easiest to make out shadows, and then the images of men and things reflected in water, and later on the things themselves. After that, it would be easier to watch the heavenly bodies and the sky itself by night, looking at the light of the moon and stars rather than the Sun and the Sun's light in the day-time. . . .
>
> Last of all, he would be able to look at the Sun and contemplate its nature, not as it appears when reflected in water or any alien medium, but as it is in itself in its own domain.[6]

Having attained this immensely increased level of perception about the relationship between reality and the sun (or the "Good") as the source of reality, this specially endowed individual—one whom Socrates calls the "philosopher-king"—must now accomplish another difficult part of his task. Having become enlightened—and "delighted" with his newfound knowledge—this noble soul realizes that if he himself is to be virtuous, he must share what he has learned. He determines that he must return to the cave to assist those still imprisoned in the darkness of illusion and shadow.

When he descends into the cave, his eyes have trouble becoming accustomed to the darkness with this sudden transition from bright sunlight into a world of darkness and shadow. To the prisoners in the cave the messenger of truth, the philosopher-king, seems clumsy and awkward to them, hardly a wise teacher returned to guide the others:

> Coming suddenly out of the sunlight, his eyes would be filled with darkness. He might be required once more to deliver his opinion on those shadows, in competition with the prisoners who had never been released, while his eyesight was still dim and unsteady; and it might take some time to become used to the darkness. They would laugh at him and say that he had gone up only to come back with his sight ruined; it was worth no one's while even to attempt the ascent. If they could lay hands on the man who was trying to set them free and lead them up, they would kill him.[7]

The allusion to the killing of the philosopher-king poignantly foreshadows Socrates' own execution for his teachings as well as the suffering and execution of the Prophets of God. But Plato's primary objective here is not to bemoan the plight of those who bring an enhanced vision of reality. Since the divisions of the state are analogous to the division among human faculties, this analogy or allegory represents a process that takes place within the individual. As we have noted, the philosopher-king most probably represents the combined mental and spiritual capacities of the individual, or possibly the soul itself from which these powers emanate. The journey of the prisoner from shadow, to object, to light, to categories of objects, to sunlight could depict allegorically the ascent of the soul by means of the rational mind as one comprehends abstractions as they are expressed in particular objects or symbols—the "names" of the physical world—and through a process of persistent investigation becomes increasingly aware of the reality behind the world of appearances.

Similarly, just as those who are still imprisoned reject the enlightened guidance of the returning philosopher-king, so it is that our appetitive nature—attached as it is to the shadowy illusions of reality—resists the dictates of the rational mind or the intuitions of the spirit. Governed by the "lower" self, we are content to accept these illusory images as a complete representation of reality and reject striving to discover the reality that these images only vaguely represent. Indeed, it is only with great willpower and persistence that the "higher" spiritual or intellectual self can persuade our lower self to relinquish our attachment to earthly concerns—the passion for sensual delight and the fleeting satisfaction derived from fame or possessions.

While the cave analogy certainly has various applications, for Plato the principal value of the parable is in dramatizing how physical creation reflects the abstract "forms" or "ideas" of the spiritual plane of existence. In this sense Plato has designated the "just" or proper function of physical reality to be its ability to give metaphoric or symbolic form to metaphysical concepts—what are called in the Bahá'í writings "divine attributes," "spiritual qualities," or the "names" of God. Plato connects this process of striving to dis-

cover the reality represented by the particular expressions of reality
to his monotheistic belief when he describes how all these attributes
or "forms" are but emanations of one primary source, "the Good."

For example, Socrates compares the Good to the sun, since the
Good illuminates or makes understandable all other realities. In his
introductory notes to chapter 23 of Book VI, translator and noted
scholar Francis Macdonald Cornford clarifies what Plato's notion
of the Good represents:

> In Greek "the Good" is normally synonymous with "Goodness
> itself." This is the supreme Form or Essence manifested not only
> in the special kinds of moral goodness, Justice, Courage, etc.,
> but throughout all Nature (for every living creature has its own
> "good") and especially in the beautiful and harmonious order of
> the heavenly bodies. . . . The knowledge of the Good, on which
> well-being depends, is now to include an understanding of the
> moral and physical order of the whole universe. As the object of
> a purpose attributed to a divine Reason operating in the world,
> this supreme Good makes the world intelligible, as a work of
> human craftsmanship becomes intelligible when we see the pur-
> pose it is designed to serve.[8]

Socrates continues in the cave analogy to describe the process by
which proximity to, or a vision of, the Good empowers and inspires the "guardian" or philosopher-king to return to the cave and
lead the other prisoners out of bondage. In terms of the individual,
the return to the world of images and "bondage" might allude to
the need to struggle for transformation of our character. If we are
to benefit from the guidance we can derive from mental and spiritual reflection about what is truly important or "real" in our lives,
we have to employ our will to extricate our rational and spiritual

faculties from our attachment to the illusory world of sensual delights and distractions—for example, the ease of the "good life."

According to Plato in this imaginative dramatization of Socratic thought, the justification of temporal reality resides in the very fabric of creation itself. The physical world is a divinely ordained teaching device through which man can ascend from the depths of blindness to the heights of enlightenment by learning to discern the spiritual values and attributes reflected in the phenomenal world. From this perspective, there is no need to reject or disdain physical reality, so long as we utilize this experience to discern the spiritual attributes it manifests.

But implicit in this dramatic analogy is the value of a gradual relinquishing of the need for physical analogs as one learns spiritual lessons. So-called Platonic love, for example, is not so much a disregard for physical love as it is a process by which one ascends from physical attraction and sexual expression of love to a recognition and appreciation of the spiritual attributes made apparent first in the physical beauty of the beloved and then in the divine attributes and virtues of the beloved.

This transformation of love from one level to another occurs when one realizes that love is not a single state of being—the flick of a switch—but an organic process that necessarily progresses from stage to stage, or else it diminishes and becomes extinguished. In the dialogue titled *The Symposium* Socrates portrays this organic growth of love as a "ladder" where each rung represents an ever more expansive expression of love. One proceeds from the love of self, to the physical desire of another, to the love of the spiritual attributes in the other, to the appreciation of the attributes in all people, to the love of creation as a whole.

From the Platonic point of view, evil or injustice in the phenomenal world, at least injustice as it is perpetrated by human beings, results from a lack of knowledge about the search for the "Good." In the dialogue titled *The Gorgias* Socrates argues that no one does evil in full knowledge because to do evil is to perpetrate injustice, and to perpetrate injustice is ultimately to injure our own soul, not the soul of those whom we attempt to harm. He goes on to argue that no one would willingly and wittingly inflict misery on himself; therefore, he argues, the solution to injustice is to teach those who would do evil that the real victim of their iniquity is themselves.

In other dialogues, Socrates repeatedly proffers the argument that learning is only valuable if it provides instruction about virtue, as opposed to that learning which merely supplies the student with power. He argues that learning which bestows power without also bestowing knowledge about the proper use of that power is tantamount to providing a villain with a weapon.

Plato's examination of justice as the process of learning the truth about reality and our relationship to reality as individuals has had a remarkable impact on the history of Western thought. And yet, for all its merit and influence, Plato's study of theodicy does not deal effectively with such matters as the relationship between the Creator and creation nor with the critical issue of how seemingly arbitrary accidents and disasters of physical life can exist in a world that is a reflection of divine justice.

THE BOOK OF JOB (CA. 500–300 B.C.)

Composed sometime between 500 and 300 B.C., the Book of Job examines justice in the physical world from the point of view of an explicitly monotheistic belief. To a certain extent the work takes up where Plato leaves off. Here God is not simply the sum total of virtue—Plato's "Good." God is the Creator, a cognitive Being. He is aware of each individual life and intimately concerned for His creation.

If we put aside the numerous disputes over composition and textual integrity, we can see in this masterpiece of world literature some issues of justice not raised in the dialogues of Plato. For example, Job examines the critical dilemma of how we can maintain and sustain belief in a just God when we are daily exposed to the appearance in the physical world of seemingly arbitrary acts of cruelty, corruption, and blatant injustice.

A didactic poem of dialogue "imbedded in a prose tale," the Book of Job recounts the story of a man who has long remained the emblem of human patience and humility in the face of untold suffering and apparent injustice.[9] The story begins with an account of Job as a prosperous and respected chieftain. But Satan contends that Job's exemplary fidelity is the result of Job's prosperity in life, not real certitude or conviction. God responds to this cynicism by giving Satan permission to test Job, wagering with Satan that Job will demonstrate the depth of his belief.

After a series of disasters that deprive Job of his possessions and most of his family, he is grief stricken, but he still praises God. Not satisfied, Satan proposes that Job suffer injury to his person, and God, still confident, gives Satan permission to inflict on Job a loathsome disease.

Job's wife can take no more. She tempts her husband to despair and to curse God. Three friends, who have ostensibly come to comfort Job, state that his misfortune is a punishment from some wrongdoing, and they accuse him of some concealed act of irreligion or iniquity. Convinced of his own innocence, Job rejects their accusations. But as his anguish mounts, Job at last pleads with God to speak to him directly that he might understand the reason for this plight.

Eventually God does speak to Job as a voice from a whirlwind. In lengthy, powerful speeches, God catalogs examples of His creative authority and omnipotence. He then asks rhetorically if Job has such power—the capacity to control the forces of the universe or the wisdom to understand the complex laws governing the stars, the animals, or the weather. Job humbly confesses that he has no such ability.

After a further vision of God's might, Job understands God's infinitely lofty station, and he enthusiastically attests to God's power and majesty. His faith has been restored. In an epilogue, God condemns the three friends, gives Job twice what he had before, returns his family, and gives him twice the normal life span.

In the New Testament, James praises Job as an example of steadfastness, as do Muḥammad in the Qur'án and 'Abdu'l-Bahá in *Paris Talks:* "Job proved the fidelity of his love for God by being faithful through his great adversity, as well as during the prosperity of his life."[10] But at the crux of the story, for our purposes, are Job's response to injustice and the story's ending.

Of course, the portrait of God literally debating with Satan is generally accepted as mythological tradition in the same way that we accept the story of Adam and Eve as symbolism or allegory, not as literal history. Thus when the tests come upon Job, they come from Satan. But in the same way that the Bahá'í writings interpret scriptural allusions to Satan as symbolic portrayals of the temptation to accede to the ego or to give in to our baser instincts (as opposed to turning to God), possibly the author of Job has intended a similar meaning. Therefore, the tests of Satan may represent Job's inner turmoil, his temptation to rebel against faith and belief, especially as others urge him to do so.

Job's response to Satan's testing is human but noble: He never denies his faith or despairs of ultimate redemption. Most important, he does not accede to his friends' assertion that the torment is somehow deserved. For example, his companion Eliphaz responds to Job's lamentation by implying that no one ever suffers unjustly:

> "Think now, who that was innocent ever perished?
>   Or where were the upright cut off?
> As I have seen, those who plow iniquity
>   and sow trouble reap the same."[11]

Job answers that he has "not denied the words of the Holy One" and further challenges his friend's rebuke:

> "He who withholds kindness from a friend
>   forsakes the fear of the Almighty.
> My brethren are treacherous as a torrent-bed,
>   as freshets that pass away,
> which are dark with ice,
>   and where the snow hides itself.
> In time of heat they disappear;
>   when it is hot, they vanish from their place."[12]

Extending this metaphor to portray further his friends' lack of steadfastness, Job characterizes his companions as fearful of sharing in his fate: "You see my calamity, and are afraid." "Teach me," he continues, "and I will be silent; make me understand how I have erred."[13]

Job knows that the reasons for his afflictions, whatever they may be, have nothing to do with retribution from God for any behavior on his part. He is confident of his own goodness. He is human and feels pain, but he never denies his faith in God. For this he is rewarded with more than he had before:

And the Lord restored the fortunes of Job, when he had prayed for his friends; and the Lord gave Job twice as much as he had before. . . . And the Lord blessed the latter days of Job more than his beginning. . . .[14]

But while Job prospers in the end, we are left with a theological enigma, to say the least. True, Job becomes the emblem of fidelity and steadfastness, but in what sense has a vision of a just God or a just physical reality been revealed?

The implicit justification contained in the closing poetic speeches by God seems to imply a power beyond the ken of men, but there is no attempt to affirm that the voice out of the whirlwind has tested Job with some purpose in mind. For the author of the closing prose epilogue (who may or may not be the author of the poetic sections), justice lies in the physical redemption of Job. He gets paid off, as it were. And yet the payoff hardly reveals a logic or justice in the testing itself, something that has caused scholars and theologians alike to speculate endlessly.

While it is not the purpose here to untangle the web of theological paradox in the poem, we can discover several themes that unify the work and give important insight into the efforts of human beings to perceive the evidence of divine justice in physical reality. First, as an *exemplum*—a narrative that conveys a moral—the story of Job works well to demonstrate that over time justice is eventually accomplished, but is it inevitably accomplished in the physical realm?

While in the conclusion of the story justice seems to be accomplished on the physical plane of existence, it may well be that Job's ultimate redemption is an otherworldly experience. After all, the story is a poem replete with symbolism and imagery. Therefore, even as the initial debate between God and Satan may be symbolic, so the rest of the story may be as well. The final restoration of Job's riches may thus represent a celestial reunion, an otherworldly reward for Job's exemplary patience in this life. For example, the extension of his life may allude to the continuation of his life in the realm of the spirit.

Second, the story focuses not on justifying God's ways to man but on proclaiming forcefully that inasmuch as this life has the essential purpose of causing us to develop spiritually, even the righteous are tested. The Bahá'í authoritative texts explain the meaning of Job's life in such a context:

> What trials, calamities and perplexities did he not endure! But these tests were like unto the fire and his holiness Job as like unto pure gold. Assuredly gold is purified by being submitted to the fire and if it contain any alloy or imperfection, it will disappear. That is the reason why violent tests become the cause of the everlasting glory of the righteous and are conducive to the destruction and disappearance of the unrighteous.[15]

From this perspective the poem is a depiction of spiritual growth. It begins with a man of position and prosperity, a good man, but a man with as yet untried potential. As Job's tests increase in severity, he ultimately gives way to despair, though he never relinquishes his faith. In the end he is rewarded not with some final or complete insight into God's actions but with a vision of God's grandeur. This new vision is something quite beyond the simplistic understanding of righteousness and justice exhibited earlier by Job's friends, and it is something more emotionally powerful and complete than Plato's allusions to the impersonal intellectual comprehension of the source of attributes that is the "Good."

After the voice describes in poetic eloquence the loftiness of the Creator, the awed Job responds meekly:

"I had heard of thee by the hearing of the ear,
    but now my eye sees thee;
therefore I despise myself,
    and repent in dust and ashes."[16]

Foreshadowing Isaiah's prophecy (Isa. 6:9–10) repeated by Christ
(Matt. 13:14–16) regarding the danger of believers' relying on others for their knowledge of the truth rather than on investigating
and experiencing beliefs for themselves, Job has concluded with a
definition of justice from his own point of view. For Job, a just
condition within the individual is the capacity to experience the
reality of God. This knowledge of God enables Job to withstand
the contrary opinions of others and the adverse personal circumstances he encounters in the physical world.

According to Old Testament scholar Selton Pollock, the justice
portrayed in the poem is thus not a cosmological vision but a purely
personal one, a profound transition in the character of Job. Instead
of acting solely out of fear of God, Job comes to act out of a love of
God's power, magnificence, and beauty:

> The progress of Job's faith can be plainly traced through the story.
> It is evident that his original piety had been largely influenced by
> motives of fear. . . . And when tragedy breaks in upon him, we
> discover the main source of his moral earnestness, for he exclaims:
> "This is what I feared—and now it has come to pass" (3:25).[17]

After Job's passage through the fire of tests, he no longer acts blindly
or unconsciously. His understanding, and therefore his faith as well,
become firmly grounded in the lessons he has learned from his tests.
He may not have a complete vision of God's plan for himself or for
humankind, but he does realize profoundly that the suffering he
has endured has resulted in his own spiritual development.

BOETHIUS' *CONSOLATION* *OF PHILOSOPHY* (CA. 522 A.D.)

About a thousand years after the composition of Job, Anicius Boethius wrote *The Consolation of Philosophy*, a work that takes an approach wholly different from Plato's and Job's treatments of justice in the physical world. Affirming the providential hand of God at work in human history, Boethius advocates abandoning our concern about the apparent lack of justice in physical reality that we might focus our attention on the more enduring effects of our spiritual development.

His examination of justice was composed under the most pragmatic of circumstances. A fifth-century Italian scholar and consul to Theodoric the Ostrogoth, Boethius was a victim of political machinations for which he was imprisoned and condemned to death. While awaiting execution, he composed *The Consolation of Philosophy* as a dialogue between a fictional persona, Boethius himself, and the allegorical figure Dame Philosophy. In the course of this dialogue, Dame Philosophy attempts to teach the distraught Boethius about God's justice, primarily in relation to individual life. Her responses to Boethius' tirades against the blatant injustice of the physical world form the basis of a Christian stoicism that had a tremendous influence on medieval Christianity.

At the beginning of the work Boethius asks Dame Philosophy the obvious question: If God is, whence cometh evil? Like Job, Boethius is beset with unjust tribulation, but beyond his own unjust circumstances, he is equally concerned with the way in which the world itself seems to fall prey to the iniquity of unjust men. Therefore, after explaining his own unjust imprisonment as one example of evil, he catalogs an array of injustices he has observed in the phenomenal world:

I see honest men lying crushed with the fear which smites them after the result of my perilous case: wicked men one and all encouraged to dare every crime without fear of punishment, nay, with hope of rewards for the accomplishment thereof: the innocent I see robbed not merely of their peace and safety, but even of all chance of defending themselves.[18]

Dame Philosophy tells Boethius that his consternation about what he perceives results from his having "forgotten what you are":

Now therefore I have found out to the full the manner of your sickness, and how to attempt the restoring of your health. You are overwhelmed by this forgetfulness of yourself: hence you have been thus sorrowing that you are exiled and robbed of all your possessions. You do not know the aim and end of all things; hence you think that if men are worthless and wicked, they are powerful and fortunate. You have forgotten by what methods the universe is guided. . . .[19]

She then proceeds to prove to Boethius that his grief is unwarranted. First she shows Boethius that he has had good fortune as well as bad. Next she reminds him of the vanity of worldly desires. The very treasures that are universally prized—riches, positions, kingdoms, earthly glory, fame, nobility of birth, lusts of the flesh—are all actually harmful and not to be desired. She then discusses the source of true happiness: a belief in and understanding of God Himself.

She quickly proves to Boethius that, inasmuch as God is absolutely good, He can do no evil. What Boethius perceives as evil is either not of God or else not completely or properly understood. In the course of further discussion Dame Philosophy distinguishes between Fate and Providence. Fate, she notes, is seemingly fickle; none of us can foresee what will occur to us in the future. But Fate, she asserts, is ultimately subject to Providence, and Providence functions at the behest of God's eternal plan:

> Thus is the world governed for the best if a directness, which rests in the intelligence of God, puts forth an order of causes which may not swerve. This order restrains by its own unchangeableness changeable things, which might otherwise run hither and thither at random. Wherefore in disposing the universe this limitation directs all for good, though to you who are not strong enough to comprehend the whole order, all seems confusion and disorder.[20]

Dame Philosophy's concept of man's limited perception of divine order lies at the heart of the Boethian consolation. It implies a stoicism, both in regard to historical events whose final implications we cannot fathom, and in regard to our own individual lives which ultimately find justice and solace only in the next world.

Boethius' primary concern is focused on the individual, and his work contends that so long as the virtuous man pursues the Highest Good, whatsoever befalls him will, in the long run, serve solely to assist him in his quest for fulfillment. In short, justice will be done: "The fortune of those who are in possession of virtue, or are gaining it, or advancing therein, is entirely good, whatever it be, while for those who remain in wickedness, their fortune is the worst."[21]

The concluding argument upholding justice in God's creation is explained by Dame Philosophy in the fifth and final book, wherein she affirms that there is no such thing as pure chance—everything occurs with purpose, with God's knowledge, and within the jurisdiction of His command. Dame Philosophy also confirms the simultaneous functioning of free will and foreknowledge: She asserts that God's foreknowledge of future events has no causal effect on our freely made decisions.

There is no substantial discussion about the relationship between our freely chosen course of action and our experience in the afterlife. Boethius simply affirms that justice will be done and that we should, therefore, be detached from the trials and tribulations of this earthly life. Neither does Boethius attempt to explain why God does not intervene in history to assist His creation, except to imply that in the long-term scheme of things, justice will eventually be done on earth even as it is accomplished in the spiritual realm.

The Consolation of Philosophy thus responds primarily to the plight of the individual and focuses on evil or injustice perpetrated by malefactors. Boethius upholds the providence and benignancy of God and affirms that in this life virtue—the pursuit of the good— is every individual's goal, the attainment of which brings its own existential or immediate rewards as well as the promise of justice and further rewards in the hereafter.

According to Boethius, the appropriate response to injustice in this life is thus patience, acquiescence, and certitude—a philosophical position that upheld the notion of *contemptu mundi* (disdain for the world), the watchword of medieval Christianity, just as the Wheel of Fortune became a key metaphor for Boethian Christianity.*

Even though this stoicism, when coupled with asceticism, might seem to imply a condemnation of God's creation, Boethian philosophy views earthly ascendancy as ephemeral, capricious, arbitrary. The wisest course of action for humankind is to disdain involvement in or attachment to the physical world and, instead, to concentrate on preparation for the next world.

---

* The Latin phrase meaning "disdain for the world" was the title of a treatise, *De Contemptu Mundi*, by Pope Innocent III. It was commonly used to convey the attitude of most medieval Church authorities that the proper activity in life is to reject temporal pursuits and prepare for the afterlife. For more on the Wheel of Fortune and Boethian Christianity, see pp. 49–50.

Boethius' work is by no means unique in its response to the question of justice in God's creation. But it was a seminal work that helped console people in the Middle Ages who daily confronted all manner of chaos and injustice, including social and economic oppression, an extremely high child mortality rate, and plagues that eradicated up to fifty percent of the population in some areas. In such an environment, asceticism or the monastic ideal that Boethius' philosophy was used to uphold no doubt seemed sane responses to a reality that offered little in the way of spiritual benefit.

MILTON'S *PARADISE LOST* (1667 A.D.)

More than a thousand years after Boethius, the English poet John Milton wrote *Paradise Lost* as an attempt to explain justice in the physical world in terms of the intervention of God through the sacrifice of His Son. In the course of this magnificent epic, Milton delineates a relatively complete paradigm of physical creation that affirms the necessity of good works coupled with knowledge and free will as empowered by the guidance and assistance of God. In this sense, Milton confirms the value of participation in the world described by Plato, vindicates the majesty of God alluded to in Job, and spells out the historical perspective that Boethius asserted but failed to explain.

Contemplating the most worthy theme to which he could devote his vast talent, Milton rejected his initial plan to write an account of the Arthurian legend and determined instead to "assert Eternal Providence, / And justify the ways of God to men."[22] To bring his theology and philosophy to life in *Paradise Lost*, Milton employed the Adamic myth to portray God's justice. So confident was he that he could present justice from God's point of view (thereby eclipsing what Boethius had done) that he dared to include God as a major character in the work.

To a certain extent *Paradise Lost* deals with the same problem that is at the heart of Boethius' work—how to account for injustice and evil in a world wrought by an omnipotent and beneficent Deity. Milton is predominantly concerned with a historical perspective, a perspective that Boethius does not presume to undertake. However, possibly the most powerful effect of Milton's efforts is his remarkably insightful treatment of the fall of Satan from heaven and the fall of Adam and Eve from Edenic grace. In his portrayal of these failures, Milton offers dramatic and credible examples of free will in motion.

The work falls short of vindicating the traditional Christian interpretation of history—that the advent of Christ is the single turning point in the redemption of humankind. But clearly Milton did not intend for his fictional poem to represent a literal recounting of history. Certainly he did not presume to know what God thought or said or what the angel Michael might have recounted to Adam and Eve. Nevertheless, a good deal of the theology and philosophy we can elicit from the work are, by and large, logically consistent and extremely helpful in fulfilling Milton's avowed purpose of justifying the ways of God to humankind.

Milton responds to the problem of the origin of evil with a doctrine of free will regarding both the inception of sin in the mind of Lucifer and the negligence of Adam and Eve when they fail to follow the clear instructions of God's law. Milton answers the question of God's providence and ascendancy by showing how humankind will, over the course of history, become redeemed in spite of human frailty. He also asserts that all evil machinations, from whatever source they may originate, will ultimately serve to uphold this process by bringing about a greater good.

Milton treats the origin of evil in the story of Satan's rebellion against God, an embellishment of the biblical myth wherein the prideful Lucifer begets sin by contemplating an unholy revolt in heaven. But Milton portrays Satan as rebelling not because he is incapable of understanding the justice and wisdom in worshiping God and God's Son (Christ before His incarnation). Satan rebels against this just authority simply because he will not submit to any authority. For example, Satan later reveals he is aware of the vanity of rebelling against an omnipotent force, but he chooses to persist in rejecting the just authority of God.

In one soliloquy the fallen Satan indicates that he sincerely misses being in heaven, that he knows God's laws are just and proper, and that his rebellion was wrong and undeserved. In this same speech he asserts that God is ever-forgiving and that God would receive him back even now should he repent. But Satan will *not* repent, because his pride will not allow him to humble himself, even though it would be proper for him to do so and even though he would be happier.

On the border of God's new creation and intent on mischief (seducing God's new creation to become fallen like himself) Satan pauses, surveys the beauty before him, and is reminded of the bounty he experienced in heaven "Till pride and worse ambition threw me down / Warring in heav'n against heav'n's matchless King."[23] At this critical juncture—at the crux of fatal choice—Satan acknowledges forthrightly God's ascendancy and justice:

> He deserved no such return
> From me, whom he created what I was
> In that bright eminence, and with his good
> Upbraided none; nor was his service hard.
> What could be less than to afford him praise,
> The easiest recompense, and pay him thanks,
> How due![24]

Yet in a magnificent study of willful evil, Milton portrays Satan as knowingly acting against his own best interest, thereby apparently confounding Socrates' assertion that no one commits evil in full knowledge.

Knowing that he can never overcome God, Satan expresses the determination to accomplish two malicious tasks: to make Adam and Eve as miserable as he is and to force God to reject and condemn His own creation. Of course, the only way for Satan to redeem himself is through submission, and that is the key to his damnation. His pride will not allow him to submit to any power, even a just one, even when he knows that it would be beneficial for him should he do so:

> Nay cursed be thou, since against his thy will
> Chose freely what it now so justly rues.

In another place he states,

> O then at last relent: is there no place
> Left for repentance, none for pardon left?
> None left but by submission; and that word
> Disdain forbids me, and my dread of shame
> Among the Spirits beneath, whom I seduced
> With other promises and other vaunts
> Than to submit, boasting I could subdue
> Th' Omnipotent.[25]

To understand the dramatic, theological, and philosophical importance of this passage, we must realize that Milton implies there is a very real possibility that Satan could repent and, what is more important, that he would be redeemed were he to do so. Furthermore, it is not even appropriate to perceive Satan's rejection of this opportunity as preordained by the nature of his character. According to the theology implicit in *Paradise Lost*, Satan consciously rejects salvation not because he is inherently evil. After all, in heaven he was a lofty archangel. Satan's choice is a conscious and willful action.

In addition to the doctrine of God's forgiveness as part of a system of divine justice, and closely related to it, Milton portrays the simultaneous existence of God's foreknowledge and omnipotence with the free will of both the angelic hosts and humankind. Instead of simply affirming this belief, Milton artfully portrays the character of God explaining why He has allowed Satan to rebel and has thereby permitted evil to invade His creation—the very crux of the issue of theodicy.

In a dialogue with His Son, God states that if beings were forced to recognize His authority, love, and beneficence, they could not be said truly to understand His nature, nor would their love or obedience be praiseworthy or authentic:

Freely they stood who stood, and fell who fell.
Not free, what proof could they have giv'n sincere
Of true allegiance, constant faith or love
Where only what they needs must do, appeared,
Not what they would? What praise could they receive?
What pleasure I from such obedience paid,
When will and reason (reason also is choice)
Useless and vain, of freedom both despoiled. . . .[26]

God states that though He foreknew the angels would rebel, even as He foreknows that man will fail in Eden, His foreknowledge of these events does not cause them to occur:

they themselves decreed
Their own revolt, not I. If I foreknew,
Foreknowledge had no influence on their fault,
Which had no less proved certain unforeknown.[27]

In the remaining books of *Paradise Lost* Milton introduces his essential proof of the justification of God's ways to man. After Sa-

tan succeeds in seducing Eve and Adam, they confess their guilt
and repent. Their punishment is banishment from Eden, and their
departure is the end of the basic plot per se.

But by no means is this the end of the epic. In preparation for
their new life, God sends the angel Michael to comfort Adam and
Eve by explaining to them the ultimate triumph of God's plan. In
the last two books of the poem the couple is shown a vision that
constitutes both a history lesson and a finishing touch for Milton's
theology and the larger plot—the ultimate triumph of good over
evil on earth. He explains that humankind will become degenerate
through sin until God, out of His mercy, sends his Son. Through
the Son's sacrifice, humankind will be redeemed to a position more
lofty than that which Adam and Eve occupied before the Fall.

Michael's vision of *felix lapsus* (the "fortunate fall") so excites
Adam that he exclaims:

> "O goodness infinite, goodness immense!
> That all this good of evil shall produce,
> And evil turn to good; more wonderful
> Than that which by creation first brought forth
> Light out of darkness!"[28]

But Michael is quick to caution Adam and Eve that their knowledge of the fortuitous and just outcome of history is not sufficient
for their own personal salvation. To this knowledge, this glimpse of
God's overall power and goodness—this "right reason"*—they must

---

* "Right reason," as Milton uses the term in Michael's discussion about reason as the
guiding faculty in spiritual growth, is defined by Douglas Bush in *The Complete Poetical
Works of John Milton* as "the philosophic conscience, the power, implanted by God in
all men, to apprehend truth and moral law (a Christian legacy from classical thought)"
(566).

add deeds, faith, and other virtues. But if they can manage this, their ultimate condition will be happier than the Edenic bliss they have lost through willful neglect:

> only add
> Deeds to thy knowledge answerable, add faith,
> Add virtue, patience, temperance, add love,
> By name to come called charity, the soul
> Of all the rest: then wilt thou not be loth
> To leave this Paradise, but shalt possess
> A paradise within thee, happier far.[29]

The conclusion of Milton's presentation of God's actions, therefore, is a clearer and more complete justification of the nature of physical reality than the view of Plato, Job, or Boethius. Unlike the God of Job, Whose justice we must guess at, and beyond Boethius' blind faith that justice in any significant way is veiled from our understanding or else reserved for the afterlife, Milton's God explains the divine rationale for the creation itself and for His relationship to humankind.

Instead of simply asserting God's historical ascendancy, Milton delineates it through a historical recounting. But, most important of all, Milton's God is neither mechanistic nor impersonal. Like a loving and wise parent, He watches His creation, knows humankind will fail, but, in order to test and teach them, He withholds intervention. Ultimately God will intervene, Milton explains, and He will guide the course of history toward its benign objectives. In the long run, even the events that presently seem destructive—the rebellion of Satan, the fall of mankind, the iniquity of the wayward—God will eventually employ to achieve propitious results.

3

A BAHÁ'Í CONCEPT OF THEODICY: SOME RESPONSES TO CLASSIC THEORIES

Inasmuch as He, the sovereign Lord of all, hath willed to reveal His sovereignty in the kingdom of names and attributes, each and every created thing hath, through the act of the Divine Will, been made a sign of His glory. So pervasive and general is this revelation that nothing whatsoever in the whole universe can be discovered that doth not reflect His splendor.

—Bahá'u'lláh

The schism between science (a rational investigation of reality) and religion (a spiritual or intuitive investigation of reality) became consolidated in Western thought in the fourteenth and fifteenth centuries. This conflict is evidently no closer to being reconciled or repaired now than it was in the mid-nineteenth century when the battle seemed to reach a pitch with Darwin's publication of *On the Origin of Species by Means of Natural Selection, or the Preservation of Favoured Races in the Struggle for Life* in 1859.

So long as neither realm of "learning" encroached on the territory of the other, the two approaches to the study of and admiration for reality could peaceably coexist in the same universe and even in the same universities. But when the findings or theories of one encroached on the territory of the other, then all was not so friendly and decorous. For example, when scientific thinkers such as Galileo and Copernicus threatened the theologically based vision of the cosmos posited by the church, ideological warfare resulted, along with more overt unpleasantness such as the Spanish Inquisition. Likewise, when Darwin began what has been called the "second Copernican Revolution" with his theory of the origin of human life as a scientific rather than a divine event, the battle between science and religion grew fiercer at every turn.

Now there is not much war going on, except for the occasional political volley at the "godlessness" of universities and the equally "godless" professors who are said to pervert the young minds of innocent youths that fall prey to scientific cynicism about religious views of creation, history, or the cosmos. But for the most part, science and religion seem relatively content to ignore one another's existence, realizing that reconciliation is not possible so long as those who study physical reality refuse to admit into their universe the existence of (let alone the influence of) a spiritual or metaphysical reality, while those who affirm a belief in spiritual reality have equal disdain for scientific study, except for the rather nice technology it provides (e.g., cell phones, computers, and high-definition plasma television sets).

But perhaps the most intriguing result of this long-time family feud is the capacity of individuals to assume both views simultaneously, relegating matters of religion to their inner life or to the social milieu of the cathedral, the church, the synagogue, the temple, or mosque, while living their workaday lives in a world described and defined by technology. Consequently, the disintegration in our study of reality is tacitly responsible for the lack of integration in our personal lives.

But there is a religion which affirms that these two realms of study need not be in conflict and that our perception of reality need not be fragmented or compartmentalized. This religion does not advocate an enforced reconciliation, nor does it propose some sort of grand synod or conclave in which scientists and theologians attend workshops to resolve their differences. Instead, it asserts that science and religion are actually examining two different aspects of a single integrated reality which happens to have both physical and metaphysical properties. In short, science and religion are already in accord, even if individual scientists and students of religion have not yet come to appreciate the essential unity of creation.

WHY BAHÁ'Í?

It is a foundational thesis and essential belief of the Bahá'í Faith that reality is one integral system that possesses both outer, visible, or physical properties, and also unseen, metaphysical, or spiritual properties. It furthermore asserts that once the integration of reality is properly understood, students of the physical properties of reality and the students of the spiritual dimension can realize that their longstanding feud was needless, that all this time they have been looking at the same reality, but from different perspectives.

Such a claim is delightful to hear but not so easy to prove. The distinction in the claims of the Bahá'í Faith regarding this unity of reality is that the Bahá'í authoritative texts offer substantial proofs of the validity of this assertion. But what is important to our discussion of theodicy and the justice and sensibleness of reality is this: If reality has indeed been created by an intelligent and well-meaning Deity Who loves us and cares about all of us individually, then the Bahá'í proofs that purport to vindicate such claims would be well worth examining. Such a study would be of particular value if it could help us come to terms with the perplexing problem of the existence of evil and injustice in a world created by this Benevolent Being.

Therefore let us begin our examination of the claims of the Bahá'í Faith about physical reality being a logical expression of a Divine Creator by determining how the Bahá'í teachings might respond to the inadequacies or incompleteness in the classic works we examined that also attempt to reconcile a belief in God with the appearance of injustice or evil in God's creation.

A BAHÁ'Í RESPONSE TO PLATO

The essence of Plato's explanation of the basis for justice in the physical world consists of two general observations. First, Plato expresses the belief that physical reality corresponds to and is a reflection of spiritual reality. To Plato this correspondence is no accident, no incidental quality of physical creation, but the essential nature and purpose of all created things. Second, Plato believes that we can, by relying on our higher self, discern the spiritual messages that physical creation has to impart. These messages consist of the spiritual qualities, the abstract virtues or attributes, that exist in an ethereal condition in the spiritual realm but which are presented to us in concrete forms so that these abstractions can be initially perceived and acquired.

According to Plato, this twofold arrangement is the basis for justice in the physical world as a whole. Individual human justice consists of the propriety, harmony, and integrity among all our faculties—each faculty or power functions precisely as it has been designed to do. The mind governs the whole, and everything else (even our passions and desires) assumes a subordinate relationship to what the "higher" self decides is the best course of action for us to take. Only when we are in this "just" condition are we able to become the best individual we are capable of becoming.

Plato's view of spiritual education is remarkably parallel to the Bahá'í concept of the divine purpose of physical creation. Bahá'-u'lláh, Prophet and Founder of the Bahá'í Faith, whose writings Bahá'ís accept as having scriptural authority, states that "every created thing is a sign of the revelation of God." He further states that every human being has the capacity to recognize the imprint of the Creator in creation itself: "He hath endowed every soul with the capacity to recognize the signs of God. How could He, otherwise, have fulfilled His testimony unto men, if ye be of them that ponder His Cause in their hearts. He will never deal unjustly with anyone, neither will He task a soul beyond its power."[1]

And yet, as rewarding and influential as Plato's work has been down through the ages, it is incomplete in its response to the question of the purpose of physical reality: How does Plato justify why human beings must endure physical experience in order to become informed about reality, especially if, as the character of Socrates asserts, our soul endures beyond the death of the body?

Another missing ingredient in Plato's description of reality is a Divine Being, a Creator Who assists creation and the individuals in it at every turn. For while Plato's concept of "the Good" clearly alludes to his monotheistic belief, Plato never really attributes to this entity any awareness, concern, or cognitive powers. The Good is described more as the amalgamation, epitome, or source of all virtue rather than as a willful designer and coordinator of created reality Who monitors the progress of his most important creation—the human being.

Certainly we could view the attributes of Plato's Good as appropriate to a Supreme God, but without some sense of willful concern for the creation that emanates from this Essence, this "source" of reality seems amorphous and unconvincing, or at least not very intimate, loving, or lovable.

True, Plato presents the ascent from the cave of ignorance to the light of knowledge as the result of attraction to, or the spiritual influence emanating from, the Good. But Plato's mystic Source of reality does not exert, so far as he discusses this process, any conscious effort to bring about the philosopher-king's transformation, nor does the Good lend any overt aid to the ascent of humankind, other than indirectly through the influence of the philosopher-kings, who, through their own effort at enlightenment, descend back down into the cave of ignorance to teach whoever will heed their observations about reality. Consequently, the journey from darkness to light seems to be the result of individual insight and determination on the part of these special souls rather than the result of a divine plan of God.

Not that Plato ever intended his work to be a study of theology, but his model of human transformation is still at variance with the concept of a God Who is aware of, concerned with, and actively intervening in our individual lives as well as in human history to assist His creation. Furthermore, even if we interpret Plato's specialized individuals, the philosopher-kings, as metaphorical representations of the Prophets or Messengers of God, the analogy fails to account for the repeated statements by the Prophets that They do nothing on Their own authority, but speak and act as God directs. In effect, where Plato's philosopher kings arise from ignorance by virtue of their own inner voice, the Manifestations clearly acknowledge that their knowledge is a gift of God bestowed on them as a means by which they might become divine Emissaries and Messengers.

And yet, in defense of what Plato might have intended with the *Republic,* perhaps the single most influential work in Western philosophy, it is certainly possible that in his own mind Plato, or his mentor Socrates, is alluding to the philosopher-kings as functioning in the capacity of intermediaries between God and ordinary humans, who need the assistance of an educator. Indeed, perhaps this is precisely what Bahá'u'lláh Himself means when He states the following about Socrates and Socratic thought:

What a penetrating vision into philosophy this eminent man had! He is the most distinguished of all philosophers and was highly versed in wisdom. We testify that he is one of the heroes in this field and an outstanding champion dedicated unto it. He had a profound knowledge of such sciences as were current amongst men as well as of those which were veiled from their minds. Methinks he drank one draught when the Most Great Ocean overflowed with gleaming and life-giving waters. He it is who perceived a unique, a tempered, and a pervasive nature in things, bearing the closest likeness to the human spirit, and he discovered this nature to be distinct from the substance of things in their refined form. He hath a special pronouncement on this weighty theme. Wert thou to ask from the worldly wise of this generation about this exposition, thou wouldst witness their incapacity to grasp it.[2]

The dedication of the Prophets of God (Whom the Bahá'í writings call "Manifestations" of God) to the instruction of humankind, even at the cost of Their own lives, might certainly parallel allegorically the suffering and rejection that the philosopher-king experiences when he descends into the cave to lead others from the world of shadows and illusion up to an ever more expansive vision of reality. But we can only guess to what extent Socrates was aware of or was alluding to this theological concept and to this process of incremental enlightenment of humankind, especially since the works of his student Plato contain only the dramatic portrayal of recollections of Socrates and Socratic thought, not Socrates' own words.

A BAHÁ'Í RESPONSE TO JOB

In the Book of Job God is portrayed anthropomorphically as a personal and cognitive Being. This ancient poem provides a wonderfully poetic vision of a Creator of power and confidence in His best work—the good human being. We also are presented with a vision of justice more complex than the concept of justice as proprietary as order set forth in *The Republic*.

But while the anonymous poet of Job creates for us a Being Who is omnipotent, self-sufficient, and cognitive, the poem does not provide us with a complete understanding or appreciation of God's plan for us individually or for humankind as a whole. At the end of the work, we are not even sure He has such a plan. As Old Testament scholar Robert Gordis notes in his study of Job, we must look elsewhere in the Bible for that:

Moreover, when God finally appears out of the whirlwind He does not assure Job of His protection and love for His suffering creature. For that theme we must look elsewhere in biblical and extra-biblical literature. Here it is the divine transcendence, the majesty and mystery of God, far removed from man and his concerns, that finds expression.[3]

To a certain extent, the ending of the Book of Job might seem to contradict Gordis's observation. Job's courageous response to his trials is rewarded with divine bestowals—whether they take place in this world or in the afterlife. Nevertheless, Gordis's point is essentially correct; the vision of God that the work reveals is of a Being Who is aware, concerned, and fully in control, yet, at the same time, a Being Who remains mysteriously beyond any significant comprehension on our part. The poem seems to imply that God may have valid reasons for allowing us to suffer and that we can be assured that justice will finally be ours, but the tests themselves may often seem unwarranted and unjustified.

The Bahá'í teachings stress the logic and justice of God's actions, yet here too we can find in various passages of the Bahá'í authoritative texts similar evidence of a Deity Who is infinitely beyond our complete or final understanding. For example, the Báb (the Herald and Forerunner of Bahá'u'lláh) states, "from everlasting God hath been invested with the independent sovereignty of His exalted Being, and unto everlasting He will remain inaccessible in the transcendent majesty of His holy Essence." Yet other passages from Bahá'í scripture make it clear that while the "holy Essence" of God is inaccessible to the comprehension of man, His qualities, assistance, and *modus operandi* are readily apparent and comprehensible: "He hath extended assistance to every wayfarer, hath graciously responded to every petitioner and granted admittance to every seeker after truth."[4]

In fairness to the poet-author of Job, this magnificent poem is unified around a single theme—maintaining acquiescence, patience, and faith in the midst of tribulation even while knowledge of the logic or benefit of our trials may be withheld from us. It does not seem to be intended by its author to be a comprehensive theological treatise. Nevertheless, after we finish the work, we are left without any satisfying appreciation of God's justice in our lives or in the evolution of human civilization in God's creation.

We do come away with insight into how suffering can induce growth, even in those who are basically upright. This is no mean accomplishment. Like Job we may come to reflect on the inscrutable majesty of God's power. But we too are left to accept divine justice as a mystery concealed from our understanding. It is appropriate, we are left to infer, that we be tested so that we may progress. But there is no sense in the Book of Job of a rational explanation for, or a systematic approach to, the purpose of physical reality in our lives.

However, we need to allude to one other vindication of what the poem does accomplish. As the Bahá'í writings note, these ancient verses are steeped in symbolic and allegorical significance. Bahá'u'lláh notes that the references in these ancient scriptures to a physical heaven and hell, as well as to a literal Satan or Devil, are all symbolic in nature, and yet no less valuable because they are poetic allusions.

In this context, we should note that the Bahá'í writings explain the allusion to Satan or Satanic forces represent the ego, the insistent self that would foil our attempt to become spiritual, selfless, kind, benevolent, and submissive before the authority of God and His laws about morality. Consequently, the testing of Job could well be explicated as the symbolic portrayal of an internal war in the character of Job between his ego (Satan) and his conviction (the character of God).

With such a symbolic or allegorical take on the poem, the specific torments or temptations can themselves be viewed as having specific symbolic meanings. The wife, as with the Adamic myth, could represent some faculty of Job's soul—his reflective or spiritual self that cries out for some logical explanation for his suffering. Likewise, the tempting by his friends to believe that he should feel guilt about some concealed sin might be Job's temptation to accede to the common view of suffering—that it is somehow merited, that suffering is a punishment for unbelief or moral wavering.

If we approach the work in this manner, the victory of Job is not merely one of endurance; it is a triumph of his spiritual self over his ego, a victory symbolized by his reunion with all he thought he had lost. In effect, the reunion is an internal unity or harmony among all Job's faculties—his reason, his spiritual sense of self, and his relationship to physical reality.

A BAHÁ'Í RESPONSE TO BOETHIUS

Boethius' vision of God and of God's justice in physical life is not that different from what we find in Job. One suffers but endures and awaits the end of suffering with noble resolve. In fact, one might infer that Boethius portrays a God Who is even more aloof from justice in the individual physical life than is the God of Job. The God implicit in *The Consolation of Philosophy* seems too concerned with long-range plans to be caught up in the physical difficulties of individuals or even with the difficulties humankind as a whole at a given point in human history. After all, according to Boethius everything in history will work itself out over time, and each individual will receive his or her due recompense in the afterlife.

From this point of view physical reality has value insofar as it informs us through our experience that everything in this life is capricious, subject to change, transitory, unworthy of our attention or desire. One major symbol of physical reality for the Boethian philosophy (which, as we noted earlier, upheld Christian stoicism) became the image of the Wheel of Fortune. According to this symbolic allusion, each of us is seated in a chair affixed to a vast wheel. Dame Fortune gives the wheel a spin, and it stops wheresoever it will, without rhyme or reason as regards our individual needs or actions. Some of us will be on top. Some of us will be on the bottom. The rest will be somewhere in between.

The meaning of the image is clear enough—that nothing in this life is secure or predictable. Consequently, from such a perspective nothing material is worthy of our concern, be it material wealth, social status, physical health, or peace of mind. For as surely as we are in a state of felicity today, tomorrow may bring us a reversal of fortunes.

This sense of insecurity about physical reality was the basis for the debate in medieval Christianity about whether it is best to retire from the physical world and devote our lives to prayer and meditation (the *vita contemplativa*) or to wage war against the forces of injustice and suffering by working in the world to assist humankind (the *vita activa*).

The Boethian philosophy does not imply that justice is nonexistent in the physical world, but Boethius does portray it as beyond our comprehension or attainment so long as we dwell within its precincts. Therefore, from Boethius' perspective the just or appropriate response to physical reality is to focus attention on the next life by preparing spiritually to enter that existence. For Boethius, physical activity not only seems lacking in any inherent spiritual value; it may also become an explicit deterrent to the just purposes of humankind, especially if we become obsessed with fame or wealth.

Whether Boethius intended it so or not, the Boethian philosophy became a bulwark for the contemplative life and the ascetic ideal and the manifesto of a Christian stoicism, which affirmed that it is best simply to endure life until death ends the drudgery and pain that are man's lot in the physical world. As the character Egeus says to his bereaved son Theseus in Chaucer's "Knight's Tale," a thoroughly Boethian story, *"This world nys but a thurghfare ful of wo, / And we been pilgrymes, passynge to and fro. / Deeth is an ende of every worldly soore."*[5] (This world is but a thoroughfare full of woe, / And we are pilgrims, passing to and fro. / Death is an end of every worldly sorrow.)

Taken out of context, some passages from the Bahá'í writings might seem to support an attitude closely aligned with the tone of Egeus' dreary assessment of physical reality and our participation in it:

> Busy not thyself with this world, for with fire We test the gold, and with gold We test Our servants.[6]

> Abandon not the everlasting beauty for a beauty that must die, and set not your affections on this mortal world of dust.[7]

> Free thyself from the fetters of this world, and loose thy soul from the prison of self. Seize thy chance, for it will come to thee no more.[8]

Likewise, in another often cited passage Bahá'u'lláh indicates that, as Boethius' work implies, we may have to await the next life before we receive justice and recompense: "Sorrow not if, in these days and on this earthly plane, things contrary to your wishes have been ordained and manifested by God, for days of blissful joy, of heavenly delight, are assuredly in store for you."[9]

But this Bahá'í passage does not stop here. It goes on to hint at a vast difference between the Bahá'í view and Boethius' implications about what should be our response to physical life: "Worlds, holy and spiritually glorious, will be unveiled to your eyes. You are destined by Him, *in this world* and hereafter, to partake of their benefits, to share in their joys, and to obtain a portion of their sustaining grace."[10] In this context wherein Bahá'u'lláh is addressing those who labor to follow His teachings and live a moral life, it is clear that spiritual endeavors bring existential rewards in this life as well as further bounty in the afterlife. Likewise, instead of implying the Manichaean view of physical reality as an inherently unspiritual reality, the Bahá'í writings repeatedly assert that all physical creation as an emanation of God bears the imprint of the Creator and has the capacity to convey some insight about the nature of spirituality.

But the Bahá'í writings are more explicit still in rejecting the stoicism implicit in *The Consolation of Philosophy*. According to the Bahá'í teachings, to reject earthly life is to neglect the divine purposes for which physical reality and our experience in this reality have been created. Therefore, withdrawal from the world is viewed as inappropriate, unjust, a dereliction of divinely ordained duty and capacity.

The Bahá'í writings do indeed caution us about the dangers of the physical world, but all are commanded to have a vocation, to earn a livelihood, and to contribute to society. Furthermore, the Bahá'í writings do not portray these as incidental or arbitrary activities—something to occupy our time and keep us out of trouble. As we will later discuss, at the heart of this exhortation is the underlying fact that only through action does our knowledge about reality become experienced and confirmed thereby.

In fact, Bahá'u'lláh strictly forbids mendicancy and monasticism. He goes so far as to command monks and priests to abandon the solitary life in order to develop themselves as human beings and to assist humankind in fostering a spiritually based society: "The pious deeds of the monks and priests among the followers of the Spirit [Jesus]—upon Him be the peace of God—are remembered in His presence. In this Day, however, let them give up the life of seclusion and direct their steps towards the open world and busy themselves with that which will profit themselves and others." In another passage He similarly observes, "Seclude not yourselves in your churches and cloisters. Come ye out of them by My leave, and busy, then, yourselves with what will profit you and others."[11]

The emphasis in the Bahá'í writings on the inextricable relationship between knowledge and action is so important that it is well worth further consideration. This tenet clearly distinguishes the Bahá'í view of the just purposes of physical reality from the views of Boethius and also from the concept of salvation through grace. particularly as this concept is commonly understood and articulated by Christian Protestantism.

The ceaseless debate among Christian theologians about whether one is "saved" by faith or by deeds is so critical to any discussion of the purpose of physical reality—even in contemporary Christian discourse—that it would be helpful here to digress and briefly review its origins and its significance. Certainly the earliest Christians were divided over this issue. Paul and James seem to argue about which has primacy, faith or deeds. Paul states that faith is the sole requisite for salvation, whereas James asserts that all should be "doers of the word, and not hearers only," and that works are the "completion of faith."[12] Stated more axiomatically from a Bahá'í perspective, faith, together with virtue of every sort, is entirely theoretical until it is expressed in dramatic form, in action.

This early division in Christianity over the issue of salvation through grace, especially as it relates to the question of whether or not Christ was God, established for all time the perception by many adherents of Christianity that Christ's martyrdom was the singular significant event in the life of Christ or in religious history as a whole. As we noted, this is Milton's point of view. From such a perspective, the Christian religion is necessarily a unique event in God's expression of His love for humankind and the sole avenue whereby God's grace can be attained.

So common a reference as the *Encyclopaedia Britannica* alludes to this early ideological division among the Disciples and among the earlier followers of Christianity, also mentioning in this connection that the Apostle Paul stressed a complete break with the Judaic emphasis on law and viewed the crucifixion as "the supreme redemptive act and also as the means of expiation for the sin of man."[13]

However the Disciple James, brother of Jesus, viewed Christ's ministry as *fulfilling* the Judaic religion, not rejecting it:

> Paul linked this doctrine [of salvation through the grace of God] with his theme that the Gospel represents liberation from the Mosaic Law. The latter thesis created difficulties at Jerusalem, where the church was under the presidency of James, the brother of Jesus. . . . the canonical letter ascribed to James opposes the antinomian (antilaw) interpretations of the doctrine of justification by faith. A middle position seems to have been occupied by Peter.[14]

Christ Himself states that He did not "come to abolish the law and the prophets; I have come not to abolish them but to fulfill them." He goes on to advise His followers that their own actions are essential to their salvation: "For I tell you, unless your righteousness exceeds that of the scribes and Pharisees, you will never enter the kingdom of heaven."[15] He then proceeds to reveal a fairly exacting code of law in which He abrogates some of the Judaic laws, confirms others, and adds some more throughout the twenty-seven remaining verses of chapter 5 and the sixty-two verses of chapters 6 and 7 in the book of Matthew.

He concludes this exegesis on law and moral behavior with the well-known admonition: "And every one who hears these words of mine and does not do them will be like a foolish man who built his house upon the sand; and the rain fell, and the floods came, and the winds blew and beat against that house, and it fell; and great was the fall of it."[16]

Paul's numerous statements de-emphasizing and even denouncing "works" and "obedience to law" as having any relevance to salvation seem strangely at odds with Christ's own advice. Paul states:

> We ourselves, who are Jews by birth and not Gentile sinners, yet who know that a man is not justified by works of the law but through faith in Jesus Christ, even we have believed in Christ Jesus, in order to be justified by faith in Christ, and not by works of the law, because by works of the law shall no one be justified.[17]

In *The Light Shineth in Darkness,* Udo Schaefer goes so far as to assert that Paul's polemic against law was from Paul's own theology, not from Christ's. He further contends that much of future Christianity would derive its system of beliefs from the teachings of Paul, not from the teachings of Christ.[18]

Because Paul's interpretation of Christ's teachings largely determined the future course of Christian thought, much of contemporary Christianity accepts the doctrine that Christ and God are the same entity and that Christ's martyrdom was sufficient payment for the salvation of humankind. For example, one Christian tract states this belief succinctly as follows: "You can do nothing to earn eternal life. It is not our work that saves us, but Faith in the Lord Jesus Christ. You do not receive Eternal life by working for it or by trying to make yourself behave. Accept the payment He has made for your sins and you can rest and be assured you have eternal life."*

Less adamant, but essentially the same, is the response of respected contemporary fundamentalist Dr. Billy Graham to the question of salvation through grace. He affirms that we cannot earn salvation or even appreciably alter our spiritual condition through deeds, but he does acknowledge that the state of salvation will inevitably be reflected in our daily actions. Answering the question of why a Christian should "bother to be good if our goodness doesn't get us into heaven," Dr. Graham has stated, "God loves you so much that his Son was willing to die for you, so you could be saved. If you really understand something of how deep God's love is for you, you cannot be indifferent to him. You will want to love him in return. And how do you show your love for him? By seeking to live the way he wants you to live."[19]

For the Bahá'í, recognizing the Manifestations of God and appreciating the absolutely essential nature of Their sacrifices for the sake of our salvation and enlightenment is extremely significant, but it is not sufficient by itself to enable us to acquire spiritual transformation. Hand in hand with recognizing the Prophets and acknowledging Their exalted station and exemplary life must go obedience to the laws and ordinances They reveal for our guidance. This relationship between belief and action is inextricable.

From the Bahá'í perspective, physical reality and our participation in it are not merely reflections of belief or embellishments of faith. Bahá'u'lláh states succinctly in the Kitáb-i-Aqdas, the book

---

* This is a portion of a tract left on my windshield some years ago. I have since lost the tract but had written down the text because it seemed to me such a forthright statement of this doctrine.

of His laws, that belief and action are inseparable constituents of one integral process: "These twin duties are inseparable. Neither is acceptable without the other."[20]

Thus the Bahá'í writings agree with the spirit of Boethius' observation that universal justice is being wrought over a period of time. The Bahá'í point of view also agrees with the idea that as individuals we may have to await the afterlife before we see justice done. But the Bahá'í perspective about the just purposes of and proper attitude toward physical reality differs radically from the views of the Christian stoics who found in Boethius' work support for rejecting the *vita activa*.

A BAHÁ'Í RESPONSE TO MILTON

Milton's examination of justice in the physical world is in many ways much more complete and complex than the perspective found in Boethius' work, and the Bahá'í writings confirm many, if not most, of Milton's fundamental conclusions.

As we have already observed, Milton's work upholds the doctrine of free will, both on the part of God and on the part of humankind. In this sense Milton's theology does not seem obsessed with the doctrine of man's fall from grace. Instead, Milton portrays Edenic bliss as inferior to the possibilities of the freely chosen ascent after the fall. He does not mean by this that disobedience is a good thing, but he does imply that struggling for spiritual perfection produces a state of development and a kind of knowledge that is superior to childlike innocence and blind acceptance. 'Abdu'l-Bahá asserts that a child is innocent from weakness while a spiritual adult is innocent from strength:

The hearts of all children are of the utmost purity. They are mirrors upon which no dust has fallen. But this purity is on account of weakness and innocence, not on account of any strength and testing, for as this is the early period of their childhood, their hearts and minds are unsullied by the world. They cannot display any great intelligence. They have neither hypocrisy nor deceit. This is on account of the child's weakness, whereas the man becomes pure through his strength. Through the power of intelligence he becomes simple; through the great power of reason and understanding and not through the power of weakness he becomes sincere.[21]

Bahá'u'lláh asserts the same principle when He states, "All that which ye potentially possess can, however, be manifested only as a result of your own volition. Your own acts testify to this truth."[22]

A second important similarity between Milton's conclusions and the teachings of the Bahá'í Faith regards the concept of sin. As a Puritan, Milton might have been expected to espouse a belief in "primal" sin, the belief that man is "born in sin" because of Adam's fall from grace—especially since Milton was writing about Adam. Indeed, the foremost theological doctrine of Puritanism as devised by Calvin derived largely from Pauline Christianity, and Paul observes that sin entered the world because of Adam and that the sole source of human salvation is accepting Christ's sacrifice.[23]

Milton, however, consistently portrays sin as a process that occurs when there is a witting rebellion against just law or authority, a failure to abide by "right reason." In the same way Bahá'u'lláh states that "every good thing is of God, and every evil thing is from yourselves." 'Abdu'l-Bahá likewise states, "in the choice of good and bad actions he [humankind] is free, and he commits them according to his will."[24]

Milton thus portrays Satan as a tempter, as a miserable spirit who wishes to make others as miserable as he. But in Milton's universe, Satan cannot be said to be the source of sin in any significant sense. Satan's own sin is born from his mind when he contemplates his rebellion against God and later when he tempts Adam and Eve to sin, but their fall results from their own choice. Therefore, like Satan's sin, theirs is born from their minds and their own character flaws, which are already there, ready to be exploited by Satan.

Eve wants to attain a higher condition, possibly to become god-like, or at the very least equal with Adam. Adam is so concerned about losing his wife and companion that he gives in to her request, fully aware that he is being disobedient. Satan, as we noted, is so full of pride that he cannot abide submitting to any authority, even a just one, despite knowing that he would be happier were he to comply.

Sin, according to Milton, is thus a process whereby some weakness makes an individual vulnerable to iniquity, and, clearly, human beings are, by definition, flawed beings replete with weaknesses. In this sense Bahá'u'lláh, like the ancient Greeks, admonishes every human being to gain a knowledge of "self": "True loss is for him whose days have been spent in utter ignorance of his self."[25] When we lack sufficient knowledge of the "self" (who we are, what our purpose is, and how best to attain that objective), we yield to desires that undermine our physical, spiritual, and mental health and well-being.

A third important similarity between Milton's theodicy and the Bahá'í justification of God's creation is found in the similar doctrines of grace or forgiveness. Milton implies that the only way God's creatures can become bereft of redemption is through a willful rejection of grace. Alone and aware of what he has lost, Milton's Satan asks himself, "Is there no place / Left for repentance, none for pardon left?" Satan answers his own query when he observes, "None left but by submission. . . ."[26] Because he refuses to submit, forgiveness is unavailable to him. Stated another way, he refuses to avail himself of grace, and God will not impose it on him.

The Bahá'í writings similarly affirm that we are never beyond redemption, whether in this life or in the afterlife, unless we persist in rejecting it: "The portals of grace are wide open before the face of all men. . . . No man that seeketh Us will We ever disappoint, neither shall he that hath set his face towards Us be denied access unto Our court. . . ."[27]

A fourth doctrine of Milton that parallels Bahá'í belief is the concept that heaven and hell are primarily internal spiritual conditions, even though Milton does offer dramatic settings to represent these spiritual realities. The angel Michael explains to Adam and Eve that if they follow his advice by adding deeds to their knowledge, they will "possess / A paradise within" superior to the Edenic bliss they must abandon.[28] Paradise is thus portrayed as an internal condition of enlightenment—proximity to God and compliance with His ordinances.

Milton's hell is also a metaphysical condition. Although hell in this fictional work is described as a physical abode, the important suffering for Satan results not from the torments of a dreadful place but from his internal anguish at being deprived of companionship with God and, of course, his lofty position as an archangel.

A number of passages in the Bahá'í writings express the same notion of heaven and hell as internal states of being. In the Tablet of Ishráqát we find the following: "They say: 'Where is Paradise, and where is Hell?' Say: 'The one is reunion with Me; the other thine own self, O thou who dost associate a partner with God and doubtest.'" 'Abdu'l-Bahá states that the "paradise and hell of existence are found in all the worlds of God, whether in this world or in the spiritual heavenly worlds."[29]

Therefore, while our experience in the afterlife may be substantially different from what we experience in the physical world, 'Abdu'l-Bahá implies that since the important criteria for assessing our felicity are internal and spiritual, the just rewards of spiritual development can be experienced during our earthly lives as well as in the afterlife. In the same way, punishment for our failure to live according to the divine guidance about what is propitious for our spiritual advancement is likewise an internal anguish that can be experienced in either reality. Milton's Satan articulates this concept when, upon waking in hell, he says, "The mind is its own place, and in itself / Can make a heav'n of hell, a hell of heav'n. What matter where I be, if I be still the same. . . ."[30]

Finally, besides agreeing with Milton's justification of God's actions through his delineation of man's free will as the agent of the downfall of humankind, the Bahá'í teachings also confirm Milton's portrayal of history as a divinely guided process by which humankind will gradually become spiritually educated and ultimately redeemed. This long-range view of history as a divine process is at the heart of Milton's theology, just as the Bahá'í belief in progressive revelation* is the cornerstone of Bahá'í theology.

As we have noted, Boethius also affirms that history is being subtly influenced by divine providence, but he implies, as does Alexander Pope some fourteen hundred years later, that the eternal process of history is veiled from the ken of humankind and is not, therefore, a proper concern for the human intellect: "Know then thyself, presume not God to scan; / The proper study of mankind is Man."[31]

---

* Progressive revelation is the belief that all the world's revealed religions down through history are really one religion—the religion of God—revealed in progressive stages, each stage being appropriate to the capacity of humankind for any given period of time.

But in Milton's theology God is not only personally aware of and concerned with the just operation of His creation, He is also beneficent and forgiving when he bids the angel Michael reveal to Adam and Eve the plan by which justice will be wrought in history. In effect, God intervenes in the present and explains how He intends to intervene in the future to bring about beneficial results from Satan's attempt to pervert and destroy His creation. Furthermore, we infer from Michael's instruction that for God (and for Milton) it is important for every human being to be aware of this indirect methodology by which God will use this same malicious act of Satan to demonstrate His love of His creation and, in particular, His love of humankind by redeeming humanity through the atoning sacrifice of His own Son.

These, then, are some of the ways that Milton's theodicy seems generally in compliance with Baha'i theodicy. It is even accurate to say that Milton takes traditional Christian theology about as far as it can go by way of justifying God's decision to have human souls begin their eternal journey in a physical world. Milton seems to portray physical reality as a place of learning and the human experience in physical reality as a means whereby human beings can recognize God's loving nature and freely express their appreciation of it through obedience to divine law and a variety of other goodly deeds.

The major difference between Milton's explanation of physical reality as an expression of divine justice and the Baha'i perspective of physical reality is that where traditional Christian belief views the appearance of Christ as the unique and only necessary intervention of God in human history, the Baha'i teachings view God's intervention in human history as a continuum. Indeed, the Baha'i belief in progressive revelation (the succession of Prophets and the progression of revealed truth about reality) is at the heart of all

Bahá'í theology. Furthermore, this concept will be seen to be the *sine qua non* for any successful attempt at theodicy.

Thus, where Milton avoids the usual Christian belief in the uniqueness of Christ, he does not avoid the myriad logical problems that result from perceiving Christ's advent as the sole and sufficient occasion in human history for the revelation of God's perfection and the redemption of humankind. Milton does not explain, therefore, why God, Who is compared by Christ to a loving heavenly Father, would give His children only one opportunity to be redeemed. Neither does Milton deal with the fact that all understanding of God ("right reason") is a progressive process, not the realization of one specific idea or set of ideas.

The Bahá'í teachings recognize the divinity and exalted station of Christ. Indeed, it would be accurate to say that the Bahá'í teachings accept all the utterances of Christ in the biblical texts as authoritative and true. But Christ Himself never stated that His advent was the unique revelation from God, nor did He ever assert that He was the last appearance of such a spiritualizing force. Indeed, He frequently chided the Jews for having perpetrated in the past what they were about to recommit by persecuting Him: "Therefore I send you prophets and wise men and scribes, some of whom you will kill and crucify, and some you will scourge in your synagogues and persecute from town to town. . . ."[32]

In fact, Christ clearly proclaims that His mission is to fulfill the revelations of the past and to set the stage for the appearance of future Prophets. Regarding the Prophets of the past He states, "Think not that I have come to abolish the law and the prophets; I have come not to abolish them but to fulfill them." Regarding the awareness of the past Prophets of His own coming to fulfill their work, Christ says, "Your father Abraham rejoiced that he was to see my day; he saw it and was glad."[33]

These and other similar statements Christ makes call to mind a number of important Bahá'í beliefs about the relationship among the Manifestations of God. For example, the Bahá'í writings affirm that the Manifestations are fully aware of each other and build upon each other's efforts. Each is cognizant of how His particular ministry takes up where the previous revelation left off. Each is likewise aware that the scope of His own revelation is limited by the capacity of His followers and that the next Manifestation will advance human understanding even further.

In effect, the Bahá'í writings discuss a principle of timeliness that applies not only to humankind as a whole but also to the growth and development of the individual. That is, one can learn only so much during a given period of time. So it is that Christ clearly indicates that another Manifestation will build upon the foundation He has laid: "I have yet many things to say to you, but you cannot bear them now. When the Spirit of truth comes, he will guide you into all the truth; for he will not speak on his own authority, but whatever he hears he will speak, and he will declare to you the things that are to come."[34]

Likewise, according to Bahá'í belief, the Prophets or Manifestations of God are immaculate in their character and infallible in Their utterance. These two conditions result from the fact that they are of another order of existence, even though They choose to take on a human persona while They live among us. Though They conceal the full scope of Their power, They perfectly manifest all the attributes of God in Their lives and speak solely what God inspires Them to utter.

As Christ often notes, He acts not on His own authority but relinquishes His own will to do the bidding of God: "The words that I say to you I do not speak on my own authority; but the Father who dwells in me does his works." Similarly He notes, "He who believes in me, believes not in me but in him who sent me." And in another instance He states, "For I have not spoken on my own authority; the Father who sent me has himself given me commandment what to say and what to speak. And I know that his commandment is eternal life. What I say, therefore, I say as the Father has bidden me."[35]

Christ makes another allusion to this continuous process of God at work in human history when He states that He existed before Abraham's appearance. Here He is alluding to another aspect of the extraordinary nature of the Prophets. They are not merely inspired, specialized, or chosen human beings. They are preexistent and are aware of their mission both before They become incarnate and after They ascend. Nowhere is this distinction in Their station made more lucid than in the following description by Shoghi Effendi of the power unleashed after Bahá'u'lláh's ascension:

[T]he dissolution of the tabernacle wherein the soul of the Manifestation of God had chosen temporarily to abide signalized its release from the restrictions which an earthly life had, of necessity, imposed upon it. Its influence no longer circumscribed by any physical limitations, its radiance no longer beclouded by its human temple, that soul could henceforth energize the whole world to a degree unapproached at any stage in the course of its existence on this plane.[36]

Likewise, explaining Christ's allusion to His own preexistence, Shoghi Effendi states plainly, "The Prophets, unlike us, are preexistent. The soul of Christ existed in the spiritual world before His birth in this world."[37]

The Bahá'í concept of the unity and continuity of prophecy deriving from the successive appearances of immaculate and di-

vinely empowered beings is the most vital and fundamental ingredient in any attempt to justify God's ways to humanity and to explain why a loving God would place His creation in a physical world.
Without such a concept no explanation of physical reality or of
God's justice can make complete or final sense. For if we accept the
notion that God has devised physical reality as a place of learning
and has further established that humankind cannot succeed without assistance, it would be ludicrous for God to deprive us of
sufficient guidance to accomplish that very task of spiritual transformation or for God to await some particular moment in history
to begin the process of human enlightenment or "salvation." Rather
it is logically essential that a just and loving God, like a loving parent, bestow that guidance from the beginning and never withhold
it or cease to expand it.

Of course, we cannot much blame Milton for believing that
Christ was God's sole revelator—he inherited this misinterpreta-
tion of religious history from over a thousand years of embedded
dogma. Most important, he, like most of Western Christendom,
was deprived of the illumination that Muḥammad's revelation shed
on this subject. One of the dominant themes of the Qur'án is the
articulation of the divine assistance that God has given to humankind through the succession of Prophets or Manifestations.

For example, in the sura of Houd, Muḥammad briefly recounts
the lives of the Prophets and then observes the pitiful irony of Their
rejection by those to whom God had sent Them as teachers and as
intermediaries between the spiritual and physical realms of reality:

> Moreover, to Moses gave we "the Book," and we raised up
> apostles after him; and to Jesus, son of Mary, gave we clear proofs
> *of his mission*, and strengthened him by the Holy Spirit. So oft
> then as an apostle cometh to you with that which your souls

desire not, swell ye with pride, and treat some as impostors, and slay others?[38]

But Muḥammad speaks most forcefully on the erroneous view that Christ is the only savior sent by God to humankind when He discusses what had become, by the time of Muḥammad's advent in the seventh century, the Christian doctrine of the trinity. Repeatedly in the Qur'án Muḥammad rebukes those who believe that Christ is God, that Christ is the Son of God in the flesh, or that Christ is of the same essence as God:

> Believe therefore in God and his apostles, and say not, "Three:" (there is a Trinity)—Forbear—it will be better for you. God is only one God! Far be it from His glory that He should have a son. . . .
> The Messiah disdaineth not to be a servant of God, nor do the angels who are nigh unto Him.[39]

The importance of the concept of progressive revelation to Bahá'í belief is partially demonstrated by the fact that, next to the Kitáb-i-Aqdas, the most important single work revealed by Bahá'u'lláh is the Kitáb-i-Íqán, an exquisitely organized and lucid exposition on this subject.* In the Kitáb-i-Íqán Bahá'u'lláh explains that all of the Manifestations are "sent down from the heaven of the Will of God, and as they all arise to proclaim His irresistible Faith, they therefore are regarded as one soul and the same person."[40]

---

* Shoghi Effendi states, "A model of Persian prose, of a style at once original, chaste and vigorous, and remarkably lucid, both cogent in argument and matchless in its irresistible eloquence, this Book setting forth in outline the Grand Redemptive Scheme of God, occupies a position unequaled by any work in the entire range of Bahá'í literature, except the Kitáb-i-Aqdas, Bahá'u'lláh's Most Holy Book" (*God Passes By*, pp. 138–39).

Still another noteworthy distinction between the implications
of Milton's theology and Bahá'í beliefs has to do with the interpretation of the Adamic myth. As 'Abdu'l-Bahá notes in *Some Answered
Questions* (122–26), many interpretations of the Edenic story are
possible, but indisputable from a Bahá'í point of view is the fact
that Adam was a Prophet of God, a Manifestation. In the Qur'án,
Muḥammad describes Adam as revealing the essentially spiritual
nature of the physical world. Although the Book of Genesis seems
to portray a literal man giving names to birds and beasts and "every
living creature," the Qur'án portrays Adam as a Prophet whose task
is to reveal to the phenomenal world the spiritual attributes (spiritual names) inherent in every created thing, a likely interpretation
of the mythical allusion in Genesis:

> They said, "Praise be to Thee! We have no knowledge but
> what Thou hast given us to know. Thou! Thou art the Knowing,
> the Wise."
> He said, "O Adam, inform them of their names." And when
> he had informed them of their names, He said, "Did I not say to
> you that I know the hidden things of the Heavens and of the
> Earth, and that I know what ye bring to light, and what ye hide?"[41]

Here Adam is not bestowing names; rather He "informs them" of
names they already possess. In so doing, He implies that the name
is not so much a literal appellation as it is a spiritual quality or
divine attribute, recalling for us our earlier examination of the doctrine Plato espoused. The Qur'ánic explanation is further suggested
in the Bahá'í writings, where use of the term *name* denotes spiritual
attributes (Bahá'u'lláh, *Gleanings*, pp. 22, 48, 65, 165) and the term
Kingdom of Names refers to physical reality (*Gleanings*, pp. 184,

195), a place where spiritual reality cannot be understood directly but is comprehended indirectly through physical dramatization or metaphorical expression:

> Inasmuch as He, the sovereign Lord of all, hath willed to reveal His sovereignty in the kingdom of names and attributes, each and every created thing hath, through the act of the Divine Will, been made a sign of His glory. So pervasive and general is this revelation that nothing whatsoever in the whole universe can be discovered that doth not reflect His splendor.[42]

In the Bahá'í writings the spiritual world is thus sometimes referred to as the "world of vision," as a reality in which the attributes no longer need be understood indirectly by being concealed in "names" (physical forms): "The Kingdom is the world of vision . . . , where all the concealed realities will become disclosed."[43]

The Bahá'í interpretation of the Adamic myth does not directly contravene anything Milton is attempting to say, but it does give a more ample explanation of why humankind is ordained to begin life in a physical environment. In Milton's interpretation the earthly home is partly punishment for Adam's transgression, but mostly, we come to understand, it is a means by which humankind will come to appreciate God's mercy and grandeur.

As we continue to examine the Bahá'í paradigm of physical reality, we will see that the Bahá'í writings portray the physical world and our experience in it as valuable in and of itself. Now that we have explored the basic problem of theodicy and the Bahá'í response to some of the major questions raised by previous attempts to discern God's justice, we are ready to assemble a model, or paradigm, of physical creation as revealed in the Bahá'í scriptures.

4

THE KINGDOM OF NAMES:
A BAHÁ'Í PARADIGM
OF PHYSICAL REALITY

The world, indeed each existing being, proclaims to us one of the names of God, but the reality of man is the collective reality, the general reality, and is the center where the glory of all the perfections of God shine forth—that is to say, for each name, each attribute, each perfection which we affirm of God there exists a sign in man.
—'Abdu'l-Bahá

Having examined the Bahá'í response to some of the major questions that arise out of traditional attempts to discover divine justice at work in physical reality, we may now have some sense of how the Bahá'í Faith explains and justifies the spiritual purposes of the physical world. But before we can further explain this understanding of how physical experience is divinely ordained and, more important, how it induces spiritual development, let us first examine more fully Bahá'í beliefs about the nature of physical reality. By assembling in logical order the essential ingredients of the Bahá'í paradigm of

physical reality, we can better appreciate why the Creator has devised physical existence as the initial stage of development for what
Bahá'ís believe to be essentially spiritual beings—human souls.

THE CREATOR

The Bahá'í paradigm of physical reality logically begins with the
concept of God as Creator. Because God is "immensely exalted
beyond every human attribute" and "will remain in His Reality
everlastingly hidden from the sight of men," we are, especially in
our physical lives, limited in what we can understand about the
Creator.[1]

Our most important information about God comes through the
Manifestations, each of Whom perfectly manifests all the attributes
of God, and through our experience with physical reality, the en-
tirety of which bears the imprint of the Creator. As perfect reflections of the qualities of the Creator, the Manifestations can be correctly understood to be flawless, dramatic expressions of godliness
expressed in human terms. Or put more simply, the Prophets of
God represent the most complete and exalted expression of God
we are able to comprehend during our physical existence. In this
sense, the Manifestations are more than mere messengers or intermediaries between God and humankind—They are perfect reflections of God to the extent that godliness can be translated into a
physical analog or material expression.

As we have already observed, every created thing in physical reality is expressive of divine attributes. Furthermore, the Bahá'í writings testify that each of us is created with an inherent love of reality
and an inborn desire to study and comprehend reality. Conse-

quently, once we understand the fundamental nature of what we are trying to discover (spiritual qualities expressed in physical terms), we can achieve an ever more complete understanding of God as we study the various branches of science.

Although our understanding of the Deity will always be limited, whether in this world or the next, the Bahá'í writings do provide a number of noteworthy observations that enhance our understanding of the essential nature of God. For example, the Bahá'í texts make it clear that the word "God" is not simply a term devised to give human expression to the sum total of universal forces and attributes. For while we can only comprehend the Creator in somewhat anthropomorphic terms, God is not a mythical invention. Indeed, the Bahá'í concept of the Deity envisions a Being Who is independent of His creation, but cognitive, caring, and concerned for His creation and its progress. Furthermore, as a loving Being, God has created humankind in such a way that we are capable becoming attracted to the divine attributes of God through His Manifestations, then gradually coming to attain an ever more complete understanding of the nature of these attributes as we manifest our knowledge in various forms of creative action.

This concept of human nature is essential to any attempt to comprehend the Bahá'í paradigm of the structure of reality. God creates us out of an expression of love, not need or loneliness. Therefore, as divine emanations from God, we are created with the capacity to understand godliness, but we are created with free will as to whether or not we choose to become godly ourselves.

In this sense, all human beings *potentially* manifest all the attributes of God: "Veiled in My immemorial being and in the ancient eternity of My essence, I knew My love for thee; therefore I created thee, have engraved on thee Mine image and revealed to thee My beauty."[2] As we have noted, everyone is invested with this potentiality because every individual has both the capacity and the opportunity to recognize the Creator through some means.

The most obvious access for knowledge about God is through the advent of the Prophets of God as each reveals teachings for a new age. The more subtle avenue for human understanding is in our relationship with physical reality itself, wherein the "names" and attributes of God are likewise manifest. Thus Bahá'u'lláh observes that while people are endowed with different capacities, God "hath endowed every soul with the capacity to recognize the signs of God."[3]

Once we attain knowledge of God through whatever means, we are then capable of establishing a personal relationship with the Creator through the various methods described by each of the Manifestations: prayer, reflection, study of reality, study of the revealed utterances of the Prophets, and so on. When we open up the channels of communication and receptivity by whatever means, we set in motion the process we discussed earlier about the reciprocal relationship between knowledge and action. We attempt to acquire the attributes as we understand them by giving them dramatic expression in our daily lives, and that action in turn deepens our comprehension of the divine attributes.

This personal relationship between God and human beings functions on both a personal and a collective level. Each Manifestation prescribes a daily regimen of personal spiritual activity and also institutes methods by which the community of believers can work together, both to form bonds with each other and to devise means of providing the community as a whole with both spiritual and material sustenance. So it is that the more we as individuals and as a community of believers study and emulate the qualities of the Creator, the more we understand the divine attributes of God. This enhanced understanding empowers us to employ more innovative patterns of action that express our knowledge of God. At the heart of this creative process of growth and development is an intriguing axiom that might at first seem abstruse and enigmatic: To know God is to know ourselves, and to know ourselves is to know God. Bahá'u'lláh writes,

> How resplendent the luminaries of knowledge that shine in an atom, and how vast the oceans of wisdom that surge within a drop! To a supreme degree is this true of man, who, among all created things, hath been invested with the robe of such gifts, and hath been singled out for the glory of such distinction. For in him are potentially revealed all the attributes and names of God to a degree that no other created being hath excelled or surpassed. All these names and attributes are applicable to him. Even as He hath said: "Man is My mystery, and I am his mystery."[4]

In the context of this simple but infinitely complex method of human instruction these teachers, the Manifestations of God, might be likened to perfect mirrors reflecting the attributes of the divine reality that is the essence of God. For to study and understand Them and Their teachings is tantamount to knowledge of and proximity to God:

> Were any of the all-embracing Manifestations of God to declare: "I am God!" He verily speaketh the truth, and no doubt attacheth thereto. For it hath been repeatedly demonstrated that through their Revelations, their attributes and names, the Revelation of God, His name and His attributes, are made manifest in the world.[5]

PHYSICAL CREATION
AS DIVINE EMANATION

The next ingredient in describing the Bahá'í paradigm of physical reality is creation itself. Here we need to recognize three major Bahá'í principles: Physical creation has always existed; physical creation is in a continual state of evolutionary change; and physical creation is an "outer" or metaphorical expression of metaphysical reality.

The first principle—that physical creation has no beginning—is controversial in light of the seemingly ceaseless debates between so-called evolutionists and creationists. This principle also seems to contradict the assertion of some cosmologists regarding the "Big Bang" as the beginning of time and the universe. The Bahá'í point of view regarding the eternality of physical existence is relatively simple. Stated plainly, the Bahá'í teachings uphold a view that logically synthesizes elements of both views, even as reality itself does. The Bahá'í writings affirm that since God has always existed, and since God is a Creator, then it follows that God has always been creating. In other words, we cannot conceive of a point in time when the Creator did not have such a desire, nor can we conceive of a Creator without a creation:

> The Creator always had a creation; the rays have always shone and gleamed from the reality of the sun, for without the rays the sun would be opaque darkness. The names and attributes of God require the existence of beings, and the Eternal Bounty does not cease. If it were to, it would be contrary to the perfections of God.[6]

As another proof of the eternality of creation, 'Abdu'l-Bahá notes that absolute existence cannot come from absolute nonexistence. Therefore physical reality has always existed in some form or another. This does not mean that the "Big Bang" theorists are wrong—that the part of the universe we can observe is not expanding. Rather the Bahá'í theory does imply that creation preceded this event and that, given an infinite universe, there may be other parts of the universe where this same process is also occurring or has occurred. In effect, from the timeless perspective of the Creator, the universe may seem like a festival of fireworks with "big bangs" going off all over the place. But regardless of what the final vision of reality ultimately will be regarding universal systems, the essential purpose of the Creator has been and always will be the same: to create a being capable of knowing or understanding the Creator—what we call a human being. Therefore it also follows that "human beings" have always existed in the created universe and always will.

We know from scientific evidence, as well as from what we can glean from religious and cultural myths such as the story of creation recounted in Genesis, that particular "worlds" (planets, solar systems, and galaxies) do have a beginning and do pass through myriad stages of evolutionary growth and development. In this sense there is, from our perspective on this planet, a beginning—a creation. And certainly we know that human beings as we presently exist did not occupy this planet from its inception—gradually we came into being and evolved to our present physical appearance and capacity.

But in creation as a whole, there have necessarily always existed planets occupied by human beings, even if we are inclined to accept some present cosmological theories that space, time, and creation itself occurred about sixteen billion years ago. But certainly during those sixteen billion years planets other than our own have had the chance to have an occurrence similar to our own, unless we really do accept the theory that the evolution of human beings on planet earth is the single propitious accident in all of creation,

thereby repeatedly violating the law of probability beyond calcula-
tion to such an extent that it would be more accurate scientifically
to call our present condition a "plan" rather than a freak accident.

But whatever in the long run turns out to be an accurate description of the universe—or the portion of it we happen to be capable of
studying right now—it is clear that our own planet has gone through
dynamic change. This brings us to the second major Bahá'í principle
regarding physical reality. According to the Bahá'í description of reality, the inherent and appropriate condition of physical reality and
spiritual reality is a state of constant and unremitting change.

All physical compositions are always coming into being or going
out of being because composite realities are inherently imperma-
nent arrangements. Therefore, when we talk of creation on earth,
we are talking about the way in which matter combined over time
to assume certain properties. What is more, because the natural
course of events for our planet should have been deterioration in
order (entropy), one can only adduce that some as yet undiscov-
ered or "outside" influence ("divine" or "metaphysical"?) caused a
constant and progressive increase in order.

In this connection 'Abdu'l-Bahá explains, "Therefore, as the Essence of Unity (that is, the existence of God) is everlasting and
eternal—it is certain that this world of existence, this endless universe, has neither beginning nor end. Yet, it may be that one of the
parts of the universe, one of the globes, for example, may come
into existence, or may be disintegrated, but the other globes are still
existing; the universe would not be disordered nor destroyed." He
goes on to observe that the planet Earth, like every other physical
composition, "must of necessity be decomposed" after it has
achieved its fruition and fulfilled its inherent and, according to the
Bahá'í paradigm, its divinely ordained purpose.

That purpose may be likened to the purpose of all other organic
entities in physical reality—gradually to reflect in successively greater

degrees spiritual properties expressed or manifested in terms of social constructs. Christ alludes to this purpose as the Kingdom of God appearing on earth, and Bahá'u'lláh refers to it as carrying forward "an ever-advancing civilization."[7]

In a significant and related explanation of universal structure 'Abdu'l-Bahá explains that minuscule particulate entities resemble in both structure and function universal expressions of the same organization, "for both are subjected to one natural system, one universal law and divine organization. So you will find the smallest atoms in the universal system are similar to the greatest beings of the universe. It is clear that they come into existence from one laboratory of might under one natural system and one universal law; therefore, they may be compared to one another."[8]

We can observe, therefore, a similarity between the evolutionary growth of a seed into a flourishing plant and the development of a human being from conception to maturity, or between the evolving physical aspect of humankind as a whole on the planet and the social, physical, and spiritual evolution of human society over time. The parallels are endless, but one of the most illuminating examples is 'Abdu'l-Bahá's comparison of the evolution of our planet to a seed growing in the matrix of the universe:

> In the same manner, it is evident that this terrestrial globe, having once found existence, grew and developed in the matrix of the universe, and came forth in different forms and conditions, until gradually it attained this present perfection, and became adorned with innumerable beings, and appeared as a finished organization.[9]

There are, of course, milestones in the process of evolution, whether we are examining the geological changes of the earth, the religious history of humankind, or our own individual progress.

Furthermore, to understand this process, we find it is useful to describe these stages of growth with certain appellations. For example, we speak of times of beginning and ending not as absolutes but as points of crucial change in relation to other events. So it was that some ancient peoples used the Adamic myth as a symbol of a milestone in the evolving of human awareness about concepts of morality.

But when exponents of religious belief interpret symbolic or mythological stories about creation as literal depictions of history, they fail to appreciate the fundamental nature of cultural myths, especially in religious scripture, which is by nature inevitably replete with metaphors, symbols, allegories, and parables.

This same observation is equally important with regard to biblical and Qur'ánic allusions to the "Day of Resurrection," the "time of the end," or the "Last Judgment." Instead of referring to the destruction of physical reality or even to the termination of our planet, these phrases most often refer to particular points of transition in the evolution of human society—the end of one phase of growth and the beginning of another, even as our birth is end of our life of gestation in the womb, and our adolescence could be considered the termination of our childhood and the beginning of the assumption of our responsibilities as adults.

The Bahá'í writings, therefore, offer the evolutionists and creationists a new definition of "creation" as it regards the origins of life on this planet and as it pertains to the continuity of the universe as a whole. Physical things have a beginning: Matter assumes a certain arrangement or combination to form the human organism, or to fashion geological structures, or to form our planet, the solar system, or the infinite galaxies that populate the universe. But creation as a whole is eternal, even if we eventually discover various points of critical change and transformation in portions of an infinite system.

The third major principle of the Bahá'í view about physical reality is that the whole of creation is an emanation from the Creator.
That is, even as rays of light emanate from the sun, so physical
reality emanates from the will of the Creator. Again, this proposition does not imply that God is dependent on physical reality for
His existence, and yet neither does this concept imply that creation
is an arbitrary or mechanical act. The Creator does not require our
success for His own well-being; rather, the reverse is true:

> The sun in its own essence is independent of the bodies which it
> lights, for its light is in itself and is free and independent of the
> terrestrial globe; so the earth is under the influence of the sun
> and receives its light, whereas the sun and its rays are entirely
> independent of the earth. But if there were no sun, the earth and
> all earthly beings could not exist.[10]

As we have already noted, an integral part of this concept of the
physical creation as an emanation from God is the idea that the animating purpose of physical creation is to manifest spiritual attributes
so that human beings might discern signs of God. This relationship of
the physical world to the spiritual world is summarized succinctly in a
Hidden Word that states: "Out of the wastes of nothingness, with the
clay of My command I made thee to appear, and have ordained for thy
training every atom in existence and the essence of all created things."[11]

Because the physical world is a reflection of the unseen spiritual
realm, we might consider it to be less in degree or spirituality. Indeed, the primacy of the spiritual world in this relationship seems
clear in a passage where 'Abdu'l-Bahá reverses our usual reference to
physical reality as the "real world" when he observes that the spiritual realm "is the real world, and this nether place is only its shadow
stretching out. A shadow hath no life of its own; its existence is

only a fantasy, and nothing more; it is but images reflected in water, and seeming as pictures to the eye."[12]

And yet we do a great disservice to physical reality if, like Boethius, we disdain it as a crass and unworthy creation. As we will discover later in our examination of the Bahá'í approach to the problem of theodicy, physical reality has a benign purpose and is as much a part of God's creation as are the spiritual or metaphysical worlds.

A most revealing passage in the Bahá'í writings makes it quite clear that physical reality is not a debased version of spiritual reality. Instead, what we term "physical reality" and "metaphysical reality" are actually aspects of a single organic, integrated reality: "The spiritual world is like unto the phenomenal world. They are the *exact counterpart* of each other. Whatever objects appear in this world of existence are the outer pictures of the world of heaven."[13]

THE FRUIT OF CREATION

Considering the organic nature of the created universe as an expression of the spiritual world, we might think it erroneous to distinguish one part of the physical world as having primacy over the other parts since the whole of creation, as the Bahá'í writings depict it, is an organic construct unified by the same animating purpose—the reflection of spiritual principles. But another critical ingredient in the Bahá'í paradigm of physical creation is the belief that the spiritual education of humankind is the essential objective or end product of this divinely created and empowered mechanism.

'Abdu'l-Bahá explains the primacy of humankind in the world of creation with several succinct and useful metaphors: "If there were no man, the perfections of the spirit would not appear, and the light of the mind would not be resplendent in this world. This world would be like a body without a soul. This world is also in the condition of a fruit tree, and man is like the fruit; without the fruit the tree would be useless."[14]

However, we misunderstand this exalted station of humankind if we conclude that we are superior to the rest of creation, that the rest of creation is merely our support system, our consumables, our source of enjoyment and entertainment. Employing 'Abdu'l-Bahá's analogy, we might accurately observe that the fruit could hardly view the tree that produced its existence as insignificant, nor could the fruit consider itself superior to or independent of the tree. While creation may culminate in our existence, we are still an integral part of that creation and should, consequently, respect every created thing as both an expression of divinity and as a means by which we can learn something about the reality it is capable of disclosing to us if we are attentive.

THE SPECIAL STATION OF HUMANKIND

While we have dealt with the issue earlier in our discussion, it would be useful here to rehearse the specific reasons why humankind has such an exalted place in the physical world. First, while all creation reflects the attributes of the Creator, only we are capable of reflecting *all* of the attributes in reality. Second, only we are endowed with the capacity to comprehend our relationship with God, to appreciate the significance of that relationship, and to decide whether or not we will fulfill our potential by incorporating divine attributes into action, thereby willfully participating in the transformation of our own character.

But what gives us the capacity to reflect those attributes? What enables us to do what animals and the rest of physical creation cannot? Is it language—our capacity to articulate these abstract concepts? Is it our ability to have those abstract thoughts that we are expressing with language? Or could it be the power of will wherewith we can determine how we will employ these superior powers of rational thought and abstract conception?

From the Bahá'í perspective, what distinguishes us from the rest of creation is the essence of our reality—the human soul. According to Bahá'í belief, the human soul is an essentially spiritual creation that emanates from God at our conception. Furthermore, it is the soul that is the cause and source of all these other powers—the capacity for rational thought, abstract conception, willpower, memory, and all other faculties and capacities that we recognize as fundamentally "human" powers. In particular, it is the soul that is the source of "self," our sense of identity or personhood, our consciousness of our own reality. Bahá'u'lláh writes,

> Know, verily, that the soul is a sign of God, a heavenly gem whose reality the most learned of men hath failed to grasp, and whose mystery no mind, however acute, can ever hope to unravel. It is the first among all created things to declare the excellence of its Creator, the first to recognize His glory, to cleave to His truth, and to bow down in adoration before Him.[15]

Because the soul is a spiritual essence, we are extremely limited in what we can know about how it functions or what it is, but we do know that this essence, animated by the Holy Spirit, is the source of all we are as individuals. We further know that alone among all created things, the human soul has a beginning but no end. The soul takes its beginning when it associates with the body at conception, and it endures eternally beyond this associative relationship.

The soul is thus not *in* the body nor dependent on the body for its existence, but so long as the body remains a fit vehicle for this associative relationship, we are constrained to understand and perceive reality largely through the intermediary of the body's faculties, which are controlled by the magnificent organ that is the brain. The logical extension of this belief is that because the brain is an intermediary between the soul and the physical world, the demise of the body and brain do not adversely affect the soul or its powers—such as rational thought, will, consciousness of self, personality, memory, emotion and so on—that emanate from it. This conclusion is confirmed in the Bahá'í writings. In effect, at death we are born into the afterlife with all the awareness and mental or spiritual capacity with which we end our experience in physical reality. After all, if the soul is a spiritual essence, it has been dwelling in the metaphysical realm all along— but this reality is purposefully veiled from human awareness so long as the associative relationship endures.

Later in our discussion we will consider precisely how such an arrangement facilitates our spiritual education, but Bahá'u'lláh entices us to ponder this enigmatic relationship with the following verse which asserts that the concealing or veiling of spiritual reality from our consciousness while we exist in an associative relationship with physical reality is a purposeful arrangement for our benefit. Were we aware of the nature of what awaits us, we would not be able to refrain from escaping from the bonds of this physical relationship and we would thus forego the benefits to be derived from this foundational period of development: "Didst thou behold immortal sovereignty, thou wouldst strive to pass from this fleeting world. But to conceal the one from thee and to reveal the other is a mystery which none but the pure in heart can comprehend."[16]

Another fundamental verity about humankind as the fruit of physical creation is the Bahá'í concept of evolution. According to the Bahá'í writings the human being has not evolved from other lower forms of life. Certainly the human physical form has evolved, even as the human embryo may at first appear to be some lesser form of being. Furthermore, someone inexperienced in embryology might, upon examining a human fetus, speculate that this incipient form might become various forms of life—a cat or a puppy. But clearly only the human embryo will, upon reaching fruition, become a human being. By the same token, the Bahá'í teachings affirm that while the human species may at one time in its evolution have appeared to be similar in form to other species, the human species has always been a distinct creation, always uniquely and inherently destined to evolve into the mature human reality:

> The beginning of the existence of man on the terrestrial globe resembles his formation in the womb of the mother. The embryo in the womb of the mother gradually grows and develops until birth, after which it continues to grow and develop until it reaches the age of discretion and maturity. Though in infancy the signs of the mind and spirit appear in man, they do not reach the degree of perfection; they are imperfect. Only when man attains maturity do the mind and the spirit appear and become evident in utmost perfection.[17]

The fact that science seems to have discovered that the human species did not evolve until after other species came into existence on the planet does not mean that we evolved from those previous specious. If we are the "fruit" of this evolving "tree," then naturally we will not appear until everything else is in place—until the "tree" has achieved sufficient maturity that it can bring forth fruit.

But there is a larger implication to this thesis. This observation about humans being the focal point of creation—the student in this divinely arranged classroom—applies not solely to the single planet on which we find ourselves, however lovely in design and propitious in location planet Earth may seem to be. The Bahá'í writings speak of this premise in universal terms. If physical creation is an expression of the will of God and thus has always existed, and if humankind is the perfection or fruit of that creation, then human beings have always existed somewhere in the physical universe. 'Abdu'l-Bahá asserts that inasmuch as "the universe has no imperfection," and since man is the "chief member" of the body of the universe, there has never been a time when man did not exist:

> We consider man . . . the sum of all existing perfections. When we speak of man, we mean the perfect one, the foremost individual in the world, who is the sum of spiritual and apparent perfections, and who is like the sun among the beings. Then imagine that at one time the sun did not exist, but that it was a planet; surely at such a time the relations of existence would be disordered. How can such a thing be imagined?[18]

Finally, as we will discuss later in more detail, we observe in the Bahá'í writings that each individual has a special part to play in the process of fulfilling human potential. Bahá'u'lláh states that the "perfection" which enables us to reflect all the attributes of God is only a perfection of capacity until we freely choose to make that potentiality a reality. In humankind "are *potentially* revealed all the attributes and names of God to a degree that no other created being hath excelled or surpassed."[19] For that potentiality to become a reality, other ingredients, both internal and external to man, must be added.

SALVATION AS MOTION

If humankind is the fruit of physical creation, the next component in our model of physical reality would logically be whatever
constitutes human fulfillment—in truth, what defines or distinguishes us as human beings. According to most religions the appropriate goal of human endeavors in physical life is the attainment of
"salvation."

What constitutes salvation varies from religion to religion, but
the most commonly held belief is the concept of a precise division
between those who in their physical lives achieve a sufficient degree
of spiritual advancement that they are eternally secure in the station or progress of their souls. In the more traditional Western and
Judeo-Christian paradigms, those who achieve this state—whether
through faith, deeds, or grace—go to heaven and those who do not
go to hell.

The variations in this paradigm are many, and it is not important to rehearse them here. But we should note several major distinctions. According to some systems of belief, salvation does not
result from individual willful action. In Calvinism, for example,
the "saved" or the "elect" are chosen from the beginning. According
to the majority of Protestant religions, which derive their ideological orientations from the Pauline letters that constituted the basis
for Luther's rebellion against the Catholic Church and instigated
the Reformation, salvation is predicated on "faith." But what constitutes faith?

According to most Christian belief systems, "faith" is ambiguously
defined, but it most often alludes to personal confidence, assurance,
or conviction in the atonement for our sins provided by Christ's martyrdom—a statement of belief that fairly well defies logical explica-

tion. Other Christian beliefs incorporate some sort of action as a requisite for salvation, even though that action may be some form of ritualistic confession or penance prescribed by clergy.

The Jewish religion has no specific concept of salvation, partly because most Jewish belief systems have no precise belief in the afterlife. In this sense, the Jewish religion is heavily based on traditional observances and an existential relationship with the Deity, rather than an obsessive concern with some single point of spiritual transformation or "salvation." We might thus accurately describe Judaism as more humanistic in its orientation than most Christian religions.

There is no less variety in the way that various Muslim sects interpret the portrait of the afterlife set forth in the Qur'án. There are some very literal interpretations about the relationship between action and salvation—some believing that specific acts, like martyrdom, effect immediate salvation, as opposed to some lengthy afterlife process akin to the Catholic notion of Purgatory. Furthermore, some fundamentalist Muslim beliefs often incorporate a vision of the afterlife as a physical place with physical and sensual rewards.

On the other hand, there are quite as many Muslims who view the afterlife as the continuation of the soul in a spiritual environment. Similarly, many likewise believe that one's station in that afterlife is dependent on one's attainment of spiritual attributes in physical reality.

But regardless of the extent to which other religions or religious philosophies posit a belief in the afterlife or the relationship between what we do here and what we experience there, the Bahá'í concept of salvation is substantially different from that of Jews, Christians, and Muslims—or at least from how these concepts are most often professed or articulated. To begin with, the Bahá'í writings affirm that human spiritual progress is not confined to the physical world. Progress in the "Kingdom of Names" (physical reality) is distinct in several ways from progress in the spiritual realm, but in either world there is no final point of attainment, no point of division between success and failure. The life of the human soul is an eternal and progressive process of growth and development.

Put another way, the Bahá'í teachings assert that all human progress or spiritual transformation is relative. What might be an exalted spiritual advancement for one soul might be regressive for another. For example, for someone who has lived a life of depraved indifference to spiritual development, a single sequence of consciously chosen altruistic acts might require immense willpower and might thus be considered an incredible breakthrough—a milestone in spiritual development and the foundation for future ascent. But for someone who has spent a life dedicated to assisting humanity and who has attended to spiritual development on a daily basis, the same action by itself might be so negligible as to constitute a regression in spiritual behavior if not coupled with a panoply of other equally righteous deeds.

Stated in this simplest of analogies, such a concept of relative development would consider it a wondrous accomplish for an alcoholic not to drink for a week, or a month, or a year. But for someone who does not drink at all, this same achievement would signify no accomplishment at all. In short, we are in competition with no one—our progress is predicated only on how well we do with the capacities we have been given and the context within which we live. Each of us advances in relation to a myriad influences, opportunities, and obstacles. A valid assessment of the spiritual achievement of any individual, even of ourselves, is thus concealed from us so long as we exist in this veiled reality.

Furthermore, since the Bahá'í beliefs contend that our awareness, our individuality, and our willful development continue in the spiritual realm from whatever point we leave off in the physical world, there is no point at which the spiritual evolution of the human soul is complete or finished.

Certainly there are a myriad important stages of attainment. For example, equivalent to the Protestant concept of having "faith" is the Baháʾí concept of attaining "certitude" or conviction. This achievement does not mean that when we "enter that city" (to use Baháʾuʾlláhʾs own metaphor for this process), we have passed beyond testing or doubt.[20] But to possess certitude or conviction does imply that we are convinced our beliefs are valid because we have tested them and found them intellectually sound, spiritually rewarding, and practically useful.

One extremely important part of this concept of salvation as motion, whether in this life or in the next, is the Baháʾí belief that however much we progress or advance, we will never exhaust the possibilities of further growth even though we will ever remain a human soul:

> Both before and after putting off this material form, there is progress in perfection but not in state. So beings are consummated in perfect man. There is no other being higher than a perfect man. But man when he has reached this state can still make progress in perfections but not in state because there is no state higher than that of a perfect man to which he can transfer himself. He only progresses in the state of humanity, for the human perfections are infinite.[21]

This is a subtle but extremely important concept, because it responds directly to the idea of salvation as a single point of attainment. In other words, if the human soul is capable of infinite progress, then it need not (indeed cannot) become something else—a Manifestation, for example.

Another significant implication of this concept of salvation as motion is that such a view implies that our physical experience is not the focal point of our existence. Physical experience is the beginning of an endless educational process. It is an important beginning, even as the period of gestation in the womb greatly affects a child's further development after birth. But it is clear in the Bahá'í writings that progress is integral to our existence in the afterlife and that advancement in the afterlife is available even for those who have failed to utilize properly the opportunities afforded them for spiritual development in physical reality:

> Are not all the people in that world the creatures of God? Therefore, in that world also they can make progress. As here they can receive light by their supplications, there also they can plead for forgiveness and receive light through entreaties and supplications. Thus as souls in this world, through the help of the supplications, the entreaties and the prayers of the holy ones, can acquire development, so is it the same after death. Through *their own prayers and supplications* they can also progress, more especially when they are the object of the intercession of the Holy Manifestations.[22]

Doubtless the method of learning and advancing changes as we progress from a physical environment to a purely spiritual environment—we cannot expect to improve ourselves by helping elderly ladies across the street. At the same time, we can imagine that we will still be capable of important action. For example, we have no trouble observing diverse methodologies for progress when we compare the education of an infant to the education of a postdoctoral student of nuclear physics. Observed out of context, we might conclude that these two methodologies had nothing to do with one another. Similarly, while we tend to think of action, particularly spiritually motivated action, as having some physical component, we can also imagine how a quadriplegic could progress through vast stages of intellectual and spiritual development without ever leaving the confines of a bed. Certainly action need not be physical to have a significant impact on our selves or on others.

HEAVEN: BE CAREFUL WHAT YOU WISH FOR

To some, the Bahá'í concept of salvation as motion might seem logical and refreshing, offering as it does an eternity of challenges and growth rather than a single leap of faith followed by the prospect of dwelling endlessly in a condition of celestial stasis. Furthermore, where most religions portray our experience in physical reality as the "real world" and the afterlife experience as but a reflection of how we did, the Bahá'í teachings completely reverse this perspective, stating that this life is merely preparation for a more expansive, more enlightening, and more delightful experience.

It is absolutely crucial to understand, however, that this idea of continuous growth and change and challenge does not imply being doomed like Sisyphus to the eternal frustration of pursuing an unattainable goal, of never being finished or finally satisfied. As we have mentioned, the Bahá'í concept of salvation portrays motion itself as the objective, a motion that is existentially rewarding even while offering the promise of endless advancement and infinitely increasing delight—the profound joy of ever renewed vistas of learning and understanding coupled with the subjective experience of becoming ever more refined in our personal reflection of godliness.

Human satisfaction or fulfillment does not, therefore, await some future point of achievement any more than gaining knowledge awaits a finished point of understanding before learning becomes exciting and enjoyable. The process of learning is enjoyable in and of itself, and our learning is always in a relative condition of progress. The initial stages of learning ("the learning curve" as it is sometimes called) may be steep and difficult—not unlike Plato's description of the initially grueling ascent from the cave of ignorance—but once we are in motion, the rewards are immediate and endless.

From such a perspective, life in heaven as it is often portrayed by the teachings of some religions—a physical place of stasis, comfort, and ease (and absolutely nothing useful to do)—would seem to be an experience quickly doomed to utter boredom. In this sense, the heaven so often heralded as the ultimate goal of every human being by various religious systems of belief is not unlike the bewildering disappointment many retirees experience when they enter the long-awaited "golden years" and find themselves aimless, bored, and lost. For most of us, perhaps, a more appealing heavenly condition would involve an endless progression of fulfillment and enlightenment and an infinite array of things to do, only without an aging body to drag around as we attempt to do them.

But in the last two chapters we will deal more explicitly with what the Bahá'í paradigm of reality can reveal about the nature of our experience in the afterlife. Before we hasten to that heavenly vision, however, let us first deal more explicitly with the method by which we employ physical exercises to get there. More particularly, let us discuss the Bahá'í theory of spiritual progress as a fundamentally autonomous exercise, a matter of applied choice. Afterwards, we can discuss the nuts-and-bolts application of that theory in a user's guide to this metaphorical classroom the Creator has devised for our initial and foundational education.

5

AUTONOMY AND WILL: FUNDAMENTAL REQUISITES FOR A SPIRITUAL EDUCATION

All blessings are divine in origin but none can be compared with this power of intellectual investigation and research which is an eternal gift producing fruits of unending delight. Man is ever partaking of these fruits. All other blessings are temporary; this is an everlasting possession. Even sovereignty has its limitations and overthrow; this is a kingship and dominion which none may usurp or destroy. Briefly; it is an eternal blessing and divine bestowal, the supreme gift of God to man.

—'Abdu'l-Bahá

The implications of the Bahá'í concept of human justice—salvation as endless motion—are extremely important to all other parts of the Bahá'í paradigm of physical reality and its purposes. For example, education in such a context cannot be based solely on fostering a single pattern of behavior to befit the condition of every individual, since every individual is distinct and dwells in a unique set of circumstances. Neither can such an educational system or methodology meet the requirements of this objective if it merely imbues us with a body of facts.

Were fixed or changeless goals the Creator's objective in creating us, then we could have been created already finished, perfected, and refined. But even as Milton portrays the spiritualization of human beings as a process, so the Bahá'í writings define our objective as independently recognizing our essentially divine origin and nature, then willfully choosing a course of action that will set us in motion, and, finally, constantly monitoring ourselves on a daily basis to ensure our continued progress.

Such an objective requires an educational system capable of ministering to us both individually and collectively, whatever our condition of knowledge or progress may be. This educational system must be infinitely flexible to minister to the requirements of constantly changing individuals. What was a just, appropriate, and fulfilling lesson for us yesterday may be unjust or inadequate for us today. By comparison, the just or appropriate rules for a five-year-old child would be unduly restrictive and inappropriate for a fifteen-year-old youth.

The same principle of a progressive and flexible educational methodology applies equally well to the institutions that minister to the needs of society as a whole, since human society, like the individuals who comprise it, is an "ever-advancing" organism that is constantly evolving in nature. Therefore, institutions whose function is to instigate and nurture the collective progress of human society must themselves be capable of growth and adaptability.

Obviously this criterion applies to our school systems, but it applies equally well to religion. In this context 'Abdu'l-Bahá notes that religion must respond to the changing exigencies of the human condition: "Religion is the outer expression of the divine reality. Therefore, it must be living, vitalized, moving and progressive.

If it be without motion and nonprogressive, it is without the divine life; it is dead. The divine institutes are continuously active and evolutionary; therefore, the revelation of them must be progressive and continuous."[1]

AUTONOMY AS A PREREQUISITE FOR SPIRITUAL DEVELOPMENT

Since motion toward perfection is the Bahá'í definition of salvation and fulfillment in both the physical and the spiritual worlds, we need to consider how that motion is achieved and sustained from without and from within. But first we need to acknowledge an essential attribute of that motion and a major ingredient in the Bahá'í paradigm of physical reality—the autonomy of human advancement.

On the simplest level we can understand autonomy by again using the example of training a child. A youth may be trained to exhibit manners, kindness, and moral behavior in all its manifestations. Certainly all parents yearn to have their progeny exhibit these attributes. But the important progress of the young soul is taking place when that motion toward human perfection becomes freely chosen, self-sustained, and autonomous.

This objective does not mean that teaching a child to mimic proper behavior is in any way wrong. One of the surest ways for us to become noble is to pretend we are and act accordingly. But this objective does imply that human justice or salvation must ultimately derive from each individual's conscious striving and willful persistence. We may be able to impose some types of moral behavior on others, but we cannot coerce someone else to *be* moral. By the same token, our own spirituality cannot be accomplished or provided for us, because, Bahá'u'lláh states, "the faith of no man can be conditioned by any one except himself."[2]

This autonomy of human ascent is the just and proper condition of the human being. It is, perhaps, precisely what Bahá'u'lláh means when He defines the attribute of justice within the individual as acquiring the capacity to "see with thine own eyes and not through the eyes of others" and to "know of thine own knowledge and not through the knowledge of thy neighbor."[3] In other words, without autonomy of progress or willful striving for forward motion, we may confuse brainwashing with conviction, blind imitation with authentic faith and belief.

To protect humanity from such mistaken attitudes about human enlightenment and education, Bahá'u'lláh ensured that each person who becomes a Bahá'í must do so by his or her own choice—one cannot inherit the Bahá'í Faith. Likewise, proselytizing is prohibited by Bahá'u'lláh—Bahá'ís are admonished not to "contend with any one" about matters of religion. In this way, if someone chooses to respond to the Bahá'í teachings, "he will have responded to his own behoof." 'Abdu'l-Bahá reiterates this principle when he writes, "Do not argue with anyone, and be wary of disputation. Speak out the truth. If your hearer accepteth, the aim is achieved."[4]

But deterrents to autonomous motion are not always externally caused, not always involuntary. Equally detrimental to independence of thought is the temptation and pressure of peers to imitate others. When we fall prey to this pervasive influence, we effectively relegate our own free choices to the opinions or decisions of others, thereby abandoning the most precious of all responsibilities, the obligation to determine for ourselves what path to follow.

So it is that the Bahá'í writings denounce imitation as the antithesis of justice and as the source of human degradation. In the Kitáb-i-Íqán Bahá'u'lláh describes imitation as one of the most persistent and pernicious evils afflicting religion: "Consider how men for generations have been blindly imitating their fathers, and have been trained according to such ways and manners as have been laid down by the dictates of their Faith." 'Abdu'l-Bahá goes so far as to cite imitation as a cause of the decline of religion itself: "Imitation destroys the foundation of religion, extinguishes the spirituality of the human world, transforms heavenly illumination into darkness and deprives man of the knowledge of God. It is the cause of the victory of materialism and infidelity over religion; it is the denial of Divinity and the law of revelation; it refuses Prophethood and rejects the Kingdom of God."[5]

As we have mentioned, Bahá'u'lláh summarizes the fundamental nature of autonomy when He states that inasmuch as each individual has the capacity to recognize divine attributes, everyone is responsible for his or her own spiritual condition: "[E]very man hath been, and will continue to be, able of himself to appreciate the Beauty of God, the Glorified. Had he not been endowed with such a capacity, how could he be called to account for his failure?"[6]

EXTERNAL ASSISTANCE

As we noted in our comparison of the Bahá'í view of physical creation with that presented in *Paradise Lost,* the most essential and distinguishing characteristic of the Bahá'í concept of a justly functioning creation is the progressive and unremitting assistance provided for human advancement. And yet, because ceaseless motion towards perfection must be independent, it might seem that external assistance would encroach on our autonomy. But while the final responsibility for spiritual growth derives from individual choice, human progress of every sort, whether individual or collective, is impossible without some sort of external guidance.

This thesis is discussed throughout the Bahá'í writings, and it is a logical one—we cannot instinctively know who we are or what we are or what objectives we should pursue without someone more educated than ourselves to set us in motion and assist us along the way. Indeed, 'Abdu'l-Bahá goes so far as to assert, "A man who has not had a spiritual education is a brute." He further observes, "Were there no educator, all souls would remain savage, and were it not for the teacher, the children would be ignorant creatures."[7]

Clearly, however, the teacher can only have an effect when there is a potential for spiritual perfections within the student, and such potentiality is the key to understanding the Bahá'í concept of this vital but subtle relationship between the educator and the educated. In one of the most often cited passages on the human condition, Bahá'u'lláh likens human potentiality to a mine rich in gems. The function of the educator is to help us discover the treasures in that mine, bring them into the light, and polish and refine them: "Regard man as a mine rich in gems of inestimable value. Education can, alone, cause it to reveal its treasures, and enable mankind to benefit therefrom." 'Abdu'l-Bahá observes the same principle, stating that "education cannot alter the inner essence of a man, but it doth exert a tremendous influence, and with this power it can bring forth from the individual whatever perfections and capacities are deposited within him."[8]

THE MANIFESTATION AS EDUCATOR

As we have already observed, principal among the educators of humankind are the Manifestations of God, Whose words and actions are expressly designed to instruct us. Later we will discuss in detail some of the methods by which They instruct us, but here we should note some of the special characteristics that render them particularly effective in bringing about human enlightenment.

For one thing, since the Manifestation is not merely an enlightened human being but a divine Emissary sent explicitly to instruct us, He has a power, a capacity, a spiritual insight that enables Him to discern precisely what lessons and methodologies would be particularly effective for humankind for a particular period in our development. In this context, Bahá'u'lláh compares the Manifestation to a wise and capable physician: "The All-Knowing Physician hath His finger on the pulse of mankind. He perceiveth the disease, and prescribeth, in His unerring wisdom, the remedy. Every age hath its own problem, and every soul its particular aspiration. The remedy the world needeth in its present-day afflictions can never be the same as that which a subsequent age may require. Be anxiously concerned with the needs of the age ye live in, and center your deliberations on its exigencies and requirements."[9] Therefore, while we as ordinary human beings assume our beginning at conception when the soul associates with the body, the Manifestation preexists in the spiritual realm, where He perceives the needs of humankind before willingly assuming a human persona wherewith He can deliver divine guidance in a manner that we can understand.

Furthermore, as we have also observed, where we must acquire learning, the Manifestation possesses innate knowledge. Here we are not referring to knowledge of the revelation itself, which begins at a particular point in the life of a Manifestation which we have come to associate with some outward sign, such as Moses' seeing the burning bush, Buddha's experience under the Bo tree, Christ's baptism in the Jordan, Muḥammad's visions in the desert, the Báb's vision of the Imám Ḥusayn, and Bahá'u'lláh's vision in the Síyáh-Chál dungeon of Tehran. Well before They begin their ministries, even during child-hood, the Manifestations demonstrate that They possess a knowl-edge that they have not acquired from any earthly source. In effect, Their education is acquired before birth into this physical reality.

One and all, the Manifestations exhibit exemplary character. As we noted earlier, inasmuch as each perfectly manifests the attributes of God, each becomes tantamount to the expression of Godliness in human terms. They are not God, nor are They of the same es-sence as God. Yet, as a perfect mirror reflects the heat and light of the sun without becoming the sun, so the Manifestations demon-strate to us God's nature in dramatic expression and through inher-ent powers without ever becoming God incarnate.

Therefore Christ could say to Philip, "He who has seen me has seen the Father" without in any sense implying that He was God in the flesh. To clarify His point, Christ explains in the same conver-sation, "The words that I say to you I do not speak on my own authority; but the Father who dwells in me does his works."[10]

Christ's response also leads us to the focal point of how the Manifes-tations are utilized by God for our instruction, the process of revelation itself. For while ordinary human beings have the capacity to manifest the attributes of God and even to become divinely inspired, some to an extremely high degree, the Manifestations are uniquely endowed with the mission of becoming a channel through which God's guid-ance for a particular period in history is revealed directly to human-kind.

'Abdu'l-Bahá explains this capacity in part when he says that the Manifestations possess a "universal divine mind" which "embraces existing realities" and "receives the light of the mysteries of God." 'Abdu'l-Bahá states that this power, unlike our own intellectual power, is not a product of "investigation and research" but is "a conscious power" unique to the Manifestations:

The intellectual power of the world of nature is a power of investigation, and by its researches it discovers the realities of beings and the properties of existences; but the heavenly intellectual power, which is beyond nature, embraces things and is cognizant of things, knows them, understands them, is aware of mysteries, realities and divine significations, and is the discoverer of the concealed verities of the Kingdom. This divine intellectual power is the special attribute of the Holy Manifestations and the Dawning-places of prophethood; a ray of this light falls upon the mirrors of the hearts of the righteous, and a portion and a share of this power comes to them through the Holy Manifestations.[11]

We can attribute great influence and capacity to certain spiritualized human beings who appear throughout history, but powerful as they may be, these inspired souls operate under the influence and auspices of the Manifestations, reflecting the light of knowledge released by Their revelations, even though we may presently be unable to detect any direct tie or apparent relationship.

The Manifestations thus have untold influence. It would not be an exaggeration to say that human history is organized around Their appearances or that human history proceeds according to this divine dynamic. And yet each Manifestation forthrightly attributes every action He takes, and every word He utters, to the power of God acting through Him. For example, according to scripture, God instructed Moses what to do and assured Him that God would provide the words: "And you shall speak to him [Aaron] and put the words in his mouth; and I will be with your mouth and with his mouth, and will teach you what you shall do." Likewise, in explaining the authority of His words, Christ stated, "For I have not spoken on my own authority; the Father who sent me has himself given me command-

ment what to say and what to speak." In the Qur'án Muḥammad
states that He cannot adapt or change the Qur'án to accommodate
the desires of His followers because He is the channel through which
God speaks to them and not the author of the words: "But when our
clear signs are recited to them, they who look not forward to meet
Us, say, 'Bring a different Koran from this, or make some change in
it.' Say: It is not for me to change it as mine own soul prompteth. I
follow only what is revealed to me. . . ."

More than twelve hundred years later, in His letter to Muḥammad
Sh̲áh, the Báb (the Herald and Forerunner of Bahá'u'lláh) similarly
described the process of revelation: "God beareth Me witness, I
was not a man of learning, for I was trained as a merchant. In the
year sixty [1844 A.D.] God graciously infused my soul with the con-
clusive evidence and weighty knowledge which characterize Him
Who is the Testimony of God—may peace be upon Him—until
finally in that year I proclaimed God's hidden Cause and unveiled
its well-guarded Pillar, in such wise that no one could refute it."
Likewise, Bahá'u'lláh confirms that His revelation is not "of Mine
own volition": "Whenever I chose to hold My peace and be still, lo,
the Voice of the Holy Spirit, standing on My right hand, aroused
Me, and the Most Great Spirit appeared before My face, and Gabriel
overshadowed Me, and the Spirit of Glory stirred within My bo-
som, bidding Me arise and break My silence."[12]

Preexistent, aware of each other, fully coordinated in Their actions
and words, the Manifestations of God educate by degrees the human
race, the fruit of creation in whom "are potentially revealed all the
attributes and names of God."[13] Gradually the Manifestations transform this inherent potentiality of human nature into the reality of
progressively more enlightened civilizations. From these primal sources
of external instruction derive other benign teachers who follow Their
example with the noble and awesome task of guiding humanity.

A less overt but nonetheless significant external source of guidance is the physical world itself with its inherent capacity to manifest the attributes of God. Properly perceived and understood, the world of nature becomes for us a textbook of divine instruction: "Within every blade of grass are enshrined the mysteries of an inscrutable wisdom, and upon every rosebush a myriad nightingales pour out, in blissful rapture, their melody."[14]

But whether the source of external assistance be the revelation of a Manifestation or some more subtle and indirect instruction, such as the inspired guidance of a parent or teacher, we may conclude that the Bahá'í paradigm clearly portrays the human being as needing assistance in order to achieve the condition of independent or autonomous striving that we have described as the purpose of human fulfillment. Because of this need for external guidance, the Bahá'í writings describe the obligation of the parents and the community to instruct its children as one of their foremost responsibilities. 'Abdu'l-Bahá, for example, states that "no nobler deed than this can be imagined."

The reason for such lofty praise is explained clearly in numerous passages. 'Abdu'l-Bahá states that without training, the human being is potentially the source of incalculable iniquity; with it the human spirit is able to become utterly transcendent: "Every child is potentially the light of the world—and at the same time its darkness; wherefore must the question of education be accounted as of primary importance."[15]

THE INTERNAL MECHANISM OF JUSTICE

Although we are dependent on external influence for education and progress, the Bahá'í writings make it clear that we are all largely responsible for our own spiritual advancement. As we have noted, this condition of freely chosen ascent is virtually a definition of human justice and an essential ingredient in the Baha'i paradigm, but it also may be the most difficult concept to grasp.

How can we ever know precisely where external guidance leaves off and our own free choice begins? We do know that without our active participation in the process, human education is impossible. We can allow ourselves to become programmed or coerced or brainwashed, but that is not true advancement or valid learning—we are memorizing what some else has learned—or think they have learned.

To understand the theory underlying this distinction between the need for external assistance and the simultaneous autonomy of our own free will, 'Abdu'l-Baha employs an effective analogy that compares human progress to a boat in water. The power of wind or steam represents those external forces that impel the boat into motion, and the boat's rudder represents our individual free will:

> [T]he inaction or the movement of man depend upon the assistance of God. If he is not aided, he is not able to do either good or evil. But when the help of existence comes from the Generous Lord, he is able to do both good and evil; but if the help is cut off, he remains absolutely helpless. . . . So this condition is like that of a ship which is moved by the power of the wind or steam; if this power ceases, the ship cannot move at all. Nevertheless, the rudder of the ship turns it to either side, and the power of the steam moves it in the desired direction. . . .
>
> In the same way, in all the action or inaction of man, he receives power from the help of God; but the choice of good or evil belongs to the man himself.[16]

The significance of our volition is implied by 'Abdu'l-Baha's allusion to this power as "a mighty will." He states that in spite of the things beyond our control, the most significant events (our moral choices), are "subject to the free will of man, such as justice, equity, tyranny and injustice, in other words, good and evil actions. . . ."[17] We may not always understand exactly when our will is operating or to what degree our decisions are truly independent, but we do know that as a faculty of the human soul, the will is independent of our capacity to feel or to know.

For example, we may choose to do that which is contrary to our desires because we realize that some long-term benefit will derive from a short-term discomfort. Likewise, we may understand that our desires or emotions are often unreliable guides to proper action. Thus we may be emotionally attracted to something, to someone, or to some course of action, and yet we may choose to ignore such feelings in order to comply with what we know in our rational mind to be a higher concern, such as compliance with a moral law or the long-range sense of health and well-being we will attain by following a path that my be difficult in the short term.

Our will is also clearly a faculty distinct from our ability to know. For example, we may know very well what is best for us, and yet we may fail to decide on a proper course of action. Or we may observe intellectually that we should follow a certain course of action but ultimately fail to transform that perception into deeds.

There is, in other words, a necessary alliance between free will and action. To exercise our will signifies more than intent—it implies the implementation of intention into a course of action. Thus when we try to determine what is fitting or appropriate for our fulfillment—what is just and fitting behavior—we come to see that it is the exercise of an entire process: to know and understand, then to determine to implement that understanding in an appropriate dramatic expression, and finally to carry out that intent. Ultimately, we need to carry out this sequence repeatedly until our response becomes habitual and reflexive, an essential aspect of our character. In short, we must respond willfully until this effort or exercise of will ultimately transforms the essential nature of our character.

'Abdu'l-Bahá refers to this very process when he states that any accomplishment is achieved through "knowledge, volition and action." Similar to the dictates of the Short Obligatory Prayer revealed by Bahá'u'lláh, which ascribes to humankind the purpose of coming "to know Thee and to Worship Thee," 'Abdu'l-Bahá's prescription for human transformation can be found throughout his writings and talks. It is at the heart of his definition of "faith" when he observes, "by faith is meant, first, conscious knowledge, and second, the practice of good deeds."[18]

Conscious choice is clearly necessary for performing any important deed, just as worship requires a decision or choice followed by action. It is not sufficient that we understand the guidance which the physical sources of education reveal to us. In the Kingdom of Names (physical reality) it is further necessary that we exercise our willpower with enough persistence to manifest our inner transformation in noble deeds.

No doubt the Apostle James had such willpower in mind when he stated that faith or belief does not exist until it is expressed in action: "What does it profit, my brethren, if a man says he has faith but has not works? Can his faith save him? If a brother or sister is ill-clad and in lack of daily food, and one of you says to them, 'Go in peace, be warmed and filled,' without giving them the things needed for the body, what does it profit? So faith by itself, if it has no works, is dead."[19]

REWARD AND PUNISHMENT: THE TWIN PILLARS OF JUSTICE

Upholding the entire system we have so far delineated is yet another essential mechanism in the Bahá'í theoretical paradigm of physical reality, the twin "pillars" of reward and punishment. Alluded to throughout the Bahá'í writings as upholding justice in all its myriad forms, this system is a bulwark of the structure of reality. Bahá'u'lláh writes, "O people of God! That which traineth the world is Justice, for it is upheld by two pillars, reward and punishment. These two pillars are the sources of life to the world."[20]

In some passages it is apparent that the system of reward and punishment represents literal institutions that uphold social order by physically restraining the iniquitous: "Justice hath a mighty force at its command. It is none other than reward and punishment for the deeds of men. By the power of this force the tabernacle of order is established throughout the world, causing the wicked to restrain their natures for fear of punishment."[21] Yet the more deeply we study the relationship of reward and punishment to the enlightenment and advancement of humankind, the more we understand the amazing subtlety and pervasiveness of this training device.

According to the Bahá'í teachings, the purpose of the system of reward and punishment, when it is applied wisely by parents and educators of every sort, is to instigate autonomous motion, not to dominate or to oppress. One obvious use of this technique, for example, is so-called "operant conditioning" employed by psychologists and teachers in modifying behavior.* Certainly parents know

---

* Extending the theories of conditioning set forth by Ivan Pavlov and later by B. F. Skinner, modern therapists have come to incorporate systems of reward and punishment to induce specific patterns of behavior, thereby modifying or eliminating an unhealthy response and creating in its place a new conditioned or "operant" response.

that it is virtually impossible to train a child without the wise application of reward and punishment on a regular basis.

But we have also recently become aware of the danger of misapplying such training. Excessive reward and punishment can have precisely the opposite effect of their intended uses—instead of instigating autonomy and self-sustained progress, they can produce a mindless adherence to rules, a sort of fanaticism that destroys human development. In short, these twin stimuli when applied properly become tools of training, not ends in themselves.

The purpose of reward, punishment, and other trainers is to initiate a response and then to transfer the responsibility for considered action to the individual. This transference is accomplished when the individual becomes enlightened about the rational and benign objectives that the teaching system upholds. For example, when we understand and adopt the benign objectives of our transformation, external guidance through reward and punishment become less and less important because we internalize the objectives for ourselves, and our own emotional sensibilities reward and punish us: we feel good when we succeed and bad when we fail.

This does not mean that our "conscience" is completely a learned or programmed response, but it does mean that this internal or inherent sense of morality requires nurture and encouragement at the early stages of development, or else it can atrophy beyond repair. Nurturing and training the conscience is accomplished through external application of training until we come to appreciate that the real rewards and punishments derive from both the immediate and the long-term benefits we receive from our own mental and spiritual advancement. The same training principles apply to the shared values we have as a society. The collective conscience can be as successfully trained and developed as the individual conscience.

Here again, we are not trying to catechize, to instigate a mindless and mechanical response to reality. The objective is to educate humankind to appreciate the essential reality of human nature so that all might work in concord in the ongoing process of fostering "an ever-advancing civilization."[22] Social justice, when understood in this light, establishes its own systems of reward and punishment and attempts to train society to achieve that motion.

Such justice is operative whether we are alluding to criminal justice systems to maintain civil order or to social norms whereby citizens in a community feel the impact of their own behavior in relation to the healthy expectation of their peers. In other words, peer pressure is bad only when the peers reflect the moral climate of a degenerate society. When the society begins to have a shared goal of moral development and spiritually based norms, peer pressure can become one of the most healthy and powerful sources of reinforcement for individual development and progress. Indeed, it might well be argued that a healthy society or community is the most forceful and effective teacher of its citizenry, a dictum the veracity of which any parent in today's society will readily attest (and lament). For when society is in moral disarray, the parent discovers the difficulty of shielding children from the omnipresent and pervasive presence of a moribund perspective and perverse mentality of a debased social milieu.

Thus if society does not comprehend and eventually internalize healthy goals, no system of reward and punishment will be powerful enough to enforce order, let alone produce an advancing civilization. Certainly, contemporary attempts at law enforcement and penology confirm this verity. As 'Abdu'l-Bahá notes, effective training cannot be accomplished in a materially oriented system of reward and punishment:

With force and punishments, material civilization seeketh to restrain the people from mischief, from inflicting harm on society
and committing crimes. But in a divine civilization, the individual is so conditioned that with no fear of punishment, he
shunneth the perpetration of crimes, seeth the crime itself as the
severest of torments, and with alacrity and joy, setteth himself
to acquiring the virtues of humankind, to furthering human
progress, and to spreading light across the world.[23]

NATURAL SYSTEMS OF
REWARD AND PUNISHMENT

In addition to the wise application of reward and punishment by
the educators of humankind, there are at least two other parts of
the physical paradigm where we can observe these twin pillars upholding the concept of justice. The first is found in our relationship with the natural world. As we have repeatedly observed, there
is in the Bahá'í writings a perception of the physical world as an
expression of spiritual attributes. This view holds true not only for
the inherent imprint of the divine reality that objects themselves
manifest—the "names" of God they reflect—but also in the various levels of relationship among physical objects.

The majority of humankind is now beginning to understand the
strategic importance of such relationships, as is evidenced most dramatically in our rapidly emerging awareness of ecology, a dramatic
expression of the essential unity and integrity of creation. We are
also beginning to understand that built into the intricate web of
relationships among physical objects as portrayed by the study of

ecology is this same law of reward and punishment. We now understand that a violation of that integration of relationships in nature is not simply a travesty against natural beauty and wildlife; it also evokes punishment upon ourselves. We breathe foul air, eat contaminated food, and drink tainted water.

When we fail to appreciate and safeguard the unity and essentially spiritual nature of physical reality, we then suffer the consequences and are trained thereby. This punishment or "karma" will force us to reexamine our response to the natural world, even if our more overt education does not exhort us to do so. Through this cause-and-effect relationship between ourselves and the physical classroom, even the strictest materialist ultimately must pay careful attention to the pragmatic exigencies of spiritual relationships within the physical world.

Another less obvious application of the twin pillars of reward and punishment lies in the practical implication of our response to moral law. Traditionally, we think of moral law and social ordinances as deriving from tradition or from human invention. As a result of this thinking, we are liable to believe that punishment will occur only if our violation of moral law is discovered by someone in authority. This common attitude explains why so many politicians consider themselves beyond the constraints of a code of behavior, other than the dictates of practicality or utilitarianism, until or unless they are "found out."

Likewise, the perpetrators of social injustice, be they individual criminals or a social institution, may perceive moral law as irrelevant to its affairs. According to Bahá'í beliefs, such perceptions are erroneous. If, as we have noted, the physical world is, in reality, but the spiritual world expressed in concrete symbols, the relationships among all constituent parts of the physical world are expressions of relationships in the spiritual realm.

More to the point, all social law is, when correctly devised and understood, an expression of moral or spiritual law. Therefore, the law is operant regardless of whether the individual or society wishes or acknowledges it to be, and since moral law is always influencing our lives, it has the weight of physical law. By analogy, if we jump from the top of a three-story building, we do not need to wonder whether or not the law of gravity will be operating that day. We know what the result of our action will be because we understand something about the laws of physics. We comprehend the end result of our action in the beginning of our decision.

Because of this certitude about physical law, the wise individual will pay heed to the possible effects of those laws on his or her well-being. Once we come to appreciate that the cause and effect relationships are no less binding with moral laws (they are always operant, always extant), we will come to have the same respect for their consequences in our lives. Stated simply, the wise individuals will have the same certitude about the inevitability of the operation of moral law that they have about the inevitability of the operation of physical laws.

If we are unjust to others, we will suffer injury to our soul as well as to the success of our mundane enterprises because moral laws governing injustice are not simply religious traditions or a social wish. Justice is operant in every aspect of reality—it is not merely a social construct or idealistic stricture relevant only to a select segment of society or the spiritual realm. For if, as we observed earlier, physical and spiritual reality are counterparts of a single integrated reality, then moral law has practical consequences and delineates the most propitious course of action in the physical world quite as much as it does in the realm of the spirit.

Nowhere are the consequences of moral laxity more evident than in the study of large-scale social injustice. History bears this out. A tyrannical social force (for example, dictatorships, feudalism, totalitarianism) may enjoy success for a time. Indeed, it may seem to succeed by virtue of its injustice. But the very same system is inevitably doomed to failure precisely because of this violation of moral law for the simple reason that unjust behavior is not simply "immoral" in some abstract sense of spiritual assessment; it is also impractical inasmuch as it does not comply with a law of reality. That is, if all people are inherently equal, then logically they should have equal rights in society. When a social system is devised based on the violation of this reality, it will over the course of time break down and cease to function because it is out of compliance with the laws of reality.

From this perspective, then, moral law describes the most efficacious and, ultimately, the most expedient means of accomplishing any objective, whether for individual or collective enterprises. Consequently, injustice will inevitably produce a negative result, a form of punishment. Therefore, if we have the wisdom to perceive this "end" result in the "beginning" as we consider our choices, we will inevitably choose a moral course of action, even when another course of action may at the time seem more expedient.

A good example of this practical or physical effect of moral law is the history of economic systems built on some form of oppression. Such immoral societies are doomed to failure because they assume that humanity is neither equal nor one organic family. Eventually, the fallacious assumption that has produced such an erroneous economic oppression will undermine the most practical affairs of such societies, as is exemplified in the decline of feudalism in medieval Europe, the decline of plantation society in the American South, and in the decline of the apartheid system in South Africa, societies that subsisted effectively on slave labor and the disenfranchisement of the majority by a discrete segment of society. This same principle of the ultimate failure of economies based on injustice has been demonstrated repeatedly in the reign of colonial regimes throughout world history.

Of course, we could extend our discussion of the practical implications of moral law to virtually every facet of human endeavor, whether we examine the manufacturing of products or the organizing of the simplest kinds of enterprises. In the chapters that follow we will discuss further the practical relationships of moral law to daily life, but for our purposes here it is sufficient to conclude that the system of reward and punishment integrated into the fabric of physical reality is not something we need to impose. The system is an inherent property of the Kingdom of Names. Indeed, Bahá'u'lláh may well have been alluding to these twin pillars of reward and punishment with the following passage: "Out of the wastes of nothingness, with the clay of My command I made thee to appear, and have ordained for thy training every atom in existence and the essence of all created things. Thus, ere thou didst issue from thy mother's womb, I destined for thee two founts of gleaming milk, eyes to watch over thee, and hearts to love thee."[24]

In addition to whatever other meanings they imply, these "founts" may well refer to the twin pillars of reward and punishment as the benign guidance that is infused into every part of the physical world to stimulate autonomy of motion toward human perfection within each individual and within society as an aggregate, organic construct.

GRACE AND MERCY

In spite of our discussion of the direct and indirect methods by which the physical world is devised to instruct humankind, our outline of the Bahá'í paradigm would be quite incomplete without a final ingredient that functions as a divine elixir to anoint the entire system—that final touch of perfection in God's justice which we call "grace."

It might seem strange to include grace as part of a system of justice since the two terms seem antithetical—the term "justice" usually connotes the exact opposite of "grace." 'Abdu'l-Bahá acknowledges this antithesis when he states that "bounty is giving without desert, and justice is giving what is deserved."[25] Therefore, since we are fallible and, from the standpoint of spiritual development, in a childlike state, if we were to be judged according to strict justice, we would surely be doomed.

Bahá'u'lláh confirms as much in the beginning of the Kitáb-i-Íqán where He describes the irony of the fact that humanity has historically rejected the very Educators sent to give us assistance: "And whensoever the portals of grace did open, and the clouds of divine bounty did rain upon mankind, and the light of the Unseen did shine above the horizon of celestial might, they all denied Him, and turned away from His face—the face of God Himself. Refer ye, to verify this truth, to that which hath been recorded in every sacred Book."[26]

But as we have already observed, the term "justice" in its most ample sense designates propriety, that which is most appropriate and fulfilling of inherent purpose. Therefore, if we liken humankind in its present stage of development to an adolescent youth, and if we further believe that God is at least as kind, loving, intelligent, and forgiving as a decent human parent, then the law of justice dictates that it is appropriate for God to have mercy and grace in His treatment of His own creation. Certainly a parent's love does not cease because a child has made mistakes, even though the parent may temporarily respond with punishment to guide the wayward child aright.

Similarly, while God is sometimes portrayed in the scriptures of world religions as a strict judge, and while even the Bahá'í writings praise the "fear of God" as laudable, all world religions teach that God is ever-forgiving and all-merciful. Of course, as we have also noted, grace and mercy cannot be imposed against our will. To receive bounty we must desire it and act on that desire. The Báb states in one prayer, "Glorified art Thou, O Lord, Thou forgivest at all times the sins of such among Thy servants as *implore* Thy pardon." Thus when the Báb writes, "verily God will not forgive disbelief in Himself," He is not necessarily describing God's retribution so much as He is delineating the logical relationship between free will and grace.[27] God will not impose forgiveness, and disbelief as a rejection of divine reality implies an explicit choice on our part, a refusal of grace.

Bahá'u'lláh implies the same thing when He writes, "Woe betide him who hath rejected the grace of God and His bounty, and hath denied His tender mercy and authority."[28] In other words, God's grace and mercy are essential to our success in the physical world because we need many chances if we are to succeed. Fortunately for us, this bounty is always available to us regardless of what we may have done. But because our own desire for it and receptivity to it are necessary, mercy, grace, and forgiveness are not automatic. To receive this redeeming balm, we must follow the same pattern required for every other spiritual effort—knowledge, volition, and action. We must recognize what we need and act accordingly by expressing our desire in prayer and in obedience to the guidance of God as revealed to us throughout our association with the Kingdom of Names.

CONCLUSION OF THE PARADIGM

To conclude, these fundamental features of the Bahá'í view of a justly functioning physical creation, we have constructed a basic understanding of how physical reality is devised to ensure the appropriate results for which it has been designed and created—"ever-advancing" individuals in the context of an "ever-advancing" civilization on this ever-evolving planet. From the larger macrocosmic perspective, we perceive an organic, universal system—eternal in the past and eternal in the future, a system in which planets evolve spiritually and contribute to the benign purposes of the whole system and then, in time, cease to exist. Viewed in this way, the universe is like a vast body of God in which the planets, like cells in the human body, come into being, develop and nourish the universal body, and then go out of being when their purpose has been accomplished. Justice in this sense is the overall integrity and propriety of the Creator's plan whereby each atom in creation has an essential part to play in the abiding purpose of creation as a whole.

And yet, satisfying as this abbreviated sketch of the larger implications of the Bahá'í vision of justice may be, such an analysis is, by itself, hardly a satisfying vision of how each one of us in our daily lives can employ the physical environment for our own advancement. We might employ this vision to become assured that creation is logically and benignly devised, but such an understanding does not by itself provide us with a clear sense of how we interact with this system to perpetrate our own salvation. We still require practical assistance in accomplishing our just and proper individual objective of coming to know and worship God Whom we cannot see and Whose action or inaction often confounds us.

6

A USER'S GUIDE TO PHYSICAL REALITY: PRENATAL EXERCISES FOR OUR SECOND BIRTH

Out of the wastes of nothingness, with the clay of My command I made thee to appear, and have ordained for thy training every atom in existence and the essence of all created things.

—Bahá'u'lláh

Having examined the Bahá'í view of physical creation as a just and logically devised system, we have responded to the first of three major concerns—the theoretical basis for a belief in some form of divine justice in relation to physical reality and our individual and collective experience in it. Our second task is to move from theory and theology to practicality—to determine how this environment assists us on a daily basis to know and to worship God.

This objective should be more immediately satisfying than the first. It would certainly seem to respond more forcefully to the questions raised by Job and Boethius if such a practical analysis could provide insight into how negative experiences and unjust suffering can ultimately lead us to positive conclusions. In short, it is all well and good to assert eternal providence or to discern a coherent and logical set of laws and principles at work in the universe, but we live our lives one day at a time with family and friends in a community where we must busy ourselves with mundane sorts of activities. It is in this context that we need to understand how what we do each day can help us have the subjective knowledge of the "end" in what sometimes seems to be a very painful and ludicrous "beginning."

THE UNITY OF HUMAN EXPERIENCE

When we let the phenomenal world become an end in itself rather than a means of gaining access to the spiritual reality it reflects, or when we let our physical or appetitive nature rule over our judgmental or volitional faculties, we are, indeed, in a state of injustice, confusion, and internal strife. In such a state the physical world does become detrimental to our success. But physical reality itself is not the cause—the culprit is ourselves when we misuse temporal reality and fail to grasp the essential unity of our physical and metaphysical experiences.

The relationship between the physical and the spiritual aspects of reality is thus at the heart of appreciating and using the physical classroom. Such a relationship, hinted at by Platonic philosophy and spelled out in detail in the Bahá'í writings, does not simply affirm that it is possible to obtain spiritual benefits from physical experience. The relationship dictates that the animating principle of creation is its reflection of the spiritual world. In this sense the physical world is a means of gaining access to the spiritual world in the same way that a periscope enables us to view a reality that is otherwise blocked or obscured from our vision.

Stated in terms of Chaucer's own analogy of life as a journey or pilgrimage, when physical reality is employed to our benefit, it is a pathway to spiritual ascent. Physical reality is detrimental only when we come to believe that physical experience is the object of our pilgrimage instead of our means of transportation. Hence we can appreciate that one of the principal and most difficult tasks of the Manifestations of God is to clarify the essential relationship between these dual aspects of our experience—to show us how to use one experience as a dramatic device whereby we can comprehend the other and thereby achieve unity and harmony in our lives, as well as in our identity as human beings.

To help relate one aspect of ourselves to the other, the Manifestation works in two capacities. As He reiterates the eternal and changeless attributes of the spiritual world, He is a revealer, an unveiler of divine reality and moral law. Accordingly, religious law as it is revealed by the Prophets is not simply an attempt to impose order on disorder. Understood from this perspective, the moral or spiritual law revealed by the Prophets assumes the same objective authority as scientific law. Even as physical laws describe predictable relationships among phenomena, so spiritual or moral laws describe predictable relationships among spiritual entities.

The laws of the Manifestations are thus descriptive as well as prescriptive. For example, we praise Newton for having discovered and formulated the mutual attraction of masses—the law of gravity—not for having contrived, invented, or imposed this property of matter. Similarly, the Manifestation does not create divine reality or the laws governing that reality. He reveals them to us and invites compliance with them. Likewise, as advances in scientific understanding render more and more complete our descriptions of the phenomenal world, so the progression of revelation by the successive Manifestations makes our understanding of spiritual reality and spiritual laws more complete and more accurate.

But the Manifestation is not only a describer or revealer. He also makes things happen. In His station as lawgiver He actively affects the degree to which the physical world reflects the spiritual world. He is the primary creative force that sets in motion the spiritual forces and creative laws that will cause spiritual reality to become actuated in the phenomenal world. Consequently, when the Manifestation instructs us how to implement spiritual law, He is carrying out both objectives simultaneously: He is describing the spiritual principles that underlie and are the logical bases for His social ordinances, and He is establishing the Kingdom of God on earth by implementing those principles in a way consonant with our increased level of human understanding and our increased capacity for action.

For example, when Bahá'u'lláh institutes the concept of the equality of men and women, He is revealing a spiritual verity that has always existed—He is not inventing a new spiritual reality. But in giving voice and legal weight to this spiritual principle, He is actuating that principle in social action by pronouncing to what extent human society can now implement and reflect that reality.

Likewise, when Bahá'u'lláh speaks of the unity of science and religion, He is revealing an objective fact about reality by pointing out that both areas of investigation probe complementary aspects of one organic creation. At the same time He admonishes scientists and religious thinkers to become aware of the unity of science and religion (physical and spiritual laws as they describe reality) so that they can put aside misperceptions about the nature of reality and work together to increase our understanding of existence and the reciprocal influence in our lives of these twin aspects of reality.

At the heart of the dual function of the Manifestation, then, is the key to the essential unity of the physical and spiritual properties of reality. By demonstrating the harmony of the two aspects of reality, the Manifestation enables us to live successfully and simultaneously in both realms. Since our soul, which is essentially spiritual, operates a physical body in a physical environment, this enlightenment can be a most valuable practical aid to the unification of our everyday experience.

THE METAPHORICAL NATURE
OF PHYSICAL REALITY

If we can accept that the physical and spiritual realms, and, consequently, our participation in them, are inextricably related, we can understand the importance of appreciating how each of these seemingly disparate and discordant aspects of reality is related to the other in the physical world. We can also start to appreciate the wisdom of setting out on our spiritual pilgrimage in physical clothes.

Perhaps the clearest statement in the Bahá'í writings about the logical basis for such a system of education is found in a passage by 'Abdu'l-Bahá:

> The wisdom of the appearance of the spirit in the body is this: the human spirit is a Divine Trust, and it must traverse all conditions, for its passage and movement through the conditions of existence will be the means of its acquiring perfections. So when a man travels and passes through different regions and numerous countries with system and method, it is certainly a means of his acquiring perfection, for he will see places, scenes and countries, from which he will discover the conditions and states of other nations. . . . It is the same when the human spirit passes through the conditions of existence: it will become the possessor of each degree and station.[1]

But what is the "system and method" with which we should approach our journey? What is the specific method by which we relate our physical lives to our spiritual evolution?

The means by which the physical world, this nether world of cave and shadow, is related to the spiritual world is the metaphorical process, and to understand this relationship, we must appreciate how metaphors work.

A metaphor is one of several kinds of analogical devices, all of which function in the same manner: They compare two essentially dissimilar things (people, situations, relationships, abstractions, material objects, and so on). Always in the comparison is an implicit or explicit statement of similarity between these essentially different subjects. But regardless of whether the analogical device is a metaphor, a simile, an allegory, a conceit, a symbol, or some other type of figure or trope, it contains three basic parts: the "tenor," or that which is being described; the "vehicle," or that which is being compared to the tenor; and the "meaning," or that area of similarity between the tenor and the vehicle.*

The term "metaphor" is often used to designate the metaphorical process in general, though strictly speaking, a metaphor is a relatively short, implicit analogical device. Sometimes the terms "figure" or "image" are also used in this general sense, "figure" denoting "figure of speech" or "rhetorical device," and "image" designating "figurative image." But whatever term one uses, and regardless of whether the device is a one-word metaphor or an elaborate parable or allegory, a particularly challenging process must occur if the device is to work effectively. One must be made to think and to become creative if one is to complete the final and most important

---

* The terms "tenor" and "vehicle" were coined by I. A. Richards in *The Philosophy of Rhetoric* (London: Oxford Univ. Press, 1936), one of his numerous studies on metaphor and language.

part of the process by determining in what way the tenor and vehicle are similar in spite of their essential difference.

Consider the simple metaphor "Jane is a lovely flower." The analogical equation is established because the tenor "Jane" is essentially different from the vehicle "flower." Had we compared Jane to Mary, the tenor and the vehicle would be essentially the same—both being girls—and no analogy would occur.

Once the equation has been established, the reader must now solve the equation for x, the missing or understood ingredient—in this case, what the tenor (Jane) has in common with the vehicle (the flower). In this sense, a creative or imaginative image forces us as readers and thinkers to become creative ourselves. We must figure out the missing link or the linchpin between the two different objects—the x-factor, the common bond that is the "meaning" of the equation.

If the metaphor is obvious or trite, our thoughts go directly from tenor to meaning without examining the vehicle, without needing to solve the equation for x. Consequently, overworked similes such as "cold as ice" or "hard as stone" require no mental examination of the equation because the vehicle offers no resistance. The mental exercise becomes short-circuited. Description has occurred, but the device has not challenged us to participate in the process of creating a mental image by contributing something of our own thought or experience.

The value of the metaphorical process is immense, for it is a useful way to explain the unfamiliar in terms of the familiar, or the abstract in terms of the concrete. It also has the power to compress a great deal of meaning into few words. Moreover, because it offers a variety of meanings, it can become an expansive description rather than a limiting or restrictive one.

But probably the most important feature of the metaphorical process is its ability to educate us. Its educative properties lie in the fact that when we are forced to examine the vehicle in order to understand the tenor, we must exercise some of our most important capacities, our faculty of abstract thought and our powers of judgment and discernment:

> Metaphor is a process of comparing and identifying one thing with another. Then, as we see what things have in common, we see the general meaning they have. Now, the ability to see the relation between one thing and another is *almost a definition of intelligence*. Thinking in metaphors . . . is a tool of intelligence. Perhaps it is the most important tool.[2]

When we attempt to decipher metaphors and images, we are, in addition to exercising our faculty of discernment, also extracting the meaning for ourselves instead of having the meaning dictated to us. The interpretation is ours. Therefore the metaphorical process is indirect and objective, rather than being direct and subjective—the writer is not imposing ideas on the reader but letting the equation stand objectively by itself to provide meaning.

Another bounty of this teaching device, then, is that the teacher is truly a facilitator of an educational process, not simply a source of data or fact. In effect, if we as students are to obtain meaning, we must exercise our volition and examine the tenor and the vehicle for ourselves. When we apprehend the meaning on our own, we will not feel as if we have been told what to think, though we may be grateful to the teacher who has been creative enough to conceive the equation that led us to a new and richer understanding.

We can hardly discuss the use of the metaphorical process as it relates to religion without mentioning one more vital asset of the device. It is a safeguard against literalism and hence against imitation and dogmatism. For example, when Christ states that He is the "bread of life," He means something positive by it, that He is valuable, essential, a source of sustenance, of spiritual nourishment.[3] Yet there is no single "correct" meaning or translation of the equation. But if we accept the statement literally at face value, if we fail to realize that Christ's statement is metaphorical, we are forced to conclude that Christ was a loaf of bread. Such a conclusion should cause those who claim that scripture should be accepted literally to reconsider their assertion.

Perhaps the most important value of the metaphorical process is its function in human development. Without the capacity for analogical thinking, humankind would not be able to transcend the physical world, even for a moment, because in our physical experience abstract thought is impossible without the use of a referent or analogy. For example, to discuss or comprehend spiritual qualities, we must first relate these ephemeral realities to concrete examples we have experienced. This essential need for using the analogical process to understand abstraction is expressed by 'Abdu'l-Bahá when He explained that

human knowledge is of two kinds. One is the knowledge of things perceptible to the senses. . . .

The other kind of human knowledge is intellectual—that is to say, it is a reality of the intellect; it has no outward form and no place and is not perceptible to the senses. . . . Therefore, to explain the reality of the spirit—its condition, its station—one is obliged to give explanations under the forms of sensible things because in the external world all that exists is sensible. For example, grief and happiness are intellectual things; when you wish to express those spiritual qualities you say: "My heart is oppressed; my heart is dilated," though the heart of man is neither oppressed nor dilated. This is an intellectual or spiritual state, to explain which you are obliged to have recourse to sensible figures. Another example: you say, "such an individual made great progress," though he is remaining in the same place; or again, "such a one's position was exalted," although, like everyone else, he walks upon the earth. This exaltation and this progress are spiritual states and intellectual realities, but to explain them you are obliged to have recourse to sensible figures because in the exterior world there is nothing that is not sensible.

So the symbol of knowledge is light, and of ignorance, darkness; but reflect, is knowledge sensible light, or ignorance sensible darkness? No, they are merely symbols.[4]

It is the metaphorical process, then, together with the faculty for inductive logic, that enables us to pass beyond the Pavlovian or Skinnerian reflex in order that we might conceptualize about ourselves and about the world around us.

As any teacher knows, this process is hardly confined to the education of adults. Wittingly and unwittingly a child collects data from daily experiences, perceives the similarities among experiences, and from this collection of images induces abstract beliefs. For example, when a child is punished or corrected for essentially different actions, he or she, at some point, may come to perceive a common link among these different experiences, the x-factor. Perhaps the similar ingredients among rules and obedience may ultimately come to represent various expressions of concern or even of love.

The child then deduces further generalizations about the concepts and may even perceive that among the variety of rules that require obedience to authority is a concept of order and justice. Furthermore, if these same rules at some point prove helpful to his or her well-being, the child may further conclude that some authority is worthy of respect and obedience.

On the other hand, if there is no consistency among the rules, no basis for their administration, the child may understandably conclude that authority is capricious, unjust, frightening, and unworthy of respect.

The child need not be aware of this process and how it works in order for it to exercise its influence on the child's development. The child may not know that the process is taking place at all, that he or she is thinking metaphorically and forming generalizations from the data collected. But the child is constantly doing it all the same.

From the initial stages of abstract thought, a child progresses without limit to more encompassing abstractions; concepts are always in a relative state of being perceived and developed. Once having observed authority dramatized in a familial relationship, for example, a child may later collect and store other dramatizations of this abstraction, perhaps from observations of a teacher or public official.

As the process continues, the child continues to collect the data and may perceive authority as a quality beyond what he or she sees embodied in specific people. A belief in the concepts or virtues of truth, honesty, or kindness may represent an authority far more powerful than any human exemplifying these attributes. Even in such instances the child is still relating the abstraction to the physical world; he or she has come to understand honesty or kindness as manifested in the physical classroom.

But there is no point at which the lesson is completed. The abstraction can always be more acutely perceived, more expansively understood, more exquisitely dramatized in the physical world. And, as we have already observed, such limitless growth is not confined to the individual. Society as the collective self can grow to understand and apply more fully abstract concepts of authority, justice, or honesty. As that collective awareness progresses, society can become capable of implementing more completely such concepts in social organization and action.

Viewed in the context of our ever-expanding comprehension of abstract concepts, the metaphorical process is an educational tool that can help provide limitless development, even if we have no precise moral code or established theological belief. However, within the context of the Bahá'í perception of man's nature and destiny, this process assumes a much greater significance. Not only does this endeavor bring immediate fulfillment and happiness by utilizing the physical metaphor as it was created to be used; it also results in the gradual improvement of the soul itself as, incrementally, particular attributes are habituated and assimilated.

Metaphor and Spiritual Education

The improvement of the soul through the metaphorical dramatization of spiritual attributes is hardly a new idea. For ages the allegorized fable has been employed in almost every culture as an effective teaching device. Such fables are particularly important in tribal cultures where oral narratives in the form of myths are used to convey moral precepts of courage, generosity, obedience, and trustworthiness.

In the medieval era in Europe the "morality plays"—a form of allegorical drama—was used to teach an unlearned and predominantly illiterate populace the essential doctrines of their faith. In fact, virtually all theater, including classical Greek tragedy, derives from religious origins and the attempt to express spiritual concepts in memorable dramatic form.

The fact that allegorical storytelling and drama have a long and widespread history does not imply that all metaphorical devices function exactly the same. But all do share essentially the same ingredients and occur according to a similar pattern. First, the audience comes to understand the nature of an abstraction (a virtue or vice) by observing it in physical action. Second, the audience realizes that every action has a similar capacity—to give dramatic form to an internal condition. Third, the audience begins to understand that this same process can be employed to acquire a virtue (by responding to reality according to a certain positive pattern of behavior) or, if one is not careful, to acquire a vice (by acting in an ignoble manner repeatedly—the message of tragedy). Third, the audience comes to realize over time that when a course of action (good or bad) is pursued with intention repeatedly, the response becomes habituated, instinctive, and assimilated into one's essential character.

As we acquire an understanding of how these patterns of metaphorical action beget change in character, we can employ this methodology to alter our own character by degrees. Of course, such change comes about only with daily vigilance and persistent effort. But the end result can be immensely satisfying, not merely because we have brought about some incremental change in our essential nature, in our soul itself, but also because we realize that with this process of assimilating attributes through our own willful action, we have the capacity to take control of our own lives and to foster and fashion our own spiritual development. In short, we have the possibility of molding ourselves into whatever we aspire to become.

But there is still more to learn about the application of this process. Once we recognize a spiritual attribute in action, we are capable of becoming attentive to the same attribute as it is reflected in ever more elaborate, ever more inclusive forms. This enhanced perception or understanding of the attribute can then be employed in reverse—we can conceive of inventive expressions by which we ourselves can apply this attribute to our daily lives. In this manner we assist our soul to progress by degrees in the acquisition of virtues without ever reaching a final or finished stage of expression of a single virtue, let alone the infinitude of all attributes: "When man reaches the noblest state in the world of humanity, then he can make further progress in the conditions of perfection, but not in state; for such states are limited, but the divine perfections are endless."[5]

Physical reality thus functions metaphorically during our earthly lives as an integral and inextricable part of our efforts to achieve spiritual development by providing both the means whereby we can begin to recognize spiritual attributes and the tools with which we can express and acquire attributes in ever more complete or expansive applications in physical action.

But there is a fascinating axiom that applies to this process so long as our soul maintains its associative relationship with the human body—that is, while, we remain in the physical part of our eternal existence: Even as we grow spiritually and are able to respond to increasingly higher levels of understanding, we never relinquish during our physical existence the need to relate our understanding to instructive metaphors. Stated another way, the reciprocal relationship between knowing and doing remains functional because our understanding of abstractions remains necessarily dependent on our relating concepts to concrete expression.

Consider the attribute of cleanliness. We may first understand this abstraction in terms of seeing the similarity among the diverse acts of cleanliness we are required to perform as children—cleaning our room, bathing, brushing our teeth, putting on clean clothes. At the outset we may perceive these as separate activities, each of which requires a discrete understanding and its own set of rules. Over time each of these distinct acts may become habitual. But at some point in our development, we will mentally assemble these separate acts as diverse expressions of a single virtue.

In short, we will have discovered the metaphorical relationship that unites these essentially different actions. Once we attain this state of awareness, we will no longer have to learn so many specific regulations—we will have grasped that there is a single principle underlying the guidance implicit in all these separate acts, the attribute or concept or virtue of cleanliness itself. Once we have acquired this knowledge, we can then become capable of applying that principle to other diverse and unrelated physical actions. We apply "cleanliness" to our speech, to our manners, to our dress. We can become inventive and creative in our application of this abstract principle to every aspect of our existence in order that we may achieve ever more expansive levels of refinement as a human being.

One of the more interesting outcomes of this process by which we grow and develop in our capacity to apply physical experience as a tool for spiritual and intellectual advancement is the largely unanticipated bounty of becoming liberated—probably the last thing we might consider as the result of habit. That is, as we manifest progressively more expanded levels of understanding into patterns of habit and discipline, we no longer have to apply a significant portion of willpower to accomplish these acts—they become instinctive. We no longer have to struggle against the natural inertia that characterizes our immature nature. Instead, we can reserve the energy needed to exert willpower to more sophisticated enterprises, to more lofty and subtle expressions of a given attribute— to cleanliness of thought and reflection, to purity of motive and intention. In other words, the acquisition of habits and self-discipline frees us to attend to the more important and lofty tasks we can assume as essentially spiritual beings trying to prepare ourselves for the continuity of our existence in a metaphysical realm.

There is another related axiom that is also well worth noting at this point—instructing children in this methodology is one of the greatest gifts parents can bestow. What has been called 'Abdu'l-Bahá's "golden rule" of education is the axiom that the early training of the child in forming habits and patterns of self-discipline is relatively easy—*relatively* being the operative word here. But as a youth approaches the age of maturity (fifteen years of age for Bahá'ís), change in essential patterns of behavior becomes increasingly arduous, for both parent and child.

Indeed, it is virtually axiomatic that without some capacity for self-discipline, a developing child cannot be released from one level of response in order to ascend to the next. Consequently, the early training of the child in the formation of good habits and in the initiation of self-discipline becomes, when properly taught (nurtured instead of being coerced), a key to the child's freedom, a truly precious gift, a profound expression of love, not, as some would have it, stifling the child's creative spirit.

Once we become accustomed to the rewards of applied habit and discipline, the less likely it is that we will be overwhelmed by the initial difficulties that inevitably occur in the struggle against the natural inertia or resistance to growth. As we will discuss in the section of chapter 7 entitled "The Metaphorical Lessons in Negative Experience," attempting spiritual growth without discomfort is like trying to become physically conditioned without enduring stress, sore muscles, and repetitious exercises.

If a child has not been trained to persist in spite of anxiety and discomfort, if he or she has not experienced analogous situations in which persistence, willpower, and repeated effort have paid off and proved rewarding, no degree of assurance about abstract spiritual rewards will likely prove sufficient impetus to ensure success in exhorting the child to change. Indeed, nothing is more frustrating to a child than to be constantly admonished to be "good" without having any concrete example of exactly what this nebulous abstract reality of "goodness" really is or how exactly it is attained.

The child needs to be aware of this initial discomfort in acquiring patterns of behavior—good habits—so that when the child begins to weigh the value of moral principles against the enticements of sensuality, what "feels good" will not be the sole index as to what is the best course of action to follow. If the child is allowed to assume this commonly held epicurean philosophy of catering to comfort, it is virtually certain that he or she is doomed from the start.

As an aside, if we think about it, this same principle holds true in our investigation of religion. If we search for a set of beliefs that does not challenge us, if our sole criterion for discovering a suitable and credible system of belief is that it "feels comfortable," we may be in danger of assuming that our current state of development is the proper touchstone, the correct standard by which to judge beliefs—that we are already in a state of perfection. Obviously the reverse should be the case—we need to assess our own progress by a standard independent of our own condition, a standard that is based on spiritual truths that describe reality, but also a standard that continually exhorts us to strive beyond our present state of stasis and achievement.

Finally, we may choose not to use the metaphorical classroom to advance our growth, but all creation, from the smallest seed to the universe itself, exhorts us to fulfill our inherent destiny, to ascend from mere physical subsistence and to soar in the heights of human perfection:

> Thus the embryo of man in the womb of the mother gradually grows and develops, and appears in different forms and conditions, until in the degree of perfect beauty it reaches maturity

and appears in a perfect form with the utmost grace. And in the same way, the seed of this flower which you see was in the beginning an insignificant thing, and very small; and it grew and developed in the womb of the earth and, after appearing in various forms, came forth in this condition with perfect freshness and grace. In the same manner, it is evident that this terrestrial globe, having once found existence, grew and developed in the matrix of the universe, and came forth in different forms and conditions, until gradually it attained this present perfection, and became adorned with innumerable beings, and appeared as a finished organization.[6]

METAPHOR IN THE TEACHING TECHNIQUE OF THE MANIFESTATIONS

Since the metaphorical process is the principal means by which spiritual growth is achieved in the physical world, it would seem logical that the process would be evident in the methods of the Prophets or Manifestations of God. That is, if the theological tenets of the world religions are correct, the Manifestations of God are perfect teachers sent to direct our spiritual development. Therefore it is reasonable to assume that They would employ perfect teaching methods. When we examine the techniques They do employ, we indeed discover that analogical methodologies are at the heart of Their techniques.

In fact, metaphorical devices constitute the core of the methodology employed by the Manifestations. Even the persona or identity of each Manifestation involves the metaphorical process, for in addition to being an Emissary from the divine realm come to inform us, the Manifestation is also an Exemplar of the very same spirituality He is trying to encourage. Put in the simplest of terms, the Manifestation is a perfect reflection of all the attributes of God insofar as these attributes can be dramatized in human expression.

This station of perfection relates directly to humanity's twofold purpose: "The purpose of God in creating man hath been, and will ever be, to enable him to know his Creator and to attain His Presence."[7] Since the Bahá'í writings depict God as essentially unknowable, the most effective means of knowing God is to know the Manifestations Who, as a prism makes visible the conceal attributes of light, reveal to us the constituent qualities of Godliness. In this sense it is clear that attaining the presence of God, as described in the scriptures of various religions, does not imply attaining physical proximity, but rather changing the spiritual condition of our souls so that we become more like Him.

Yet, as we have already seen, acquisition of spiritual attributes cannot take place without understanding. In effect, knowing God and attaining His presence are two aspects of one process. In this regard Bahá'u'lláh points out in the Kitáb-i-Aqdas that we cannot sever the recognition of the Manifestation from obedience to His laws: "These twin duties are inseparable. Neither is acceptable without the other."[8]

Recognition of the Manifestation is, therefore, a necessary prerequisite for spiritual advancement; it is not sufficient simply to follow a pattern of behavior. But this is not an arbitrary requirement. Recognition of the Manifestation of God implies more than perceiving the validity of His description of the universe, the pragmatic value of His ordinances, or even the value of His sacrificial life. It involves perceiving the way in which the Manifestation "metaphorizes" or dramatizes God for us.

In this way, the Manifestation is clearly distinct from all other spiritual teachers, no matter how astute their teachings, no matter how wise their laws. To know God is to know the Manifestation, and to know the Manifestation is to understand the way in which He manifests the qualities of God. So it is that in responding to Philip's request to see the mysterious "Father" about Whom Jesus had said so much during His ministry, Christ responds, "Have I been with you so long, and yet you do not know me, Philip? He who has seen me has seen the Father; how can you say, 'Show us the Father'?"[9]

In considering Christ's response to Philip, we must not confuse the tenor with the vehicle by accepting the metaphor as having literal significance. Instead, we are challenged to extract the meaning by discerning the similarity between the two essentially distinct components. In this important passage, we are challenged to discern the similarity between Christ (the vehicle) and God (the tenor) while realizing that each is in "essence" distinct from the other.

Clearly the similarity between these two essentially different entities is not physical, since the Manifestation is not necessarily physically impressive and since God is not a physical being. Neither is the similarity in physical power, since none of the Manifestations aspire to earthly ascendancy or accept it if it is proffered to Them. The commonly shared qualities are spiritual powers and capacities. To confuse the literal or physical nature of the vehicle (the person or personality of the Manifestation) with the tenor He represents (the nature of God) is to do more than mangle an analogy. To miss the metaphorical nature of the relationship between the Manifestation and God is to misunderstand completely the nature of the Manifestation, to fail to understand God Himself, and to confuse the whole educative process by which the Manifestation is attempting to instruct us.

No doubt it is because of the tendency to confuse the vehicle with the tenor that the Manifestations expend extensive effort in making this metaphorical relationship clear. For example, even though Christ states that no one can understand God except by first understanding Christ, He explains that He is essentially *different* from God: "'I am the true vine, and my Father is the vine-dresser.'"[10] Furthermore, throughout His teachings He explains that He is not the ultimate source of authority behind the revelation, but a reflection of the Deity Who is:

> "He who believes in me, believes not in me but in him who sent me."[11]

> "For I have not spoken on my own authority; the Father who sent me has himself given me commandment what to say and what to speak."[12]

> "The words that I say to you I do not speak on my own authority; but the Father who dwells in me does his works."[13]

In a similar manner, Bahá'u'lláh explains the relationship of the Manifestation to God and repeatedly articulates the same theme—that He is an instrument God has employed to educate men:

> This thing is not from Me, but from One Who is Almighty and All-Knowing. And He bade Me lift up My voice between earth and heaven. . . .[14]

> This is but a leaf which the winds of the will of thy Lord, the Almighty, the All-Praised, have stirred.[15]

> By My Life! Not of Mine own volition have I revealed Myself, but God, of His own choosing, hath manifested Me.[16]

One example of the disastrous results of not recognizing the metaphorical process at work in the nature of the Manifestations is evident in the far-reaching effects of the vote taken at the Council of Nicaea in 325 A.D. The followers of Athanasius, an Egyptian theologian and ecclesiastical statesman, asserted that the tenor and the vehicle are one—that Christ and God are the same essence. The followers of Arius, a Christian priest of Alexandria, believed Christ is essentially inferior to God and was sent to do God's bidding.

Subsequent to heated debate, a ballot was cast and Arius lost. The institution of the church sanctioned the theology of Athanasius, condemned as heresy the views of Arius, and effectively severed itself from Christ's fundamental teaching for all time. As Muḥammad pointed out to the Christians three hundred years later, to equate Christ with God is to add gods to God—in effect, to believe in more than one God as did the idolaters of Muḥammad's day:

> Infidels now are they who say, "God is the Messiah, Son of Mary;" for the Messiah said, "O children of Israel! worship God, my Lord and your Lord." Whoever shall join other gods with God, God shall forbid him the Garden, and his abode shall be the Fire; and the wicked shall have no helpers.[17]

The use of metaphor is also the key to unlocking the meaning of the physical acts of the Manifestations. Since none of the Manifestations aspire to physical authority or dominion, any expression of physical power by Them clearly has limited importance. In healing the sick, Christ was not attempting to rid the land of disease or to demonstrate an innovative medical technique. 'Abdu'l-Bahá explains that the miraculous acts of the Manifestations have as their primary purpose the metaphorical or analogical dramatization of a spiritual truth:

The outward miracles have no importance for the people of Reality. If a blind man receive sight, for example, he will finally again become sightless, for he will die and be deprived of all his senses and powers. Therefore, causing the blind man to see is comparatively of little importance, for this faculty of sight will at last disappear. If the body of a dead person be resuscitated, of what use is it since the body will die again? But it is important to give perception and eternal life—that is, the spiritual and divine life. . . .

. . . Wherever in the Holy Books they speak of raising the dead, the meaning is that the dead were blessed by eternal life; where it is said that the blind received sight, the signification is that he obtained the true perception. . . . This is ascertained from the text of the Gospel where Christ said: "These are like those of whom Isaiah said, They have eyes and see not, they have ears and hear not; and I healed them."

The meaning is not that the Manifestations are unable to perform miracles, for They have all power. But for Them inner sight, spiritual healing and eternal life are the valuable and important things.[18]

It is with obvious wisdom, therefore, that Bahá'u'lláh and 'Abdu'l-Bahá exhort Bahá'ís not to place any emphasis on the miracles associated with Bahá'u'lláh. As 'Abdu'l-Bahá points out, the act is valuable only to those who witness the event, and even those witnesses may later doubt what they thought they observed:

I do not wish to mention the miracles of Bahá'u'lláh, for it may perhaps be said that these are traditions, liable both to truth and to error. . . . Though if I wish to mention the supernatural acts of Bahá'u'lláh, they are numerous; they are acknowledged

in the Orient, and even by some non-Bahá'ís. . . . Yes, miracles
are proofs for the eyewitness only, and even he may regard them
not as a miracle but as an enchantment.[19]

There is also an obvious temptation on the part of the followers of
a Manifestation to believe in Him or to worship Him because of
what they perceive to be impressive or miraculous physical deeds.
When they do so, they perceive Him as a figure of temporal power
instead of spiritual authority. It is understandably easier for the followers to become attracted to the vehicle—the personalities of the
Prophets or the literal acts They perform—than to recognize the
spiritual powers and attributes They manifest.

One of the clearest examples of such a mistaken perception, besides the almost inevitable attachment to the physical person of the
Manifestation, is the incident of Christ's feeding of the five thousand. After He performed the miracle of feeding the masses with
only five barley loaves and two fishes, the people suddenly became
assured that He was indeed a Prophet. When Christ saw that they
wanted to take Him by force and make Him king, He fled to the
hills. He explained the reason for His action to His disciples the
next day when they found Him on the opposite side of the Sea of
Galilee:

"Truly, truly, I say to you, you seek me, not because you saw
signs, but because you ate your fill of the loaves. Do not labor for
the food which perishes, but for the food which endures to eternal life, which the Son of man will give to you; for on him has
God the Father set his seal."[20]

When the people failed to understand the metaphorical meaning or
inner significance of His act and wanted to become His followers
because of the miracle He seemed to have performed, He became

disconsolate and left them. The importance He placed on their grasping the "inner" significance of His physical actions is further evident in the patience with which He continued His explanation:

> "Our fathers ate the manna in the wilderness; as it is written, 'He gave them bread from heaven to eat.'" Jesus then said to them, "Truly, truly, I say to you, it was not Moses who gave you the bread from heaven; my Father gives you the true bread from heaven. For the bread of God is that which comes down from heaven, and gives life to the world." They said to him, "Lord, give us this bread always."
>
> Jesus said to them, "I am the bread of life; he who comes to me shall not hunger, and he who believes in me shall never thirst."[21]

If we think that Christ belabors the imagery of the bread from heaven, we are wrong. Even when He repeats and extends the conceit, the Jews do not appreciate the metaphorical intent of His actions or of His words:

> "I am the living bread which came down from heaven; if any one eats of this bread, he will live for ever; and the bread which I shall give for the life of the world is my flesh."
>
> The Jews then disputed among themselves, saying "How can this man give us his flesh to eat?"[22]

Having been raised in a legalistic religious tradition, the Jews had difficulty understanding teachings that were communicated through metaphor and symbol, even though their own rituals had originated in the symbolic or metaphorical expression of spiritual concepts.

Thus, in a very real sense the actions and teaching methods of Christ were precisely aimed at breaking through the literalism of His primary audience, the Jewish people. He was teaching them to think "spiritually" or metaphorically, to sense the inner significance of His words and their own scripture, as well as the meaning underlying the outer forms of their religious practices. For example, one of the most powerful symbolic acts Christ performed became for Christians the most important sacrament, the sacrament of the Eucharist.

As one of His last actions among His disciples, Christ once again employed the metaphor or symbol of nourishment when He spoke of the wine and the bread imagery at the Last Supper:

> Now as they were eating, Jesus took bread, and blessed, and broke it, and gave it to the disciples and said, "Take, eat; this is my body." And he took a cup, and when he had given thanks he gave it to them, saying, "Drink of it, all of you; for this is my blood of the covenant, which is poured out for many for the forgiveness of sins."[23]

In this case, a verbal metaphor was not sufficient. Christ had His own disciples act out the metaphor. And yet, despite the clarity of this teaching exercise, the Christian church in the thirteenth century adopted the doctrine of transubstantiation—the belief that the wine and bread when blessed by the priest literally become the blood and body of Christ (though there are variations on how this doctrine is explained).

The life of Bahá'u'lláh also contains many actions replete with obvious metaphorical value. The conference at Badasht in 1848 is among the most intriguing. The purpose of the occasion was, according to Shoghi Effendi, to implement the revelation of the Báb by a sudden, complete, and dramatic break with Islam—"with its order, its ecclesiasticism, its traditions, and ceremonials."[24] In order to act out this transition metaphorically, Bahá'u'lláh rented three gardens—one for Himself, one for Quddús, and a third for Ṭáhirih.* According to a prearranged plan, Quddús and Ṭáhirih publicly quarreled during the conference, Quddús advocating a conservative view that the followers of the Báb not dissociate themselves from the religion of Islam, and Ṭáhirih asserting that the Bábí movement was a new revelation and urging the Bábís to break with Islam:

> It was Bahá'u'lláh Who steadily, unerringly, yet unsuspectedly, steered the course of that memorable episode, and it was Bahá'u'lláh Who brought the meeting to its final and dramatic climax. One day in His presence, when illness had confined Him to bed, Ṭáhirih, regarded as the fair and spotless emblem of chastity and the incarnation of the holy Fáṭimih, appeared suddenly, adorned yet unveiled, before the assembled companions, seated herself on the right hand of the affrighted and infuriated Quddús, and tearing through her fiery words the veils guarding the sanctity of the ordinances of Islám, sounded the clarion-call, and proclaimed the inauguration, of a new Dispensation.[25]

This dramatic event no doubt had many metaphorical meanings, not the least of which was a transition from one "garden" (Islam) to a completely new "garden" (the Bábí revelation). We may also find symbolic value in the fact that Bahá'u'lláh occupied a third "garden"—possibly a symbol of His own revelation, in the same way that one of the Hidden Words employs a garden image to represent that revelation:

---

* Quddús and Ṭáhirih were prominent Bábí leaders and teachers.

> Proclaim unto the children of assurance that within the realms
> of holiness, nigh unto the celestial paradise, a new garden hath
> appeared, round which circle the denizens of the realm on high
> and the immortal dwellers of the exalted paradise.[26]

Not all the actions of the Manifestations and Their followers are so clearly symbolic or metaphorical, though one can hardly ignore the overall dramatic and metaphorical tenor of the entire Heroic Age* of the Bahá'í Faith. But, strictly speaking, all the actions of the Manifestation demonstrate God's love for man through dramatic physical expression.

Possibly the most obvious use of metaphor as a teaching device by the Manifestations is in Their use of language. Whether it is in from of the allegorical myths of the Old Testament, the parables of Christ, or the exquisite poetic imagery of Bahá'u'lláh's verses, the language of the Manifestations relies on figures drawn from the phenomenal world in order to translate abstract concepts into terms that humanity can more readily understand. To render a comparative analysis of the types of imagery used by the successive Manifestations would require countless volumes, but several general observations will be sufficient for our purposes to demonstrate how essential metaphor is in the language of these Teachers.

As Bahá'u'lláh explains in the Kitáb-i-Íqán, the Manifestations do not always use language that is veiled, allusive, or metaphorical. The type of language They employ depends on the purposes of the work and the exigencies of the situation:

---

* The Heroic Age of the Bahá'í Faith is the period of Bahá'í history that spans the ministries of the Báb, Bahá'u'lláh, and 'Abdu'l-Bahá. It began with the Báb's declaration of His mission in 1844 and ended in 1921 with the passing of 'Abdu'l-Bahá.

It is evident unto thee that the Birds of Heaven and Doves of Eternity speak a twofold language. One language, the outward language, is devoid of allusions, is unconcealed and unveiled; that it may be a guiding lamp and a beaconing light whereby wayfarers may attain the heights of holiness, and seekers may advance into the realm of eternal reunion. Such are the unveiled traditions and the evident verses already mentioned. The other language is veiled and concealed, so that whatever lieth hidden in the heart of the malevolent may be made manifest and their innermost being be disclosed. . . . In such utterances, the literal meaning, as generally understood by the people, is not what hath been intended.[27]

One illustration of Bahá'u'lláh's statement might be the distinction we would make between the language with which the Manifestation reveals His laws and the language with which He inspires and explains spiritual verities and attributes.

There are no exact rules about when a Manifestation will speak metaphorically and when He will not. As we study the Old Testament, we can only guess how literally the followers of Abraham or Moses perceived the anthropomorphic descriptions of God and the physical evidences of His intervention in the lives of the peoples of that day. But two major uses of metaphorical language seem relatively consistent, as in the revelations of Christ, Muḥammad, and Bahá'u'lláh.

One recurring use is the portrayal of spiritual concepts. Christ employed the parable almost exclusively. Like other metaphorical devices, the parable forces the listener to participate, to decide the meaning. But being an extended analogy in the form of a story, the parable has the further advantage of working on various levels with multiple metaphoric equations. It is also able to hold the interest of the audience because on the literal level it contains a dramatic narrative.

Thus while Christ was establishing a degree of intimacy with His audience by telling a literal story that depicts characters and situations familiar to His listeners (a prodigal son, laborers in a vineyard, a merchant discovering a pearl of great worth, sowers of seed), He was also teaching His followers to think abstractly, to escape the literalism of their inherited beliefs, and to understand the spiritual or inner significance of His words. Instead of an elaborate canon of law (though He did reveal an abundance of laws as well), He bequeathed to His believers a treasury of memorable stories, each one of which had the capacity to challenge the most humble and the most erudite among his followers. Any seeker, the highest or the lowest, the learned as well as the untutored, could appreciate Christ's parables in a different way. But those entrapped in their literalism could not penetrate the shell of the metaphorical lesson, neither could they grasp the figurative implications of their own Messianic teachings and thereby recognize Christ as having fulfilled the symbolic prophecies of their own scripture:

> Then the disciples came and said to him, "Why do you speak to them in parables?" And he answered them, "To you it has been given to know the secrets of the kingdom of heaven, but to them it has not been given. For to him who has will more be given, and he will have abundance; but from him who has not, even what he has will be taken away. This is why I speak to them in parables, because seeing they do not see, and hearing they do not hear, nor do they understand."[28]

Christ later told His disciples, "the hour is coming when I shall no longer speak to you in figures but tell you plainly of the Father."[29]

Certainly Muḥammad fulfills this promise in the Qur'án. He speaks openly and forthrightly about the sequence of Prophets God has sent and about how humankind has rejected each of them. As we mentioned earlier, He also blatantly chastises the Christian clergy who had distorted the teachings of Christ to imply that Christ was God incarnate, stating that Christ was no less divine because He was a Prophet or Apostle of God and not God Himself.

7

METAPHORICAL SOLUTIONS TO THEODICY: WHY GOD WANTS US TO THINK

O My Servant! Thou art even as a finely tempered sword concealed in the darkness of its sheath and its value hidden from the artificer's knowledge. Wherefore come forth from the sheath of self and desire that thy worth may be made resplendent and manifest unto all the world.

—Bahá'u'lláh

In the Kitáb-i-Íqán, a highly structured work that discusses the importance of learning to understand the symbolic and metaphorical language of scripture, Bahá'u'lláh asserts that one of the primary reasons the Prophets down through the ages have been rejected has been the inability of religious leaders to understand the veiled or metaphorical meaning of the prophecies in the utterances of the previous Manifestation.

To prove His point, Bahá'u'lláh devotes the first hundred pages or more of this treatise to explicating the meaning of Christ's prophe-

cies about the coming of Muḥammad as foretold in Matthew 24:
29–31. He elucidates the meaning of the verses to demonstrate to
His largely Muslim audience that their inability to convince Christians that Muḥammad had fulfilled Christ's promise was not, as
some Muslim clerics had claimed, the result of the corruption of
the scriptures. Rather, He points out, the Muslim teacher had
failed to show Christians how to perceive the metaphorical and
symbolic meaning of their own scripture, the same plight, he notes,
that prevented Jewish scholars from recognizing Christ as the
messiah.

He goes on to note that their own scripture, the Qur'án, clearly
foretells the advent of the Báb in fulfillment of prophecies regarding the Qá'im (Arabic for "He who shall arise"). As a demonstration of this thesis, Bahá'u'lláh continually cites abstruse Qur'ánic
passages and interprets their metaphorical meaning to show how
they prepare Muslims for the events that—by the time of Bahá'-
u'lláh's revelation of the Kitáb-i-Íqán in 1862—had already occurred.
He concludes this remarkable work about language and the progressive nature of revelation by admonishing the Bábís (the followers of the Báb) that they too would be tested in precisely the same
way when the succeeding Manifestation of God (Whom the Báb
revealed to be Bahá'u'lláh Himself) would appear in fulfillment of
prophecies in the writings of the Báb regarding "Him Whom God
Will Make Manifest."

But in addition to teaching us how to read scripture, Bahá'u'lláh
Himself employs imagery magnificently in those passages and works
where such poetic technique is warranted and useful. For example,
in His meditative writings, in most of His prayers, in the Persian
Hidden Words, in the Súriy-i-Haykal, and in various other works,
Bahá'u'lláh bequeathed a vast storehouse of figurative imagery and
symbols, the interpretation of which challenge even the most as-

tute minds. In fact, in describing those utterances in which "the
literal meaning, as generally understood by the people, is not what
hath been intended," Bahá'u'lláh states,

> Thus it is recorded: "Every knowledge hath seventy meanings,
> of which one only is known amongst the people. And when the
> Qá'im shall arise, He shall reveal unto men all that which
> remaineth." He also saith: "We speak one word, and by it we
> intend one and seventy meanings; each one of these meanings
> we can explain."[1]

However, the fact that the Manifestation can explain all the meanings does not mean He will. Like Christ with His parables,
Bahá'u'lláh most often does not explicate His own imagery but tests
our sincerity and determination to think for ourselves by forcing us
to extract the inner essence of His teachings.

Obviously it would be pretentious and, for our purposes here,
unnecessary to attempt any sort of general survey of Bahá'u'lláh's
utilization of imagery in His revealed writings. His uses are as var-
ied as the styles and purposes of His hundreds of tablets. But a few
examples of this technique will illustrate the importance of understanding the metaphorical process when we are studying the writings of Bahá'u'lláh.

One of the most notable examples of an extended metaphor is
found in the Seven Valleys, a richly allusive and highly imagistic
discussion of the pathway to spirituality. Written in the form of a
mystical treatise (similar in structure to *The Conference of the Birds*,
by twelfth-century Ṣúfí poet Farídu'd-Dín 'Aṭṭár), the work employs as its organizing principle a journey through seven symbolic
valleys as a metaphor for seven stages in the process of spiritual
development.

The idea of life as a journey or of spiritual ascent as a path or pilgrimage was not new in itself. Chaucer used a literal pilgrimage to symbolize the spiritual journey to the "New Jerusalem,"* and John Bunyan depicted salvation allegorically as a journey in *The Pilgrim's Progress*. Nevertheless, Bahá'u'lláh's application of this frame is particularly useful as an allegorical device. For example, for the first several valleys there is a symbolic "steed" to carry the wayfarer—for the Valley of Search it is the steed of Patience, for the Valley of Love it is the steed of Pain, and so on. Each horse, of course, symbolizes the primary capacity or attribute that the seeker must possess in order to traverse the valley successfully. Within each valley Bahá'u'lláh employs elaborate analogies and allegorical anecdotes, the most familiar of which is the story of Majnún and Laylí. He also alludes to various traditions, poems, Qur'ánic verses, and a variety of other poetic devices to describe the essential nature and purpose of each stage in the spiritual ascent.

In a more subtle utilization of metaphorical technique in His writings, Bahá'u'lláh will often employ a predominating image in His revealed prayers. For example, the morning prayers, while certainly appropriate to recitation during the literal morning time, also employ the repeated image of the morning time as a period of spiritual awakening during the early stages of the dispensation of a Prophet. For the same reason, the early Bábí martyrs were designated "Dawn-Breakers."

Metaphorically, the morning prayers play off the notion of sleep as a state of spiritual decline or obliviousness. For example, in one of the Hidden Words Bahá'u'lláh addresses the "Bond Slave of the World" over whom "many a dawn hath the breeze of My loving-

---

* At the end of the pilgrimage to Canterbury the Parson says, "And Jesus, by his grace, send me wit / To show you the way, on this journey, / To that same perfect glorious pilgrimage / Which is called the celestial city of Jerusalem." My translation is based on the Fisher edition (348: X, 48–51).

kindness wafted" and "found thee upon the bed of heedlessness fast asleep."[2] Each "dawn" can represent the successive appearance of the Manifestations, signifying that those attached to the mundane world have been oblivious to the coming of more than one Prophet. The Sun, of course, represents the Manifestation. The light is the truth He brings, and the cycle of the day is the Prophet's dispensation.

Having established some of the possible meanings of "dawn" as a metaphor, we can discover a deeper level of meaning to a morning prayer by penetrating its literal surfaces. For example, let us see what happens in two paragraphs from the following "morning" prayer of Bahá'u'lláh if we approach the words with these symbols in mind:

> I give praise to Thee, O my God, that Thou has awakened me out of my sleep, and brought me forth after my disappearance, and raised me up from my slumber. I have awakened this morning with my face set toward the splendors of the Daystar of Thy Revelation, through Which the heavens of Thy power and Thy majesty have been illumined, acknowledging Thy signs, believing in Thy Book, and holding fast unto Thy Cord.

> I beseech Thee, by the potency of Thy will and the compelling power of Thy purpose, to make of what Thou didst reveal unto me in my sleep the surest foundation for the mansions of Thy love that are within the hearts of Thy loved ones, and the best instrument for the revelation of the tokens of Thy grace and Thy loving-kindness.[3]

The prayer continues, but this passage is the heart of the metaphoric use of morning time. To interpret the prayer on a literal level would seem to imply that we should try to recall something about a dream we have had—and, in fact, 'Abdu'l-Bahá does admonish us to pay attention to our dreams. But probing beneath these literal surfaces we find another and perhaps more significant level of meaning.

If sleep is a state of heedlessness, we are praising God for having made us spiritually aware. But how can we assume that we are aware? Of course, the fact is that we are praying the prayer—why else would we be praying unless we were aware? As we pray, we may literally be facing the point of the sun's rising as we turn to the Qiblih (the point of adoration), but we are figuratively turning our attention to the "Daystar of Thy Revelation," Bahá'u'lláh Himself. Furthermore, the speaker, by acknowledging that he has "disappeared," implies that he had been awake before but had gone to sleep again, a possible allusion to the fact that most of us fail to maintain absolute constancy in following the light of truth. Even at our best, we have good days and bad days. Therefore the articulation of our own return from our "disappearance" is an affirmation of our determination to do better than we have been doing.

But what was it that was revealed to us in our sleep that "brought me forth after my disappearance"? What reminded us of who we are and what our purpose is? Perhaps for each of us it is something different. For example, in the Long Obligatory Prayer of Bahá'u'lláh we give thanks to God "that Thou hast aided me to remember Thee and to praise Thee. . . ."[4] In this instance, it is our obligation to pray the prayer that has awakened us from spiritual slumber or lethargy and caused us to reaffirm our essential purpose in life—our "just" state of being. One implication of this statement, then, is that without the ordinance that we pray, we might pray only when we feel extremely grateful to God or extremely oppressed, downhearted, or fearful.

With a morning prayer it may be the same thing that has awakened us—our sense of obligation to pray. But if we are praying and

struggling to attain spiritual growth, something has aided us to arrive at that condition, and whatever it might be has revived us and
renewed our awareness of the metaphorical morning time in which
we live.

Besides the prayers and meditations of Bahá'u'lláh, some of His
most frequently noted extended metaphors occur in the Persian
Hidden Words. The Persian language is, by tradition, a poetic language. This often happens with a language that does not have so
rich a vocabulary as do English or Arabic. For without words of
precision, connotation and imagery enable the speaker to express
subtleties. But the fact is that poetic traditions emerge early in the
history of a people for reasons that may have more to do with other
cultural orientations and less to do with vocabulary per se.

Regardless of the reason, it is enough to note that the Persian
section of the Hidden Words abounds in imagery. Some of the
metaphors are simple and easily understood, though no less powerful because they are accessible: "In the garden of thy heart plant
naught but the rose of love, and from the nightingale of affection
and desire loosen not thy hold."5 Other verses in the Persian Hidden Words are long, complex, and extremely difficult. But almost
all illustrate well the importance of metaphor in understanding the
many levels of meaning in the writings of Bahá'u'lláh.

One Hidden Word that is particularly well suited to illustrating
the mechanics of metaphor employs an extended image with three
main vehicles—a sword, a sheath, and an artificer, or sword-maker:

O My Servant! Thou art even as a finely tempered sword concealed in the darkness of its sheath and its value hidden from the
artificer's knowledge. Wherefore come forth from the sheath of
self and desire that thy worth may be made resplendent and
manifest unto all the world.6

Here Bahá'u'lláh has given us a start by filling in one of the three missing tenors in this equation; He tells us the sheath is "self and desire." Moreover, since the passage is addressed to a "servant," we can assume, perhaps, that the sword is a Bahá'í—a follower of Bahá'u'lláh. We can also assume that the "artificer" is God or the Manifestation of God (that is, God as Creator or the Manifestation Who has, in effect, recreated us on God's behalf).

But the equation is still not really solved because we do not know why the sword, the sheath, and the artificer are compared or what the metaphor is meant to demonstrate until we consider more carefully the tone and nature of the comparison. The servant is being criticized for remaining in the "sheath of self and desire"—that much we can understand—but why a sword, and a finely tempered one at that?

A sword, especially when finely tempered, is a practical instrument, a weapon of war. The servants of God are also meant to be practically useful—no longer monks in monasteries, but active in the world, warring against iniquity and injustice. To make themselves known to God, they must act, must use the perfections that lie dormant.

Here we may be reminded of the many passages that extol the lofty possibilities of the human spirit. When this potential is manifest in physical action, the spiritual capacity latent within all men becomes "manifest unto all the world." This is a particularly plausible interpretation since this passage is near the end of the volume, where we find similar exhortations for the "servant" to act: "Ye are the trees of My garden; ye must give forth goodly and wondrous fruits, that ye yourselves and others may profit therefrom."[7] But a more subtle and perhaps more refined interpretation is that the sword represents the tongue, an image that Bahá'u'lláh employs elsewhere.

The passage then becomes an exhortation for the believers or followers of the Prophet not to keep silent about what they have discovered, but to busy themselves teaching the good news to the rest of humankind, even as Bahá'u'lláh commands His followers: "Say: Teach ye the Cause of God, O people of Bahá, for God hath prescribed unto every one the duty of proclaiming His Message, and regardeth it as the most meritorious of all deeds."[8]

Relevant to our previous discussion, however, is the continuation of this exhortation in which Bahá'u'lláh states that such teaching will have no effect unless the teacher manifests the truth of his utterance in his own actions: "Such a deed is acceptable only when he that teacheth the Cause is already a firm believer in God, the Supreme Protector, the Gracious, the Almighty. He hath, moreover, ordained that His Cause be taught through the power of men's utterance, and not through resort to violence."[9]

These images from the Seven Valleys, the morning prayer, and the Hidden Words are but a few examples of the variety of uses of metaphorical language found in the writings of Bahá'u'lláh, each with its own possibilities for meaning. Not that we need become students of literature or poetry to understand or appreciate the writings of Bahá'u'lláh, but we must have something of a poetic soul to grasp the inner essence of what the Prophet means, if by "poetic" we mean the capacity to "see with thine own eyes and not through the eyes of others."[10]

But even more important regarding understanding the utterances of the Manifestations is Bahá'u'lláh's observation that the capacity to understand is actually more of a matter of spiritual attitude or purity of heart than it is the result of an intellectual exercise:

The understanding of His words and the comprehension of the utterances of the Birds of Heaven are in no wise dependent upon human learning. They depend solely upon purity of heart, chastity of soul, and freedom of spirit. This is evidenced by those who, today, though without a single letter of the accepted standards of learning, are occupying the loftiest seats of knowledge; and the garden of their hearts is adorned, through the showers of divine grace, with the roses of wisdom and the tulips of understanding.[11]

But it is not only in the more poetic tablets that Bahá'u'lláh uses imagery. Even in the Kitáb-i-Aqdas, the primary repository of Bahá'u'lláh's laws, there appears image upon image. Sometimes these figures may be a mere word or phrase, but often the figures are several lines in length. We need glimpse only a few of the numerous examples from the early passages of the Kitáb-i-Aqdas to appreciate the importance of figurative language in this work. In the following examples Bahá'u'lláh compares His laws to lamps, to keys, to choice wine, and to the sun:

Know assuredly that My commandments are the lamps of My loving providence among My servants, and the keys of My mercy for My creatures. . . .
    Think not that We have revealed unto you a mere code of laws. Nay, rather, We have unsealed the choice Wine with the fingers of might and power.[12]

In another place He has written,

Whenever My laws appear like the sun in the heaven of Mine utterance, they must be faithfully obeyed by all, though My decree be such as to cause the heaven of every religion to be cleft asunder.[13]

METAPHOR AND PROPHECY

As we have noted, Bahá'u'lláh particularly emphasizes the importance of understanding metaphor and symbol in the language of prophecy in the utterances of the Manifestations of God. Many Christians are still trying to discover the key to the symbols and figurative imagery in Christ's allusions to His return, and speculation abounds regarding the intricate symbolism of the Book of Revelation. Likewise, many Muslim scholars have devoted themselves to interpreting the veiled traditions regarding the Promised Qá'im or the Mihdí, while many Jews still await the fulfillment of the Messianic prophecies.

Perhaps because prophecy is such an important link from one revelation to the next, Bahá'u'lláh devotes a substantial portion of the Kitáb-i-Íqán to discussing the nature of prophecy. More specifically, when Bahá'u'lláh explicates the passage from Matthew 24:29–31, He explains in great detail the meaning of vehicles such as "sun," "heaven," "clouds," "smoke," and "angels." He also discusses some of the reasons for the intentional concealment and obfuscation that this symbolic language creates.

For example, He states that one reason that the Manifestation alludes to the time, place, and personhood of the succeeding Manifestation in symbolic terms is to test the sincerity and spirituality of those who await the advent of the Prophet. If people were allowed to discover the Manifestation by a name or physical sign only, they would not be required to understand or ascertain the spiritual nature of what it is they seek. Furthermore, some might turn to the Manifestation to achieve fame or to use His power for their benefit. What is more, those who possess temporal power and authority might view the Manifestation as a threat to their positions and might attempt to destroy Him, as did Herod with Christ.

But because the identity of the Manifestation is concealed in prophecy, humankind must be spiritually aware to understand the inner meaning of prophetic allusions and discover the Prophet's identity. For example, if we comprehend power and authority only in literal or physical terms, we will probably look for a physically impressive figure or someone who has achieved political power or importance. In short, we will be totally oblivious to the identity of the Manifestation.

LAW AS METAPHOR

Another important application of imagery occurs in the laws of the Manifestation. In addition to the figurative language in which the law itself may be expressed, there is often a metaphorical significance to the specific actions the laws require of us. For while the laws may have the obvious benefit of offering pragmatic responses to existential dilemmas, they also force us to act out dramatically in the physical world what we are trying to accomplish in the spiritual world.

The correlation between healthy actions and spiritual growth may not be so apparent with the laws that are basically restrictive and prohibitive in nature, but it is there all the same. For example, the Jews may have thought the Mosaic dietary laws arbitrary, but they followed them anyway as a demonstration of their faith in the authority of Moses and their obedience to the laws of God. But as they practiced this reverence for divine authority, they received the ancillary benefits of the fact that the creator of the law knew something about health that they did not. Now that science has discovered how various diseases are contracted, we can understand the scientific or practical basis underlying the dietary laws of Moses and realize how these "restrictions" were actually a source of liberation—from disease or even death.

Therefore, in perceiving the divine logic in the laws governing physical action and learning to follow the conduct prescribed by the Manifestations, we are training ourselves to have faith in the long-term benefits that the ostensible restriction imposes. It is then possible for us to apply this lesson to our compliance with other spiritual laws, and we can begin to accept the laws of the Manifestation as benign guidance and a loving gift. From such a perspective, the word "law" takes on an entirely new connotation.

Like their counterparts in the phenomenal world—laws that describe physical reality—God's divine ordinances are thus pragmatic, logical, and beneficial. Furthermore, as we act out the divine ordinances, we are gradually enabled to appreciate ever more profoundly the beneficence of God in educating us:

> Say: True liberty consisteth in man's submission unto My commandments, little as ye know it. Were men to observe that which We have sent down unto them from the Heaven of Revelation, they would, of a certainty, attain unto perfect liberty. Happy is the man that hath apprehended the Purpose of God in whatever He hath revealed from the Heaven of His Will, that pervadeth all created things.[14]

Understood in the light of this statement by Bahá'u'lláh about "true" liberty (as opposed to the concept of total license that currently passes for liberty), the laws of the Manifestation never prevent the full and complete utilization of the physical experience that is our participation in this foundational part of our eternal lives. On the contrary, even those laws that imply restriction in some physical enterprise ultimately encourage the most fulfilling use of it. Stated another way, the laws of the Manifestation enable us to experience the metaphorical value of the physical world, even when we as followers are unaware that we are doing anything other than obeying divine authority.

The laws that provide creative use of our physical lives reinforce the metaphorical value of that experience perhaps even more obviously than the laws of admonition and prohibition. The laws governing our physical lives change from one Manifestation to the next so that they accurately describe the relative progress in the stages of development of humankind. This progress of the human body politic is itself essentially metaphorical in nature in that a society acts out literally a figurative or spiritual understanding and perception.

For example, when law creates institutions, organizational structures, and codes of behavior that foster advancement, the law becomes an integral part of our efforts to dramatize spiritual progress. Thus, in addition to the long-range benefit of laws governing our physical lives, such laws have the immediate effect of creating for each individual an spiritual atmosphere through a social environment that is conducive to moral development.

One of the best examples of this relationship can be witnessed in our rapidly changing (deteriorating) environment. We are only beginning to understand the profound influence that every aspect of our physical environment has on our mental, emotional, and spiritual conditions. On the most basic level, we mammals require air, water, nourishment, and fellowship. We presently cannot depend on any of these. The air is polluted, often a source of disease, even as is the chemically treated water, the inorganic and chemically preserved foodstuffs, while the society which should provide us with safety and assistance in constructing a healthy family, seems bent on tearing at the very fabric of familial and community life.

But the Manifestations have always understood this relationship, and They have poignantly reflected that understanding in Their laws, whether the law describes how we conduct human relationships, organize our lives, care for our bodies, or associate with other human beings. Consider the following passage about the inner or spiritual effects of the simple outward attention to physical cleanliness:

> External cleanliness, although it is but a physical thing, hath a great influence upon spirituality. For example, although sound is but the vibrations of the air which affect the tympanum of the ear, and vibrations of the air are but an accident among the accidents which depend upon the air, consider how much marvelous notes or a charming song influence the spirits![15]

As the obedience to the laws of the Manifestation for each age gradually enhance the capacity of humankind to manifest spiritual concepts in social structure, we discover that these laws assist in bringing about the most encompassing and most strategic metaphorical exercise that exists, the gradual but unrelenting establishment of a planetary spiritual community. When understood from this perspective, the entire Bahá'í administrative order, its institutions, and its procedures are dramatic expressions of this process:

> The emergence of a world community, the consciousness of world citizenship, the founding of a world civilization and culture—all of which must synchronize with the initial stages in the unfoldment of the Golden Age of the Bahá'í Era—should, by their very nature, be regarded, as far as this planetary life is concerned, as the furthermost limits in the organization of human society, though man, as an individual, will, nay must indeed as a result

of such a consummation, continue indefinitely to progress and develop.[16]

Finally, many of the laws themselves are metaphorical exercises. When Christ wished to teach the abstract concept of the brotherhood of humankind to His followers, He ordained a law to help them act out that concept in a daring, dramatic change in Mosaic law:

> "You have heard that it was said, 'An eye for an eye and a tooth for a tooth.' But I say to you, Do not resist one who is evil. But if any one strikes you on the right cheek, turn to him the other also; and if any one would sue you and take your coat, let him have your cloak as well; and if any one forces you to go one mile, go with him two miles. Give to him who begs from you, and do not refuse him who would borrow from you.
>
> ". . . For if you love those who love you, what reward have you? Do not even the tax collectors do the same?"[17]

Likewise, while Bahá'u'lláh teaches abstract concepts such as the unity of humankind and the equality of women and men, He also provides humankind creative laws and dramatic institutions that enable us to act out spiritual principles in similar creative physical exercises. Many of the laws of the Manifestations are thus dramaturgical in nature, metaphorical devices by which we express with actions the spiritual attitudes we are attempting to develop. Sometimes understanding of the attitudes precedes the dramatization; sometimes the reverse is true. The point is that in studying the nature of the Manifestation Himself, His actions, His use of language, or the laws He institutes, we can observe the metaphorical tie between spiritual growth and physical performance as each reinforces the other in a pattern of continuous growth.

THE METAPHORICAL LESSONS
IN NEGATIVE EXPERIENCE

It would be erroneous to imply that all spiritual growth results from the willful application of the metaphorical process. A substantial portion of our experience is beyond our control. In addition, many of our most memorable experiences in life center on negative events, whether they be injustices suffered at the hands of others or simply the myriad unfortunate accidents that are the lot of mortal beings. But though such experiences may not result from our intentional application of the metaphorical process, we can still extract from them some of our most significant spiritual lessons.

To begin with, negative experience can be generally classified in three broad categories. First, there are accidents like those suffered by Job, events we might describe in terms of chance, natural disasters (ironically termed "acts of God"). Second, there are negative experiences resulting from the iniquity, malice, or injustice of others, the sort of experience that provoked Boethius to write his treatise. Third, there are the negative experiences that result from our own ignorance of, or refusal to abide by the guidance bestowed by the Manifestations—those moral laws that we cited earlier as having the same relationship to our lives as do physical laws of cause and effect.

The traditional problem in understanding experiences of the first category is an obvious one. If God loves us and has the power to prevent such events, why does He not do so? Or, following what we have observed about the benign intent of physical reality, what is the metaphorical value of such experience? If accidents are not part of the punishment inherent in the system of rewards and punishments, how do we account for the death of the innocent? Furthermore, if God has foreknowledge, then He is aware that a chance disaster is going to occur. And if He is aware that it will occur, it must occur (so traditional reasoning goes). Therefore, are not these foreseen events unavoidable or predestined?

In the face of such reasoning and the unfortunate events that often befall humankind, many have found it extremely difficult to believe in a loving Deity. The solution for some is to recreate God in an image that makes Him exist but not be responsible because He is constrained by the laws of nature that He has created: In effect, God "is limited in what He can do by laws of nature and by the evolution of human nature and human moral freedom."[18]

Juxtaposed to wars and other unspeakable sorts of inhumanity, our view of physical reality as a just and exquisite teaching device may indeed seem to falter and fail. To respond even briefly to these concerns, we first need to clarify what we mean by "evil," because we tend to classify experience quite broadly.

We tend to categorize as evil all things that we perceive as negative at a given point in time and from a given point of view. These "negative" events might include human immorality, lightning, floods, disease, political tyranny, insects, sharks, and fast food. Our tendency to apply the broad rubric of "negative" or "evil" to such unparallel and diverse experiences is understandable—we naturally assume that whatever occurs in God's universe is directly or indirectly His responsibility. He is logically guilty of either malfeasance or nonfeasance while operating heavy machinery (our planet and the rest of the universe).

As we noted earlier, from a Bahá'í point of view there is only one sort of occurrence that can appropriately be designated as "evil"— our willful rejection of our divine purpose. Bahá'u'lláh states that "the source of all evil is for man to turn away from his Lord and set his heart on things ungodly."[19] This is very specific. Yet "evil" in this sense does not include the failure to recognize the Manifestation as a result of our having an improper or inadequate education or our falling prey to other forces beyond our control:

> But in a place where the commands of a Prophet are not known, and where the people do not act in conformity with the divine instructions, . . . from the point of view of religion they are excused because the divine command has not been delivered to them.[20]

Stated another way, there is no evil inherent in God's creation except for those events that proceed from humanity's willful rejection of goodness. Thus when 'Abdu'l-Bahá states that "in creation there is no evil; all is good," he means that there is no *source* of evil.[21] Terms such as "sin," "Satan," "evil," and "wickedness" appear in the Bahá'í writings, even as they have appeared in the scriptures of previous revelations, but they designate an action or causal relationship, not an "essence."

The term "Satan," for example, is employed most frequently as a metaphor for the temptations of the "self"—to be self-centered or self-absorbed, to glory in one's own accomplishments or personality. But these are willful actions, or inactions, not a failure that results from the subtle seduction of an evil spirit. 'Abdu'l-Bahá states, "God has never created an evil spirit; all such ideas and nomenclature are symbols expressing the mere human or earthly nature of man."[22]

Evil is thus the absence of goodness in the same way that darkness is the absence of light or cold is the absence of heat. Nevertheless, there are *very* significant effects caused by the absence of light or heat or goodness. Turning away from the source of all life can cause changes in condition that can be momentous and devastating. Consequently, because we strive to understand clearly and to describe accurately these events and their consequences in our lives, we use powerful and vivid metaphorical terms to portray these effects.

By analogy, were we to travel to the Arctic wastes without proper clothing, we might admit intellectually that the absence of heat was causing us to freeze to death. But the effect of being remote from the direct rays of the sun produces the subjective experience of an active force, the force of ice and snow and bone-chilling wind. Clearly we would find it unsatisfying and ludicrous to announce to our companions as we freeze to death, "Say, fellows, this absence of energy from the sun's rays is certainly causing my feet to become black from frostbite!"

How can an essentially nonexistent force destroy our very lives? Therefore we need words, powerful and vivid images to portray the operation of these laws in our lives. Thus we might say that Hitler and the destruction he wrought resulted from his rampant violation and rejection of the laws of God, obedience to which is the source of all positive forces. And yet we desperately need to portray adequately the wretched and heartrending results that this active rejection of moral truth caused.

There are effects, and these effects have the appearance and feel of a negative energy, as if they were emanating from some evil source. Consequently, we resort to inventive metaphorical expressions to describe this appearance in history of such an obvious source of iniquity, injustice, and human suffering. Of course, history also teaches us that these immoral responses to the source of energy, these sorts of blatant injustice, are all ultimately doomed to failure, but we still need to describe these events and the ravages they have wrought.

The Manifestations of the past, wishing to convey spiritual states of being, have thus resorted to metaphors for evil, not because the Manifestations wished to portray a distorted image of reality, but because such devices were the best means by which humankind could at the time understand these abstract concepts of cause and effect and appreciate the peril resulting from ignoring or actively rejecting moral law. The Prophets thus frequently describe pride in terms of an iniquitous tempter, a "Satan." Likewise, they portray spiritual existence in the afterlife where one is freed from the injustice of tyranny or physical ills in terms of an idyllic pastoral abode, a paradise or Heaven. Similarly, spiritual degeneration and the resulting effects on a soul once it has come to realize how it has willfully perverted its opportunities to develop are portrayed in vivid sensual terms, a place of physical torment, a "hell":

Even the materialists have testified in their writings to the wisdom of these divinely-appointed Messengers, and have regarded the references made by the Prophets to Paradise, to hell fire, to future reward and punishment, to have been actuated by a desire to educate and uplift the souls of men.[23]

In one sense, then, evil is the result of man's willful acts; Bahá'u'lláh writes, "were men to abide by and observe the divine teachings, every trace of evil would be banished from the face of the earth."[24] And yet not all events that we term "evil" can be defined as the logical, direct consequences of our turning away from goodness. How do we account for the suffering of the innocent and for tests that befall us which seem to have no relationship to anything we have done? While not "evil" according to our precise definition, these events are still negative, unfortunate, unjust, or at least unmerited.

SUFFERING OF THE INNOCENT

There are several major principles in the Bahá'í writings that urge us toward a solution to these substantial dilemmas. For example, God is not restricted to this physical life in rectifying the injustices we have suffered in our individual lives, nor is God limited to a certain span of time for working out justice in history, as we have noted earlier.

This observation may seem obvious, but it is the single most critical factor in coming to terms with theodicy because it means that we cannot possibly evaluate or judge what befalls us or anyone else in terms of what they endure in their earthly experience. Whether suffering ultimately results in justice or injustice, something beneficial or harmful, would be similar to our attempting to assess how someone will fare in their chosen profession while they are still in a formative stage within the mother's womb.

Since our fruition is destined for another plane of existence, we can hardly assess what does and does not benefit that process any more than a fruit tree could evaluate the beneficial results of its own pruning. From our limited point of view, the death of an infant seems pointless and unjust, as does the suffering of the innocent. Yet it is clear in the Bahá'í writings that these infants are cared for, as are all who suffer innocently:

These infants are under the shadow of the favor of God; and as they have not committed any sin and are not soiled with the impurities of the world of nature, they are the centers of the manifestation of bounty, and the Eye of Compassion will be turned upon them.[25]

As to the subject of babes and infants and weak ones who are aicted by the hands of oppressors: This contains great wisdom and this subject is of paramount importance. In brief, for those souls there is a recompense in another world and many details are connected with this matter. For those souls that suffering is the greatest mercy of God. Verily that mercy of the Lord is far better and preferable to all the comfort of this world and the growth and development of this place of mortality.[26]

In other words, while those of us who have the opportunity to make use of our physical existence are encouraged, even obliged to do so, those who for whatever reason are deprived of this opportunity are provided with other means of being prepared for their continued existence in the realm of the spirit.

Properly comprehended, then, true suffering in relation to what we consider to be the "premature death" or "unjust suffering" of other souls is experienced on the part of those of us who remain behind, deprived of their companionship. From their own perspective, justice has been accomplished because they progress without hindrance. They are in no way impaired because they were prevented from participating fully in this life. Likewise we are assured that those who, because of mental or physical illness, no longer seem to us to be progressing spirituality are actually not negatively affected such experience:

> man is exalted above, and is independent of all infirmities of body or mind. That a sick person showeth signs of weakness is due to the hindrances that interpose themselves between his soul and his body, for the soul itself remaineth unaffected by any bodily ailments.[27]

To fail to grasp the essential realization of the Bahá'í paradigm that life is a continuum and not limited to the physical world is to see as ludicrous most martyrdoms and all the indignities that the Manifestations Themselves willingly endure:

> How could such Souls have consented to surrender themselves unto their enemies if they believed all the worlds of God to have been reduced to this earthly life? Would they have willingly suffered such afflictions and torments as no man hath ever experienced or witnessed?[28]

But we are still left with a dilemma regarding God's intervention. If God foreknows our suffering, is He not somehow responsible? Why does He not intervene to prevent our suffering so that we can reap the benefits of the metaphorical classroom He has so creatively devised for our education?

To a certain extent this subject transcends the purpose of this discussion, but several important responses resolve a major portion of this issue. We have already noted that God's foreknowledge of a thing is not the cause of its occurrence any more than our knowledge of the operation of a physical law causes that law to be enforced. But once foreknowing our suffering, why does God not prevent it?

The most important response to this essential question of theodicy is that God *does* intervene! He intervenes repeatedly, consistently, progressively, even daily on a personal basis if we choose to be aware of that intervention and take full advantage of the opportunities it affords us. For example, in the larger context of human history on this planet, God precisely directs the course of history, sending successive Manifestations according to the ancient Covenant between God and humankind, not because we deserve such bestowals, but because God is loving, forgiving, and intent on assisting us to develop as individuals and as a global community.

The Bahá'í writings confirm this perspective by asserting that human history is a spiritual dynamic and that without God's intervention through the Intermediaries Who are the Manifestations, there would be no human history:

> The enlightenment of the world of thought comes from these centers of light and sources of mysteries. Without the bounty of the splendor and the instructions of these Holy Beings the world of souls and thoughts would be opaque darkness. Without the irrefutable teachings of those sources of mysteries the human world would become the pasture of animal appetites and qualities, the existence of everything would be unreal, and there would be no true life. That is why it is said in the Gospel: "In the beginning was the Word," meaning that it became the cause of all life.[29]

This same divine intervention is also at work in our personal lives. We are assured that whatever assistance we need is available in our personal lives if we but ask for it: "God is merciful. In His mercy He answers the prayers of all His servants when according to His supreme wisdom it is necessary."[30]

Of course, what God as divine physician deems an appropriate response to our behests may not always accord with our present desires or personal estimation of what would be propitious for our growth and development. In this sense, we cannot always predict when or how God will intervene in our lives or in what way He will respond to our entreaties. We know only that intervention will occur if we earnestly seek it, if it is beneficial for us, and if we develop the perception to recognize it when it occurs. And that is a big "if"! For how do we know when something occurs following our supplication whether or not it is divine intercession or simply some random event?

The answer is that in this life we can never know for certain. Consequently, our best course of action is always to assume that what occurs is meant to teach us something about ourselves, and if we strive to discern what that lesson is, we will inevitably discover a lesson there, because all of our experiences during our physical existence are endowed with the power to educate us spiritually.

This observation brings us to a second axiom about the question of why God does not prevent our negative experience. More often than not the events we perceive to be negative have immense capacity to educate us. Such tests are part and parcel of the whole metaphorical scheme by which we are spirituality transformed by our physical experience. To understand the merits or rewards of such negative experiences, we can return to our earlier analogy of the athlete.

To an athlete, stress, even stress to the point of pain, is not perceived as negative. The intelligent athlete is aware of the objective of training and knowledgeable about how the seemingly negative experience of daily stress will in the long run gradually increase strength and power. The athlete perceives the "end" in the "beginning." As a result, the well-trained athlete comes to view training as exhilarating, beneficial, and often even enjoyable.

For our own education in the metaphorical classroom of physical reality, all testing and suffering is similarly crucial. The Bahá'í writings are replete with discussions affirming this principle:

Tests are benefits from God, for which we should thank Him. Grief and sorrow do not come to us by chance, they are sent to us by the Divine Mercy for our own perfecting.[31]

The mind and spirit of man advance when he is tried by suffering. The more the ground is ploughed the better the seed will grow, the better the harvest will be.[32]

As to tests, these are inevitable. Hast thou not heard and read how there appeared trials from God in the days of Jesus, and thereafter, and how the winds of tests became severe? Even the glorious Peter was not relieved from the claws of trials. He wavered, then he repented and mourned the mourning of a bereaved one. . . .[33]

The teachings of Bahá'u'lláh thus respond to the questions raised by both sorts of negative experience and thereby resolve the dilemmas presented in the Book of Job and in *The Consolation of Philosophy*. As an integral part of the metaphorical acting out of virtue, testing assays the degree to which we have truly understood and habituated spiritual attributes: "Were it not for tests, pure gold could not be distinguished from the impure."[34]

Doubtless it is for this reason that "the tests and trials of God take place in this world, not in the world of the Kingdom." And yet, even though we are assured that through suffering we "will attain to an eternal happiness" and that "soon (God) thy Lord will bestow upon thee that which shall satisfy thee," we are also told that our refusal to recognize our weaknesses ensures that we will be subjected to the same test recurring with ever greater severity until we learn how to respond appropriately:

Tests are a means by which a soul is measured as to its fitness, and proven out by its own acts. God knows its fitness beforehand, and also its unpreparedness, but man, with an ego, would not believe himself unfit unless proof were given him. Consequently his susceptibility to evil is proven to him when he falls into the tests, and the tests are continued until the soul realizes its own unfitness, then remorse and regret tend to root out the weakness.

The same test comes again in greater degree, until it is shown that a former weakness has become a strength, and the power to overcome evil has been established.[35]

WHY IS PHYSICAL EXPERIENCE NECESSARY?

Assuming, then, that we can accept even the negative experiences as part of the divine plan for educating us, we are still left with a final question that encompasses the whole process: Why is a physical existence necessary in the first place? For even if the process of spiritual development and enlightenment works as planned, why could there not be a simpler, easier, less painful method of accomplishing the same task? If God is omnipotent and can create us in whatever way He wishes, why did He not create us already spiritualized, already in a state of understanding?

If the question seems presumptuous, it is not. Bahá'u'lláh deals with this very issue when He explains that God could have made things simpler, but His purpose is to force us to search independently, to choose for ourselves the path that is the source of our advancement:

> He Who is the Day Spring of Truth is, no doubt, fully capable of rescuing from such remoteness wayward souls and of causing them to draw nigh unto His court and attain His Presence. "If God had pleased He had surely made all men one people." His purpose, however, is to enable the pure in spirit and the detached in heart to ascend, by virtue of their own innate powers, unto the shores of the Most Great Ocean, that thereby

they who seek the Beauty of the All-Glorious may be distinguished and separated from the wayward and perverse.[36]

To create already spiritualized beings would be to produce automatons incapable of progressing any further on their own or of appreciating what they are because they would not have discovered it for themselves, nor would they have experienced any alternative experience with which to compare their relationship with God. Furthermore, were spiritual reality and its laws more obvious to us on this plane of existence, we might not develop our sense of perception, since the meaning of reality would be obvious to all alike.

By veiling spiritual reality in a metaphorical physical garb, and thus removing the essential reality of things one step from the vision of humankind, God has enabled us to have every opportunity to attain spiritual knowledge together with the bounty of experiencing personal recognition of reality. At the heart of this exercise, of course, is the gradual discovery of the distinction between illusion and reality. And this transition we experience as we emerge from darkness into light, from ignorance into the realm of understanding, will provide us with more than a few moments of elation and reward. This experience will provide us with the spiritual impetus to strive for continued progress and the tools of discernment with which to carry out the objective of our spiritual evolution.

But as we will see more completely in chapter 8, the most important justification for having to learn initially about spiritual reality indirectly or periscopically through physical metaphors is that we must each learn from our physical classroom the method of maintaining progress in our existence beyond this world. Were there only two levels of existence in the next world, a heaven for those who succeed and a hell for those who fail, or even if there were various strata within these categories, possibly God could have created man sufficiently spiritualized for a heavenly existence, and we would not have lost much.

But the Bahá'í writings reveal that there is no static existence in this world or the next, no relegation of the soul to an eternal abode within some fixed category of existence. Whether in this world or in the next, we are constantly changing, and the point of transition and transformation we call "death" does not terminate the process of our spiritual development, nor does it end our need to utilize the spiritual faculties we have developed in this life.

The distinction between the Bahá'í view of the afterlife and the traditional conceptions maintained by other belief systems is, as we will see, a critical one. Were it our destiny to attain one static or changeless state of being, one explicit level of growth (or salvation), such development could conceivably be accomplished without the metaphorical classroom, or else with an exacting canon of rules and guidelines to program us for growth. But because it is our nature as human souls, whether in this life or in the next, to be continually evolving, what may have been adequate guidance for us at one time in our development may be totally inadequate for another.

Furthermore, since no two people are exactly the same or have the same experiences, each individual's plan of spiritual development must be distinctly tailored to the conditions of his or her soul. Therefore, what we need to develop are faculties of discernment and judgment so that each of us has a degree of spiritual autonomy, coupled with the desire to foster our own spiritual advancement, together with the tools wherewith to carry out that progress. We must be capable of choosing on a daily or even minute-by-minute basis that point of balance or moderation—the Aristotelian mean between the extremes. We must choose the courage that lies between foolhardiness and cowardice, the joy that lies between insipid frivolity and oppressive seriousness, the wise guidance that lies between calculating judiciousness and mindless permissiveness.

The objective of our education, then, is not blind adherence to dogma. Bahá'u'lláh admonishes us to evaluate our progress daily and, with each new assessment, decide what will be a progressive goal for us. Yet this objective must not be so far beyond our grasp that we will frustrate our own determination to strive, and certainly reflecting on the lessons we can extract from negative and painful experiences is an integral and vital part of this daily exercise of self-evaluation.

No handbook on personal conduct could do this for us because no code of conduct, however exacting, could take into account the myriad exigencies of each individual life. Perhaps it is for this reason that Bahá'u'lláh revealed relatively few laws regarding personal behavior. Instead, He mandated a course of conduct that stresses the development of the faculty of discernment for each individual. Likewise, He ordained decision-making institutions for human society, institutions with the capacity to consider all the variables in a given situation and to make appropriate decisions about a course of action based on those considerations rather than on a canon of law.

DETACHMENT

It becomes clear, then, that our spiritual development is largely contingent on the development of spiritual faculties by means of metaphorical exercises provided for our advancement. It is equally clear that to learn how to use our metaphorical classroom, we must rely on our own volition and, at least in the initial stages of our

growth, participate actively, enthusiastically, and wisely in the phenomenal world.

But as we participate, we must be wary of one final and absolutely critical requisite for the proper and healthy use of our ingenious instructional device—the attribute or attitude of detachment.
As a quality, the term "detachment" denotes the capacity to use
physical metaphors without becoming overly attracted to, infatu-
ated with, or involved in the literal teaching device. As a process,
the term implies a gradual relinquishing of our reliance on physical
processes for achieving spiritual development.

Our use of physical metaphors is purposely short-lived. Like water
that primes a pump, physical lessons serve to instigate the process of
spiritual understanding and growth. But as our growth progresses,
we should become less and less dependent on the physical metaphor
in order to understand the abstraction and to set ourselves in motion.

In the beginning we may well feel inseparable from the literal
vehicle (our body) through which our soul finds expression. Our
self-image and self-respect are usually inextricably bound up in our
sense of physical well-being and our physical appearance: Do we
feel okay? Do we look okay? Are we too tall, too short, too fat, or
too thin? Are we sufficiently beautiful, popular, and strong?

But the Bahá'í writings admonish us to learn over time as we mature to relinquish our dependency on our physical selves and our
physical circumstance as the primary index to our well-being. In time
we come to evaluate ourselves in terms of the spiritual qualities we
have attempted to express through the vehicle of the body. And over
time we strive to transcend the need to relate to spiritual reality entirely through the intermediary of the phenomenal metaphor.

We are told in the holy writings of all religions that one of the
most dangerous impediments to spiritual advancement is the love
of self. Metaphorically, this love is expressed through excessive at-

tachment to the vehicle for the self, the physical body. When we become obsessed with our physical appearance, we may be forgetting that our essential reality is our soul, which temporarily expresses itself through the body. If we love the physical temple for itself or come to accept this metaphorical vehicle that is our body as being synonymous with the tenor that is our soul, we quickly lose touch with the foundational purpose which caused God to create physical reality in the first place.

To safeguard against just such a misuse, the Creator has provided us with a number of metaphorical reminders of our true nature. Clearly the most ingenious and clever of these is the aging process. The Creator has arranged our lives so that at almost the precise period in our lives when our physical self has reached its peak of perfection (age twenty or so), we are as intellectual and spiritual beings just beginning to develop. Then, as we make progress in striving for spiritual and intellectual development, our metaphorical self begins to disintegrate before our eyes.

Thus, if we have missed the point of our earthly assignment and have become too attached to the metaphorical vehicle that is the physical body, the divinely ordained aging process will soon teach us the truth about our reality—that our attachment is doomed. In due time we will become detached from the metaphorical self whether we like it or not. But if we follow our lessons well in this "great workshop" that is physical reality, the deterioration of our physical selves, together with the decrease in our ability to utilize the physical classroom, will parallel a corresponding increase in our spiritual faculties. The end result of this inverse relationship will be that at the moment of transition from the terrestrial world to the "real world"—our final detachment from our worn-out metaphorical self—will occur at precisely the same instant that we no longer need it or even desire it:

The purpose underlying their revelation hath been to educate all men, that they may, at the hour of death, ascend, in the utmost purity and sanctity and with absolute detachment, to the throne of the Most High.[37]

And what will be the nature of our experience in that life after death? How will our efforts here affect our experience there?

This is naturally the most intriguing question of all. For if our purpose here is to transform ourselves in preparation for our birth into spiritual existence, should we not presume that what we do in the physical world has a direct and dramatic bearing on our success in the afterlife?

8

THE ETERNAL CONSEQUENCES OF OUR PHYSICAL PERFORMANCE: HELL, HEAVEN, OR "NONE OF THE ABOVE"

Didst thou behold immortal sovereignty, thou wouldst strive to pass from this fleeting world. But to conceal the one from thee and to reveal the other is a mystery which none but the pure in heart can comprehend.

—Bahá'u'lláh

If one point has become clear thus far in our examination of the nature and purpose of physical reality, it is the forceful emphasis in the Bahá'í writings on the strategic relationship in our physical lives between our actions and our spiritual development.

The Bahá'í teachings are very existential in this regard. In no sense is physical life viewed merely as a period of waiting until we enter a spiritual realm. The physical world, properly understood, is an integral part of spiritual reality, indeed, a precise expression of that world. But if our actions greatly affect our spiritual progress during our physical existence, we might reasonably assume that our overall performance on earth might likewise have a significant effect on our spiritual existence in the afterlife.

Therefore, the critical question of the nature of that relationship between our earthly lives and our eternal spiritual destiny is our final concern in examining the spiritual purpose of physical reality.

THE FEAR OF DEATH

As we have noted, in the Bahá'í paradigm of divine justice our departure from the physical world is not portrayed as a separate venture, not really an "afterlife," but a continuation of the same life, at least in terms of our soul and conscious self. While noble aspirations and actions in the physical world are extremely important in determining our spiritual condition when we enter the next stage of our life, the afterlife according to the Bahá'í paradigm of reality is not, in any ordinary sense, merely an experience based on the result of our efforts made in the physical phase of our eternal existence. For if our physical life has its primary objective the development of spiritual faculties and the incremental improvement of our soul in preparation for a more expansive life and a more complete encounter with reality, we can be assured that the continuation of our life has these same objectives.

Of course, belief in a continuation of life after the soul dissociates from the physical body is not necessarily comforting. After all, this continuity might imply that all the arduous efforts we have made at spiritual transformation in our physical life lead only to further challenges in the next stage of our existence. But perhaps the most startling realization we come to as we consider this promise of future existence is the simple fact that there is ultimately no escape from ourselves!

This is a matter well worth pondering for a moment or two, for if we are unhappy or dissatisfied with who or what we are now, will we not likely be just as disappointed after death? Certainly the nature of the challenges we will face in an entirely spiritual realm will be significantly different from the trials we presently confront, and that's comforting. After all, physical difficulties probably account for the greater part of our struggle in this life—aches and pains, dentist appointments, financial hardships, car repairs, and the like. All these mundane concerns will have vanished.

We can only guess at how our lives will proceed in the next world insofar as a regimen of spiritual development is concerned, but in the Bahá'í teachings we can discover some profound and important realities about that existence and, more to the point, about the relationship between this life and the next. In particular, we are able to discover the relationship between what we do in the physical part of our existence and what we experience in life beyond this world, a source of great concern for the followers of many systems of belief.

On the one hand, the Bahá'í writings seem totally comforting in this regard. Repeatedly in His writings Bahá'u'lláh emphasizes that were we to understand adequately the operation of God's creation, we would cast aside all fears of death: "I have made death a messenger of joy to thee. Wherefore dost thou grieve?"[1] Nevertheless, most of us continue to fear death, and for many understandable reasons. If we do not believe in the continuity of the soul and our consciousness after death, we may dread the prospect of nonexistence. If we do believe in a continuation of our lives, we may be concerned about what sort of judgment awaits us. If we are dissatisfied with who we are or what we have become, we may fear the inability to escape from our own consciousness, in which case the prospect of nonexistence might seem appealing.

But if there is nothing to fear—if, as Bahá'u'lláh says, death is "a messenger of joy"—we cannot help asking why so little is revealed to us about that existence. Why, in other words, are we not given ample detail about how our development will continue so that we can accept this assurance, become comforted by it, and approach our physical tasks with relief and enthusiasm?

One hindrance in responding meaningfully to what would seem to be a legitimate desire is the difficulty the Manifestation of God would have in portraying a dimension for which we have no frame of reference. In the same way, we ourselves might find it impossible to describe to a child in the womb of its mother the reality of this world. We could talk about trees and birds and swing sets, but the words would evoke no meaningful mental images, and nothing useful would have been imparted.

Thus far we can also conclude from our examination of the metaphorical nature of physical reality that concealment of the afterlife serves to teach us by testing and stretching us, something wise teachers are wont to do by withholding answers to problems in order to motivate students to acquire the essential tools for further advancement. For example, were a math teacher simply to write a math problem on a board and tell the students to memorize the answer, the students might recall that answer in the future—should they ever happen across that particular problem again. But how much more valuable it would be for the teacher to help the students acquire the knowledge necessary to solve the problem so that the student could independently solve an entire panoply of similar problems.

Bahá'u'lláh states explicitly that another purpose in concealing the reality of the afterlife is to protect us. He explains that were we adequately informed about the life to come, we would find it so appealing that we would not be able to restrain ourselves from attaining that next stage in our existence. We would become so distracted and so desirous of abandoning this life that we would no longer be able to concentrate on the spiritual development we need to acquire to prepare for the transition from this life to the next: "If any man be told that which hath been ordained for such a soul [one who is 'sanctified from the vain imaginings of the peoples of the world'] in the worlds of God, . . . his whole being will instantly blaze out in his great longing to attain that most exalted, that sanctified and resplendent station. . . ."[2]

THE EFFECTS OF "NDE" ON CONTEMPORARY ATTITUDES ABOUT THE AFTERLIFE

But in spite of such reassurances about the next stage of existence, it is easy to fall prey to prevailing attitudes regarding death. In the forward to Elisabeth Kübler-Ross's work *Death: The Final Stage of Growth,* Joseph and Laurie Braga observe, "death is a subject that is evaded, ignored, and denied by our youth-worshipping, progress-oriented society. It is almost as if we have taken on death as just another disease to be conquered."[3]

When in the 1970s a number of books began to be published that attempted to document the afterlife experiences of patients who had experienced "clinical" death, we might have thought that attitudes about death would have been dramatically affected—that the fear of death would have vanished and that we would all become immensely more dedicated to attending to the health of our immortal soul. After all, such studies seemed to confirm belief in the continuation of the soul. Furthermore, most of the earlier works seemed to portray the afterlife as a totally positive experience.

For example, Elisabeth Kübler-Ross, perhaps the most widely acclaimed pioneer in the then emerging field of death counseling, stated in one interview that there is no need to fear death since God does not judge us—our earthly performance has no bearing on how we are received:

> Discussing the aspects of an afterlife as described by patients, Mrs. Kübler-Ross remarked that those involved in the research were puzzled that there seemed to be no fear or punishment connected with death.
>
> "It seemed that a Hitler and a Mother Theresa got the same treatment. Then, we realized that God is not judgmental. We are the ones who discriminate."[4]

Views such as those of Kübler-Ross might make us wonder if we are not being provided with the knowledge to which Bahá'u'lláh alludes when He states,

> In the treasuries of the knowledge of God there lieth concealed a knowledge which, when applied, will largely, though not wholly, eliminate fear. This knowledge, however, should be taught from childhood, as it will greatly aid in its elimination. Whatever decreaseth fear increaseth courage.[5]

When Shoghi Effendi, grandson of 'Abdu'l-Bahá and authorized interpreter of Bahá'í texts, was asked about this passage, his secretary replied on his behalf, "Unfortunately it would seem that the knowledge 'which could largely eliminate fear' has not been disclosed or identified by Bahá'u'lláh, so we do not know what it is."[6] Clearly, then, we cannot ascertain with any certainty what knowledge Bahá'u'lláh intended, but the remarkable courage of Bahá'í martyrs who have eagerly submitted to their executioners might seem to indicate that they possessed such knowledge.* Perhaps the acquiescence with which martyrs sacrificed their lives when they refused to recant their faith resulted from certitude they possessed about the continuation of their lives. Perhaps they had no fear because they were given a clear vision of the joyous reality that lay before them only minutes away.† Certainly their resolve—choosing to pass through that portal—still required immense courage and staunch faith, but perhaps such a divine bestowal helped them endure the terror, humiliation, torture, and mutilation of themselves and of their own families.

Interestingly, this fearlessness when facing death is reflected in and somewhat corroborated by the collected accounts of people who have acquired such knowledge through what is commonly referred to as the NDE (Near Death Experience)—an account by an individual who has been clinically dead but who, after being revived, describes in detail the experience of what they believe to be a glimpse of the afterlife.

One of the best known early compilations of these experiences was Raymond A. Moody's *Life After Life*, published in 1975. In this work he discusses how the subjects who had undergone the NDE speak of an inner peace and a fearlessness about life as a consequence of what they perceive to be their personal experience in the afterlife. In addition, these subjects no longer seem worried about the prospect of death itself.

---

* Such stalwart courage was demonstrated both in the midst of the so-called Heroic Age of the Bahá'í Faith between 1848 and 1850 when more than twenty thousand souls were tortured and slain and in the era since the revolution in Iran in 1979.

† This observation comes to me secondhand but is purported to have been suggested by A. Q. Faizí.

Elisabeth Kübler-Ross in a work also published in 1975 indicated as a result of her observations from dealing with terminally ill and dying patients that an accurate understanding of death would reveal nothing to fear in the transition to another stage in our continuing existence: "Death is the final stage of growth in this life. There is no total death. Only the body dies. The self or spirit, or whatever you may wish to label it, is eternal. . . ."[7] Death, in this context, may be viewed as the curtain between the existence that we are conscious of and one that is hidden from us until we raise that curtain.

But even if we are assured that further existence awaits us, our fears are not assuaged unless we are also confident that such an existence will inevitably be a positive one. For if there is even a possibility that it will not be, if we continue in much the same condition that we now experience, then if we are not content with life in general or with ourselves in particular, we might, like Hamlet, feel "the dread of something after death, / The undiscover'd country from whose bourn / No traveller returns." And like Hamlet, we might decide that it is better to cling to this life, to "bear those ills we have / Than fly to others that we know not of."[8]

Our primary concern, then, is the nature of that afterlife experience as it relates to our physical lives—the correlation between our physical performance—the metaphorical acting out of spiritual attributes—and our eternal well-being. For if there is a causal relationship, naturally our feelings about the physical plane of existence would be profoundly affected by this knowledge, as would be our anticipation of our future existence in the spiritual realm.

THE PASSAGE TO THE NEXT WORLD

While Bahá'u'lláh withholds from us any complete portrayal of the afterlife experience, the Bahá'í writings contain a logically consistent portrait of the passage to the next stage of our existence. By comparing the Bahá'í paradigm of this passage with the experiences reported in Moody's work, a pattern that has since been verified by literally millions of other such reports, we can begin to understand something about what the initial stages of the afterlife might be like and what the purpose of physical reality is in relation to that initial afterlife experience.

At the outset of *Life After Life* Moody presents a composite description of the afterlife experience, a synthesis of the elements that most commonly occur in the NDE, though not all individual experiences follow exactly the same pattern:

A man is dying and, as he reaches the point of greatest physical distress, he hears himself pronounced dead by his doctor. He begins to hear an uncomfortable noise, a loud ringing or buzzing, and at the same time feels himself moving very rapidly through a long dark tunnel. After this, he suddenly finds himself outside of his own physical body, but still in the immediate physical environment, and he sees his own body from a distance, as though he is a spectator. He watches the resuscitation attempt from this unusual vantage point and is in a state of emotional upheaval.

After a while, he collects himself and becomes more accustomed to his odd condition. He notices that he still has a "body," but one of a very different nature and with very different powers from the physical body he has left behind. Soon other things begin to happen. Others come to meet and to help him. He glimpses the spirits of relatives and friends who have already died, and a loving, warm spirit of a kind he has never encountered before—a being of light—appears before him. This being asks him a question, nonverbal, to make him evaluate his life and helps him along by showing him a panoramic, instantaneous playback of the major events of his life. At some point he finds himself approaching some sort of barrier or border, apparently representing the limit between earthly life and the next life. Yet, he finds that he must go back to the earth, that the time for his death has not yet come. At this point he resists, for by now he is taken up with his experiences in the afterlife and does not want to return. He is overwhelmed by intense feelings of joy, love, and peace. Despite his attitude, though, he somehow reunites with his physical body and lives.[9]

Before Moody rehearses some of his collected accounts that describe particular parts of this pattern, he issues several caveats that become important when we compare his findings with the afterlife experience as depicted in the Bahá'í writings. First, he observes that no two experiences are exactly the same. Usually an individual does not experience all parts of the model, and, conversely, no single part of the model seems to occur in every recorded experience. In addition, the sequence of the experience—the order of the parts of the model—varies from one subject to another. Another interesting observation he makes is that the clarity of the experience increases in proportion to the length of time the subject is clinically dead, though not everyone who has been clinically dead recollects an afterlife experience.

Perhaps the most important remark Moody makes prior to his presentation of the particular accounts in *Life After Life* is his statement qualifying the shortcomings of his sampling technique: His sampling is limited primarily to those experiences that *support* the pattern he had already begun to observe. In fact, in the main body of this work, Moody does not discuss or even *mention* those who had negative experiences.

Moody admits that his sampling is also limited with regard to the number of people interviewed and to the lack of cross-cultural cases: "In fact, one of the many reasons I say that my study is not 'scientific' is that the group of individuals to whom I have listened is not a random sample of human beings. I would be very interested in hearing about the near-death experience of Eskimos, Kwakiutl Indians, Navahos, Watusi tribesmen, and so on."[10] The fact is that in the three decades since this work was published, many cross-cultural studies have been made, and, in fact, they do support Moody's findings, so long as the reader heeds the "fine print" in the back of Moody's work.

Still another contributing variable in the uniformly positive nature of these experiences—something Moody failed to note in the main body of his work—is the fact that his samples are taken from those who wished to talk about their experiences. In his succeeding study, *Reflections on Life After Life*, Moody admits that people with *negative* experiences would obviously be less enthusiastic about sharing their story, especially since a negative afterlife might seem to incriminate their performance in this life.

Moody organizes the life-after-death accounts into the fifteen parts of his model. These begin with the initial stages in which one might hear his or her death pronounced by attending physicians, and they end with statements about how the afterlife experience affects the physical life of the revived subject after the event. The paradigm created by Moody's assembling of these fifteen parts of the NDE is positive and—something essential to our present concern—the sequence is corroborated at almost every turn by the description of our transition to the afterlife as portrayed in passages from the Bahá'í writings.

Part 1: Dissociation of Soul and Body

In the first part of the experience, subjects describe the dissociation of the mind or conscious self from the body, and many speak of how detached they felt in viewing their own lifeless body from some objective perspective:

I was out of my body looking at it from about ten yards away, but I was still thinking, just like in physical life. And *where* I was thinking was about my normal bodily height. I wasn't in a body, as such.[11]

I kept bobbling up and down, and all of a sudden, it felt as though I were away from my body, away from everybody, in space by my-self. Although I was stable, staying at the same level, I saw my body in the water about three or four feet away, bobbling up and down.[12]

While nothing in the Bahá'í writings specifically describes the sensation of dissociating from the body, there are several passages, some of which have been cited earlier, that describe a similar relationship between the conscious mind (which is a property of the soul and, therefore, continuous) and the physical body. These passages indicate that, since the soul is not attached to or dependent on the physical body, one does not cease to have self-consciousness after death:

That a sick person showeth signs of weakness is due to the hindrances that interpose themselves between his soul and his body, for the soul itself remaineth unaffected by any bodily ailments. Consider the light of the lamp. Though an external object may interfere with its radiance, the light itself continueth to shine with undiminished power. In like manner, every malady afflicting the body of man is an impediment that preventeth the soul from manifesting its inherent might and power. When it leaveth the body, however, it will evince such ascendancy, and reveal such influence as no force on earth can equal.[13]

But the mind is the power of the human spirit. Spirit is the lamp; mind is the light which shines from the lamp. Spirit is the tree, and the mind is the fruit.[14]

The rational soul, meaning the human spirit, does not descend
into the body—that is to say, it does not enter it, for descent
and entrance are characteristics of bodies, and the rational soul
is exempt from this. The spirit never entered this body, so in
quitting it, it will not be in need of an abiding-place: no, the
spirit is connected with the body, as this light is with this mirror.
When the mirror is clear and perfect, the light of the lamp will
be apparent in it, and when the mirror becomes covered with
dust or breaks, the light will disappear.

... The personality of the rational soul is from its beginning;
it is not due to the instrumentality of the body. . . .[15]

These descriptions of the relationship of the body to the soul and
of the continuity of consciousness after the death of the body do
not allude to viewing one's body as an inevitable part of the dissociation of the soul from the body; but, given the nature of the
relationship as it is here depicted, we can readily accept the feasibil-
ity of such an experience.

PART 2: AWARENESS OF OTHER SOULS

A second parallel between the accounts in *Life After Life* and the
discussions in the Bahá'í writings concerns the encounter with other
souls shortly after the initial sensation of departure from the body.
Moody's subjects describe a sense of comfort and companionship
resulting from this experience. In most cases there is the specific
recognition of other souls who have already passed on, individuals
the subjects have known in their earthly existence:

I realized that all these people were there, almost in multitudes it seems, hovering around the ceiling of the room. They were all people I had known in my past life, but who had passed on before. I recognized my grandmother and a girl I had known when I was in school, and many other relatives and friends. It seems that I mainly saw their faces and felt their presence. They all seemed pleased. It was a very happy occasion, and I felt that they had come to protect or to guide me. . . . It was a beautiful and glorious moment.[16]

Several weeks before I nearly died, a good friend of mine, Bob, had been killed. Now the moment I got out of my body I had the feeling that Bob was standing there, right next to me. I could see him in my mind and felt like he was there, but it was strange. I didn't see him as his physical body. . . . He was there but he didn't have a physical body.[17]

I had the feeling that there were people around me, and I could feel their presence, and could feel them moving, though I could never see anyone. Every now and then, I would talk with one of them, but I couldn't see them. And whenever I wondered what was going on, I would always get a thought back from one of them, that everything was all right, that I was dying but would be fine.[18]

The Bahá'í writings describe essentially the same experience of recognizing deceased individuals, but these passages give additional insights. There seems to be implicit in Bahá'u'lláh's descriptions a qualification for the soul that experiences the companionship of other departed souls, or at least an indication of who those companions will be:

Blessed is the soul which, at the hour of its separation from the body, is sanctified from the vain imaginings of the peoples of the world. . . . The Maids of Heaven, inmates of the loftiest mansions, will circle around it, and the Prophets of God and His chosen ones will seek its companionship. With them that soul will freely converse, and will recount unto them that which it hath been made to endure in the path of God, the Lord of all worlds.[19]

Know thou that the souls of the people of Bahá,* who have entered and been established within the Crimson Ark, shall associate and commune intimately one with another, and shall be so closely associated in their lives, their aspirations, their aims and strivings as to be even as one soul.[20]

From these statements by Bahá'u'lláh, one might infer that only particular souls will experience companionship in the next life, souls who are "sanctified" and souls "of the people of Bahá." Furthermore, the companionship is depicted in more detail. The newly deceased will recount what they have accomplished and will converse with other spiritually eloquent souls. But in another passage from the Bahá'í writings it becomes clear that such an experience is not confined to people of the Bahá'í Faith or to those who have attained all wisdom:

As to the question whether the souls will recognize each other in the spiritual world: This (fact) is certain; for the Kingdom is the world of vision (i.e., things are visible in it), where all the concealed realities will become disclosed. How much more the

---

* Followers of Bahá'u'lláh.

well-known souls will become manifest. The mysteries of which man is heedless in this earthly world, those will he discover in the heavenly world, and there will he be informed of the secret of truth; how much more will he recognize or discover persons with whom he hath been associated.[21]

PART 3: PANORAMIC REVIEW

A third parallel between *Life After Life* and the Bahá'í writings concerns the panoramic review of one's life, an experience consistent with the vast majority of the subjects Moody interviewed as well as with the myriad subjects who have discussed the NDE in works published in the thirty years since Moody's work. This assessment, evaluation, or retrospective of one's earthly performance is described as being instigated by a nonverbal query from a "being of light." And yet the purpose in this review does not seem to be to rebuke, humiliate, or shame the individual, but rather to enable the soul to evaluate the accomplishments and failures of the physical existence. According to most accounts, the purpose is to instruct the subject in a most loving and gentle manner so that, having gained this insight, further progress may be accomplished:

> When the light appeared, the first thing he said to me was "What do you have to show me that you've done with your life?", or something to this effect. And that's when these flashbacks started. . . .
> Now, I didn't actually see the light as I was going through the flashbacks. He disappeared as soon as he asked me what I had done, and the flashbacks started, and yet I knew that he was

there with me the whole time. . . . He was trying to show me something in each one of these flashbacks. It's not like he was trying to see what I had done—he knew already—but he was picking out these certain flashbacks of my life and putting them in front of me so that I would have to recall them.

. . . There wasn't any accusation of any of this, though. When he came across times when I had been selfish, his attitude was only that I had been learning from them, too.[22]

Bahá'u'lláh describes precisely the same procedure, not for one category of soul only, but for every departed individual: "It is clear and evident that all men shall, after their physical death, estimate the worth of their deeds, and realize all that their hands have wrought." Furthermore, since we never know when we ourselves shall be faced with this examination of our performance on earth, Bahá'u'lláh commands us to evaluate ourselves each day so that we might be prepared for a frank assessment at our life's end, whenever it may come: "Bring thyself to account each day ere thou art summoned to a reckoning; for death, unheralded, shall come upon thee and thou shalt be called to give account for thy deeds."[23]

PART 4: THE INEFFABLE NATURE OF THE EXPERIENCE

In the accounts of the subjects in Moody's study, particularly in the accounts of those who seem to have had an extended experience, other parallels between the NDE and the description of entrance into the afterlife in the Bahá'í writings are evident. For example, all of Moody's subjects acknowledge the ineffable nature of their near-death experiences. They find language totally inadequate to convey the reality of that existence:

> Now, there is a real problem for me as I'm trying to tell you this, because all the words I know are thee-dimensional. As I was going through this, I kept thinking, "Well, when I was taking geometry, they always told me there were only three dimensions, and I always just accepted that. But they were wrong. There are more." And, of course, our world—the one we're living in now—*is* three-dimensional, but the next one definitely isn't. And that's why it's so hard to tell you this. I have to describe it to you in words that are three-dimensional. That's as close as I can get to it, but it's not really adequate. I can't really give you a complete picture.[24]

Bahá'u'lláh likewise indicates the indescribable difference between the two planes of existence. He further notes that even were it possible to describe this experience, He would not do it because it would be unwise for Him to give us this insight: "The nature of the soul after death can never be described, nor is it meet and permissible to reveal its whole character to the eyes of men. . . . The world beyond is as different from this world as this world is different from that of the child while still in the womb of its mother."[25]

PART 5: THE PURPOSE OF LIFE

Moody's subjects and the Bahá'í writings are also in accord regarding the purpose of physical experience and the progress of the human soul—incremental spiritual development through a process of learning, something Moody discusses more elaborately in *Reflections on Life After Life.*

One of Moody's subjects states that in the course of his experience he came to understand that, according to the "being of light," the attainment of knowledge is the purpose of life: "He seemed very interested in things concerning knowledge, too. He kept on pointing out things that had to do with learning, and he did say that I was going to continue learning, and he said that even when he comes back for me (because by this time he had told me that I was going back) that there will always be a quest for knowledge. He said that it is a continuous process, so I got the feeling that it goes on after death."[26]

We noted in chapter 2 the emphasis in the Bahá'í writings on education as the purpose of physical reality. The Bahá'í definition of justice for the individual is to know and then to do. As we have also noted, the sort of knowledge and learning that is most praiseworthy is that which leads to spiritual progress. In fact, Bahá'u'lláh states that the acquisition of knowledge is essential if the soul is to fulfill its potential: "Regard man as a mine rich in gems of inestimable value. Education can, alone, cause it to reveal its treasures, and enable mankind to benefit therefrom."[27]

What is more, there are many statements in the Bahá'í writings indicating that our education continues in the next stage of our existence in the realm of the spirit: "Know thou of a truth that the soul, after its separation from the body, will continue to progress until it attaineth the presence of God, in a state and condition which neither the revolution of ages and centuries, nor the changes and chances of this world, can alter." 'Abdu'l-Bahá likewise affirms that during such progress, the departed souls will discover the "mysteries of which man is heedless in this earthly world."[28]

PART 6: PEACE AND JOY

Perhaps the most striking, and for our purposes the most significant parallel between *Life After Life* and the Bahá'í writings is the similarity in tone between the description of the total peace and joy that Moody's subjects experience, and the delight that the Bahá'í writings portray as our experience in the afterlife.

All of Moody's subjects affirm that they did not want to return to physical reality and their physical lives, and many imply that they themselves had a volitional role to play in determining whether or not they would remain in the spiritual realm, or return to their physical existence. Those who stated that they "decided" to return explained that they did so only because they felt an overwhelming sense responsibility to some unfulfilled duty—children to raise or some equally important mission. But all of them uniformly describe the "afterlife" as preferable to this life:

all I felt was warmth and the most extreme comfort I have ever experienced.[29]

I began to experience the most wonderful feelings. I couldn't feel a thing in the world except peace, comfort, ease—just quietness. I felt that all my troubles were gone. . . .[30]

As I went across the line, the most wonderful feelings came over me—feelings of peace, tranquillity, a vanishing of all worries.[31]

I didn't want to go back, but I had no choice, and immediately I was back in my body.[32]

When I had this wonderful feeling, there in the presence of that light, I really didn't want to come back. But I take my responsibilities very seriously, and I knew that I had a duty to my family. So I decided to try to come back.[33]

This same sense of joy, exuberance, release, and transcendence is corroborated in numerous passages in the Bahá'í writings, but with a significant and consistent qualification:

Every pure, every refined and sanctified soul will be endowed with tremendous power, and shall rejoice with exceeding gladness.[34]

Every soul that walketh humbly with its God, in this Day, and cleaveth unto Him, shall find itself invested with the honor and glory of all goodly names and stations.[35]

Know thou, of a truth, that if the soul of man hath walked in the ways of God, it will, assuredly, return and be gathered to the glory of the Beloved.[36]

They that are the followers of the one true God shall, the moment they depart out of this life, experience such joy and gladness as would be impossible to describe. . . .[37]

Unlike the implications of Moody's model that every deceased soul experiences this sensation—even as Kübler-Ross asserted that everyone has the same experience—the Bahá'í writings qualify the category of souls that experience this utter detachment and otherworldly delight. The Bahá'í writings describe the category of soul who has this sense of release, elation, detachment, and complete joy as consisting of "every pure, every refined and sanctified soul," "every soul that walketh humbly with its God," "the soul of man that hath walked in the ways of God," and "they that are the followers of the one true God."[38]

Of course, it is extremely important to note that Bahá'í writings do not imply that this standard is a fixed point of achievement nor a category circumscribed by dogmatic or doctrinaire standards, even as we have noted in discussing the issue of "salvation" previously. Doubtless there are myriad degrees of distinction within this broad category and, we must assume, myriad particularized experiences appropriately designed for each soul.

Nevertheless, we can hardly ignore that while we cannot determine precisely who might be appropriately depicted by such appellations or qualifications, we most certainly can admit that we have encountered in our lives individuals for whom such descriptions would not be appropriate. Indeed, we would be less than honest with ourselves if we did not wonder whether we ourselves could be accurately depicted with these phrases.

PART 7: NEGATIVE EXPERIENCES

As we read in the Bahá'í writings those passages that portray the pure joy and utter delight souls experience upon being released from their associative or indirect relationship with physical experience, we suddenly encounter related passages indicating why this sense of release and relief are qualified. For while these passages, taken out of context, do not seem to deny that a pleasant afterlife experience would not be available to souls who do not meet these qualifications, other passages in the Bahá'í writings clearly indicate that unpleasant afterlife experiences do await some souls, at least in the initial stages of that experience. Therefore, to have a valid understanding of the Bahá'í paradigm, we need to comprehend the basis for such a negative experience.

The unmistakably clear implication of Moody's *Life After Life* is that all alike receive a uniformly blissful experience in the afterlife. And yet such is not the case, not merely as portrayed in the Bahá'í writings, but because even a single alternative experience reported by Moody might have indicated a totally distinct paradigm—one that Moody might have neglected to emphasize because his initial purpose was to corroborate and share the positive pattern, an understandable objective.

But the fact is that Moody himself *does* acknowledge in his first work that at least one consistent alternative model exists. Relatively unnoticed in a final section on "miscellaneous questions" is a significant and unexpected observation by the author. He notes that those who had the NDE as the result of suicide seemed to have a uniformly *negative* experience:

I do know of a few cases in which a suicide attempt was the cause of the apparent "death." These experiences were uniformly characterized as being unpleasant.

As one woman said, "If you leave here a tormented soul, you will be a tormented soul over there, too." In short, they report that the conflicts they had attempted to escape were still present when they died, but with added complications. In their disembodied state they were unable to do anything about their problems, and they also had to view the unfortunate consequences which resulted from their acts.

A man who was despondent about the death of his wife shot himself, "died" as a result, and was resuscitated. He states:

> I didn't go where [my wife] was. I went to an awful place.
> . . . I immediately saw the mistake I had made. . . . I thought,
> "I wish I hadn't done it."

Others who experienced this unpleasant "limbo" state have remarked that they had the feeling they would be there for a long time. This was their penalty for "breaking the rules" by trying to release themselves prematurely from what was, in effect, an "assignment"—to fulfill a certain purpose in life.[39]

Moody's reference to an "unpleasant limbo" experienced because of "breaking the rules" has a profound impact on the entire validity of what *Life After Life* seems to imply with regard to the central paradigm the book discusses.

Clearly there is not merely one category of experience after all, something that even variations with the positive model indicate. More to the point, there is at least one category of experiences that is not positive.

PART 8: ACCOUNTABILITY

These alternative paradigms that are negative and that are alluded to in the Bahá'í writings, as well as in the scriptures of all other religions, have tremendous importance insofar as the portrayal of the overall afterlife experience is concerned. Succinctly stated, there emerges in this alternative category of experience an explicit relationship between our performance in the physical part of our lives and what we will experience in the continuation of our lives in the afterlife, at least in the initial stages of that experience.

This observation or axiom is quite different from the paradigm posited by Kübler-Ross in her statement that all receive the same joyous experience—that a Hitler and a Mother Theresa receive the same treatment after death. It would seem that God (the "Being of Light," as the subjects often allude to this sense of a guide) does judge us, or perhaps more accurately stated, causes us to be capable of judging or assessing ourselves.

This alternative experience, then, is not really an aberration, a deviation from the norm that Moody, Kübler-Ross, and others describe. Indeed, this implication that there is an explicit relationship between how we perform in this life and what we experience in the continuation of our lives would seem to corroborate statements by some of Moody's subjects—that after the NDE, they came to believe that this life is an "assignment," that tests in this life fulfill "a certain purpose in life," and that the initial afterlife experience is an appropriate response to the evaluation of one's efforts.

PART 9: A LOVING AND FORGIVING GOD

It would appear, then, that assurance of an afterlife is by itself hardly a sufficient reason to relinquish a fear of death, since few of us can be absolutely certain how well we have performed at that point. The Bahá'í writings pointedly confirm the validity of such concern. In numerous passages the initial stages of a negative experience are described, and the basis for this experience defined:

[T]hey that live in error shall be seized with such fear and trembling, and shall be filled with such consternation, as nothing can exceed.[40]

The souls of the infidels, however, shall—and to this I bear witness—when breathing their last be made aware of the good things that have escaped them, and shall bemoan their plight, and shall humble themselves before God. They shall continue doing so after the separation of their souls from their bodies.[41]

If it [the individual soul] be faithful to God, it will reflect His light, and will, eventually, return unto Him. If it fail, however, in its allegiance to its Creator, it will become a victim to self and passion, and will, in the end, sink in their depths.[42]

At first we might be tempted to consider that what Moody's subjects categorize as the consequences of "breaking the rules" might correspond to what Bahá'u'lláh designates in these passages with such epithets as "infidels," "they that live in error," and those who "become a victim to self and passion." And yet these phrases hardly seem appropriate to those who, in despair or in the ravages of clinical depression, take their lives. Furthermore, it is not at all clear from these passages what exactly Bahá'u'lláh means by such phrases as "infidel," especially since there is nothing in the Bahá'í writings to indicate that spirituality or godliness is conditioned on belonging to any particular group or adhering to any particular belief system.

Certainly it would appear that for God to provide only two alternatives—a positive experience for the spirituality elite and a negative experience for failures—is hardly more just or appropriate than the allusions to "heaven" and "hell" of other religions. Furthermore, this bifurcation of the afterlife experience is only slightly more just and logical than for everyone to receive a uniformly blissful experience since, as we have noted previously, God's ultimate purpose for us is not judgment but the education and development of our souls as we gradually evolve through an ever more complete understanding of reality and act out that understanding in an ever more creative and selfless response to that knowledge.

For while there seems to be a relationship between one's performance in the physical world and one's continued progress in the next life (and therefore an explicit meaning and purpose in the way we conduct our physical lives), it hardly seems appropriate that fallible souls should be condemned perpetually for mistakes made over a relatively short period of an eternal existence. Put another way, it seems improbable and inconsistent that a wise, just, and loving Deity would be incapable of making finer distinctions in judging us than creating only two possible responses to our performance in this initial stage of our existence, especially since no two souls are exactly the same and no two lives are identical. Surely a just and loving God is capable of making each afterlife experience fit precisely the unique exigencies that pertain to the life of each soul.

PART 10: SELF-JUDGMENT

We can begin to discern a more enhanced paradigm of the afterlife experience by examining what Moody himself discovered as he investigated further what had appeared only as an aberration of the model in his first work—the unpleasant experiences of the suicides. In *Reflections on Life After Life* Moody presents several distinct categories of afterlife experiences, all of which differ dramatically from the pattern he emphasizes in his initial study.

One such category is a variation on the "unpleasant limbo" model. This, too, is a negative experience, but it results from a sense of judgment that occurs during the panoramic replay. The subjects in this category do not seem to be in an explicitly negative environment, nor are they in the sort of "holding pattern" described by those in the "unpleasant limbo" state. However, they do seem to have committed enough negative acts—or to have *omitted* committing enough positive acts—that the replay of their lives makes them feel immense shame and guilt:

> Then it seemed there was a display all around me, and everything in my life just went by for review, you might say. I was really very, very ashamed of a lot of the things that I experienced because it seemed that I had a different knowledge, that the light was showing me what was wrong, what I did wrong. And it was very real.[43]

Moody himself speculates that a mode of experience most closely approximating the mythic hell of scripture might be this same model as experienced by someone who had perpetrated horrendous acts upon others. Moody notes importantly that the subjects he interviewed were, after all, guilty of only minor transgressions, and yet they experienced great remorse.

Moody thus surmises that were the emotions evoked by such a recounting proportionately greater for more grievous acts, he could imagine no worse punishment than to go through such a review after having committed truly horrendous acts upon innocent victims: "If what happened to my subjects happened to these men, they would see all these things and many others come alive, vividly portrayed before them. In my wildest fantasies, I am totally unable to imagine a hell more horrible, more ultimately unbearable than this."[44]

PART 11: BEWILDERED ONES

Of course, to experience "hell" depends on the spiritual sensitivity of the departed soul, which is something we cannot necessarily take for granted. If one is spiritually insensitive in this life and has, through a process of willful choices, become inured to guilt, it might well be that such a one could remain spiritually complacent or oblivious after this life, at least for some appropriate duration. Moody describes a related model of experience that might well account for these heedless souls, as well as for those subjects in his first work who, while having experienced clinical death, could not recall an afterlife experience. This is a realm of "bewildered spirits," a condition in which souls seem trapped between the physical and spiritual worlds of existence.

According to accounts by Moody's subjects, these spirits seem oblivious, heedless, dulled. They are physically dead but are still emotionally attached to the physical world: "First, they state that these beings seemed to be, in effect, unable to surrender their attachments to the physical world. One man recounted that the spirits he saw apparently 'couldn't progress on the other side because their God is still living here.' That is, they seemed bound to some particular object, person, or habit."[45] Like the subjects who experienced the "unpleasant limbo," these souls were not doomed to dwell in a condition of bewilderment eternally; they were to be there only until they resolved whatever problem, difficulty, or attachment was keeping them in that perplexed state.

Unlike the subjects in the "unpleasant limbo," and unlike the subjects who experienced the guilt and shame during the panoramic replay, these "dulled spirits" do not seem to be in a state of guilt or regret; they are, instead, oblivious to what has happened to them, "not knowing who they are or what they are." They are thus between worlds, unable to return to the physical realm but uninterested in finding out what is in store for them. They are insistently attached to the physical existence in which they can no longer participate, or else they are spiritually blind, unable to perceive the world of the spirit. Some even try "unsuccessfully to communicate with persons who were still physically alive."[46]

With the enhanced portrait of negative afterlife experiences offered in *Reflections on Life After Life*, Moody dramatically alters the dominant impression created by his first work and gives a kind of empirical confirmation for the principles governing the "initial" unpleasant afterlife experiences mentioned in the Bahá'í writings. For example, Moody's evidence clearly demonstrates a relationship between one's conduct in the physical world and one's subsequent experience in the afterlife. The evidence also implies a more complex response to the individual life than the two-part division of a heaven and a hell. In fact, Moody correctly asserts that there is no reason to doubt that there are endless possibilities:

> I want very much for others to avoid taking my list of common elements as being a fixed, exhaustive model of what a near-death experience *must* be like. There is an enormously wide spectrum of experiences, with some people having only one or two of the elements, and others most of them. I anticipate that the list I have developed will be added to, modified, and reformulated.[47]

SOME CONCLUSIONS ABOUT THE AFTERLIFE EXPERIENCE

Obviously we are somewhat limited in what we can conclude from the anecdotal evidence collected from near-death experiences. We may observe in these accounts some valid similarities with what we find set forth in the Bahá'í writings about the initial stages of our entrance into the next world. But because NDE subjects all reenter this life before they spend too much time in the afterlife, we cannot infer with certainty a great deal about what happens beyond this initial experience, assuming we accept these accounts as accurate portrayals of the afterlife and not merely illusions that the dying brain devises to console itself, a somewhat ludicrous conclusion if we accept the materialist view that the "self" and "consciousness" are but products of a three-pound organ containing approximately a hundred billion neurons.

Nevertheless, Moody's additional categories of experience do support some important principles in the Bahá'í writings that serve to allay our fears and to show us that spiritual progress beyond the physical world not only is possible, but the primary function of the continuation of our lives.

AN INFINITY OF "HEAVENS"?

Perhaps the major Bahá'í principle supported by Moody's assertion of the possibility of an infinite variety of experiences is that divine justice is operant in the afterlife even as it is in physical reality. Stated axiomatically, if we can acknowledge that there are an infinite variety of experiences in the physical part of our lives, we can certainly accept that there are also an infinite variety of experiences possible in the afterlife, each one of which is fashioned to assist the educational needs of each individual soul.

In short, we can certainly assume that an omnipotent Creator is capable of enabling us to experience precisely what is appropriate to our individual spiritual condition at the time of our transition. God is hardly limited by our imagination or by some predetermined categories of response when He assists us in reviewing and evaluating our successes and failures in preparing ourselves for further growth and development. Indeed, if the objective of our continued life is spiritual progress, we can be certain that our personal experience in the afterlife will be constructed so as to ensure that we are assisted in every way possible, even as we have been assisted in this life, little as we may be consciously aware of that sometimes concealed guidance. In fact, if we are to assert that God is infinitely just and infinitely loving and infinitely forgiving, no other response would be just or appropriate on His part.

9

DIVINE SUSTENANCE:
MERCY, PITY, PEACE, AND LOVE

The Prophets and Messengers of God have been sent down for the sole purpose of guiding mankind to the straight Path of Truth. The purpose underlying Their revelation hath been to educate all men, that they may, at the hour of death, ascend, in the utmost purity and sanctity and with absolute detachment, to the throne of the Most High.

—Bahá'u'lláh

Moody's observations, as well as those offered by subsequent NDE collections, support the Bahá'í concept of salvation as described in the paradigm in chapter 4—that there is no final point of development. The purpose of human life is spiritual education and development, and inasmuch as human life is infinite, so is the possible progress we can make.

But as we were careful to note earlier, this concept of human advancement as endless does not mean that the joy of salvation is eternally or even temporarily delayed. The joy of our existence is to be making progress on an endlessly rewarding journey. As opposed to many traditional theological descriptions of the afterlife, the Bahá'í writings describe our condition as always being in a state of relative advancement.

Doubtless the joy, release, and sense of fulfillment that is the initial lot of some souls would accurately be described as a veritable heaven, but 'Abdu'l-Bahá says that "as the perfections of humanity are endless, man can also make progress in perfections after leaving this world."[1] Consequently, we can imagine this "heavenly" reward as a succession of ever more progressive experiences of learning and delight.

The Bahá'í teaching that learning and spiritual development continue after death is also supported in the NDE accounts by subjects in their description of a "Vision of Knowledge," an afterlife experience in which "they got brief glimpses of an entire separate realm of existence in which all knowledge—whether of past, present, or future—seemed to co-exist in a sort of timeless state."[2]

Other subjects describe a moment of enlightenment when they seem to have complete knowledge—though obviously that "completeness" would be relative to what they understood prior to that point. Nevertheless, they describe this experience as a condition wherein they are aware of universal secrets, as if they were in a school or library where knowledge is readily available, where whatever they want to know is made suddenly accessible.[3]

We have already noted that belief in the continued education and progress of the soul after death is likewise an essential part of the Bahá'í paradigm. But there are also numerous passages that similarly extol life after death as a reality in which learning will become accelerated because the verities that are concealed in this life will be apparent in the "realm of vision":

Consider how a being, in the world of the womb, was deaf of ear and blind of eye, and mute of tongue; how he was bereft of any perceptions at all. But once, out of that world of darkness, he passed into this world of light, then his eye saw, his ear heard, his tongue spoke. In the same way, once he hath hastened away from this mortal place into the Kingdom of God, then he will be born in the spirit; then the eye of his perception will open, the ear of his soul will hearken, and all the truths of which he was ignorant before will be made plain and clear.[4]

ETERNAL GRACE AND PARDON

Another Bahá'í principle ostensibly reflected in the accounts of NDE subjects has to do with grace and pardon in the next life. This principle of forgiveness is expressed in a variety of ways in the Bahá'í writings. For example, Bahá'í law forbids suicide, and NDE subjects consistently report negative results attached to that act. And yet we can infer from a tablet of 'Abdu'l-Bahá to a bereaved widow that hope is hardly lost for such a soul:

That honorable personage has been so much subjected to the stress and pain of this world that his highest wish became deliverance from it. ... Thus it is seen that some, under extreme pressure of anguish, have committed suicide.

As to him rest assured; he will be immersed in the ocean of God's pardon and forgiveness and will become the recipient of bounty and favor.[5]

It may well be that this individual experienced an initial "unpleasant limbo" before being comforted by the "ocean of pardon and forgiveness"—the purpose of God, after all, is to educate. But the passage suggests that, even though suicide is strictly forbidden in

Bahá'í law, the ultimate destiny of a suicide is not to be wretched, but to be nurtured and assisted.

THE POSSIBILITY OF FAILURE?

The assurance that every soul continues to grow after death also has a more weighty significance. It means that growth is possible not only for those souls who have an initially positive experience but also for souls who have entered the next life in a "sinful" state and yet at some point—possibly immediately upon realizing what they neglected—desire to become transformed. Possibly the initial negative experience may endure for a period—albeit we are discussing a reality in which the physical property of time is no longer operant. Nonetheless change and progress are not only possible, but perhaps even probable, at least for those who actively desire it.

In this connection, 'Abdu'l-Bahá writes that all movement of the soul in the afterlife is progressive:

> All creation, whether of the mineral, vegetable or animal kingdom, is compelled to obey the law of motion; it must either ascend or descend. But with the human soul, there is no decline. Its only movement is towards perfection; growth and progress alone constitute the motion of the soul.[6]

> In the world of spirit there is no retrogression. The world of mortality is a world of contradictions, of opposites; motion being compulsory everything must either go forward or retreat. In the realm of spirit there is no retreat possible, all movement is bound to be towards a perfect state.[7]

Taken singly and out of context, these passages from the talks of 'Abdu'l-Bahá might seem to imply that no matter what we do in our physical life, we are ultimately destined to progress, a thesis that might seem to support the observations already cited from the writings of Elizabeth Kübler-Ross about there being no judgment. However, other passages from 'Abdu'l-Bahá reveal the possibility of the soul's decline after death:

> Know that nothing which exists remains in a state of repose—that is to say, all things are in motion. Everything is either growing or declining. . . .
>
> Thus it is established that this movement is necessary to existence, which is either growing or declining. Now, as the spirit continues to exist after death, it necessarily progresses or declines. . . .[8]

In this same discussion 'Abdu'l-Bahá clarifies the nature of the soul's decline when he states, "In the other world, to cease to progress is the same as to decline. . . ." For, according to 'Abdu'l-Bahá, a soul that is "deprived of these divine favors, although he continues after death, is considered as dead by the people of truth."[9]

To understand further the principle of the soul's progress and decline, we can consider what 'Abdu'l-Bahá states about the progress of the soul in general—whether in this life or the next. 'Abdu'l-Bahá affirms that all souls take their beginning in a state of spiritual equality, but they soon become differentiated from one another by virtue of their efforts, though it is clear that in no sense are we in competition with other souls.

In other words, as distinct from other theologies, the Bahá'í system of belief denies the concept that souls are brought into this life in a state of predetermined salvation (the Calvinistic concept of the "elect") or preexistent sinfulness (one of the concepts of Mormonism that relates to skin color derived from the "mark of Ham"):

> As for what is meant by the equality of souls in the all-highest realm, it is this: the souls of the believers, at the time when they first become manifest in the world of the body, are equal, and each is sanctified and pure. In this world, however, they will begin to differ one from another, some achieving the highest station, some a middle one, others remaining at the lowest stage of being.[10]

As we noted in chapter 4, according to the Bahá'í paradigm of physical reality, God has "singled out for His special favor the pure, the gem-like reality of man, and invested it with a unique capacity of knowing Him and of reflecting the greatness of His glory." As we also noted, Bahá'u'lláh attests that God "hath endowed every soul with the capacity to recognize the signs of God."[11]

And yet as we also noted, Bahá'u'lláh says in the Kitáb-i-Aqdas (Most Holy Book) that recognition alone is not sufficient unless we act in accordance with that understanding: "These twin duties are inseparable. Neither is acceptable without the other." Therefore, according to Bahá'u'lláh, every soul has a chance at progress, but that progress still depends on some sort of effort, some manner of employing free will: "Success or failure, gain or loss, must, therefore, depend upon man's own exertions. The more he striveth, the greater will be his progress."[12] Logically, then, it is crucial to examine the role free will plays in the development of our souls after the death of our bodies.

FREE WILL AND PROGRESS
IN THE AFTERLIFE

Given that a soul's motion in the next world is always forward, stagnation is equivalent to regression. We have observed that a soul which has not fulfilled its potential may be as if it were dead compared to the souls which have developed. The question then arises as to whether such souls are doomed to remain in that condition, whether the physical life is the only part of our development wherein we have the opportunity willfully to affect our own salvation. In short, can the soul initiate its own progress in the next life? If it can, how does it accomplish such a change without opportunities for physical action?

Of course, the inability to perform *physical* action per se does not imply that there will be no ability to act or, if we have the duty there of assisting those who are in the physical stage of their existence, to influence the outcome of physical events. Nevertheless, the Bahá'í principles governing the progress of the soul in the afterlife seem occasionally misunderstood.

Obviously we are not tested to discern concealed realities in the next life—the associative relationship with reality that we have described as a metaphorical relationship will no longer exist for us. Thus, reality and knowledge of reality will no longer be veiled or concealed in symbolic disguise:

When the human soul soareth out of this transient heap of dust and riseth into the world of God, then veils will fall away, and verities will come to light, and all things unknown before will be made clear, and hidden truths be understood.[13]

In such a context, we may presume that life's purpose will be apparent to all alike, or at least to all who have developed spiritual faculties sufficient to perceive it. Even so, knowledge, if readily available, is always in a relative condition of being comprehended by us.

Perhaps there would no longer be as much merit in discerning spiritual verities if we no longer have to struggle to perceive these properties of reality. And since we must further assume that no physical exercise is needed in the process of learning, how then might the soul strive? What could we *do* to foster our own advancement if *doing* implies action? And if no effort is required to learn and no physical action is required as an indication of our understanding, how will our souls be said to have free will?

It is abundantly clear in numerous passages in the Bahá'í writings and in the NDE accounts that the soul, once it is dissociated from the body, is *not* merely an amorphous entity oblivious to its own identity, urged along by forces beyond its control or understanding. The soul after physical life has the selfsame identity it had in the physical world and can initiate thought and action, albeit not physical action per se, though there are indications that those who have ascended to the spiritual realm can assist the souls of those who remain in the physical realm to accomplish physical tasks. Furthermore, though knowledge may be readily available, we can still imagine that we would have a choice as to whether or not we would choose to pursue it and, having advanced more completely our understanding about reality, determine to assist in advancing or serving that reality. As we have noted, action does not have to be physical in order to be action. Some of our most important actions as human beings are internal transformations that result from meditation, reflection, prayer, and willful change of heart.

However, one often cited passage from the writings of 'Abdu'l-Bahá might seem to refute the idea that the soul will have the abil-

ity to think and act willfully and independently. In this passage
'Abdu'l-Bahá describes three methods by which we can advance in
the afterlife: "through the bounty and grace of the Lord alone, or
through the intercession and the sincere prayers of other human
souls, or through the charities and important good works which are
performed in its name."[14] Taken out of the context of other equally
important statements made by 'Abdu'l-Bahá that explain more aptly
what "bounty and grace" involve and how we participate in receiv-
ing forgiveness, this passage could be understood to imply that the
soul is powerless in the afterlife to instigate action or even its own
change. We might infer that we will have no free will in that condition, that the sole means by which we will be capable of progress
will be through the prayers or deeds of those still in the physical
world, or else by the chance intervention of God—Who may or
may not decide to help us out.

In sum, such a misguided and unfortunate interpretation virtually recreates the anathema of the fundamentalist heaven in which
the condition of the soul is determined solely as a result of performance in the physical world and that condition remains fixed without one of these three events occurring outside the soul's control.
Therefore, the soul would be presumed to have no ability to influence its own salvation once it has become dissociated from the body.

To believe that the soul is powerless with regard to its development
in the hereafter is understandably discomfiting, even as it is totally
illogical and inconsistent with the Bahá'í teachings and with any belief
in a just Creator. Such a view conveys an image of the afterlife as a
realm of souls that function more or less mechanically, much like pro-
toplasmic globs that drift around at the whim of God or else are moved
about by supplications or deeds of those in the physical world.

The most illogical and absurd property of such a view is that it
effectively recreates creation so that the whole scheme of things is

reversed. Physical reality becomes the "real world," and the afterlife is merely a static condition of relative nonexistence—no will, no action, no effective human powers. In other words, such an interpretation implies that physical life is the focal point of our existence—the exclusive opportunity for us to have any vital or dramatic part to play in the divine plan of God—and the afterlife merely a judgment about whether or not we succeeded.

Such an inference is particularly illogical and unfortunate when we consider that those who have had no opportunity to be tested in the crucible of physical reality—those who pass on prematurely or who have been deprived of an opportunity to develop—would totally circumvent the process by which others are adjudged. To put it simply, while clearly those of us who have opportunity to participate actively in our spiritual development while we exist in the physical realm are obliged to take advantage of the special opportunity we are afforded, how is it just that those who seem to botch things up or simply not do quite as well as they might have, should be pitted against those who were never even tested?

THE IMPORTANCE OF OUR PERSONHOOD IN THE AFTERLIFE

'Abdu'l-Bahá makes it unmistakably clear that in the continuation of our life our soul in the next world will have individuality, free will, and the opportunity for instigating personal change. He further observes that we will be capable of communicating with others, will be able to pray for other souls (regardless of the realm in which they dwell), and, if our soul dissociates from the body in a condition of sin and unbelief, we will still have the opportunity to instigate our own reformation and progress:

As we have power to pray for these souls here, so likewise we shall possess the same power in the other world, which is the Kingdom of God. Are not all the people in that world the creatures of God? Therefore, in that world also they can make progress. As here they can receive light by their supplications, *there also* they can plead for forgiveness and receive light through entreaties and supplications.[15]

We can hardly fail to recognize and appreciate that to supplicate, to plead, to make entreaties are, one and all, personally instigated actions. Consequently, each is an action that requires free will. It is true that the capacity to do this is indeed the result of the "bounty and grace of the Lord alone." But—and this is the most important insight into this passage—*all* progress we make in every stage of our existence is the result of the "bounty and grace of the Lord alone," whether we are considering our advancement as individuals or collectively as an "ever-advancing" civilization.

As the discussion of the paradigm of physical reality demonstrates in chapter 4, human advancement, whether individually or collectively, inevitably depends upon the bounty of God. As we noted, were it not for His grace and bounty, God would hardly continue to send His Manifestations to humankind in spite of our horrible mistreatment of these divine and selfless Emissaries, who come to us as teachers and saviors.

When we take passages out of context and misinterpret them to infer that physical existence is our one opportunity for growth, or at least for the soul to take an active part in its own development, we fail to recognize that other forms of volitional activity can abound in a spiritual realm. Furthermore, by perceiving the willful progress of the soul as confined to the physical stage of life, we fail to recognize that the forgiveness of God is not so confined.

Clearly we can imagine that there remain in effect the next world all the spiritual laws we cited earlier—for example, the requisite that we recognize our need for grace and pardon and then act accordingly by beseeching God for His forgiveness. But if we can pray or beseech God for this pardon, we have to be free to choose that course of action. After all, a prayer that is not self-actuated is really not a prayer at all.

Similarly, if we continue to have self-consciousness and individuality—and the Bahá'í writings assert in numerous passages that such will be the case—then certainly we will be capable of thought, reflection, meditation. And if we can carry out these most crucial of human activities, then we can assess ourselves, determine to understand more, and effectuate that understanding in whatever sort of myriad activities one can accomplish in the infinite realms of spiritual reality to assist the progress of creation.

SOME FURTHER CONCLUSIONS

To appreciate the logic and distinctive nature of the Bahá'í paradigm of the afterlife and its relationship to the physical life, we must recognize that we can initiate our spiritual growth in both worlds. Certainly there is a significant and indisputable emphasis in the Bahá'í writings on the utilization of the physical life to ensure spiritual growth, because that's where we are when we read these writings—in the physical stage of our existence. Consequently, it is only logical that while here, we should be repeatedly cautioned about the perilous dangers of not taking advantage of this crucial opportunity for development, even as we can imagine we will be in the afterlife if we aren't doing well there.

This means that we cannot afford to be cavalier about our opportunities for growth in the challenging classroom of physical reality. For while we are never beyond God's grace or forgiveness unless we put ourselves in such a position, each occasion for growth and development has its own special characteristics and challenges. And since this physical experience has been specifically designed by the Creator as an appropriate classroom for our initial development and will not be repeated, we dare not ignore a single day's lesson in this metaphorical course about spiritual reality, let alone drop out of the program altogether.

Bahá'u'lláh emphasizes this point when He observes, "Seize thy chance, for it will come to thee no more."[16] Other opportunities for development may occur, but each particular opportunity is unique and, once lost, is eternally lost.

At the same time we should not mistakenly regard the physical life as the only occasion for our development or even as the focal point of our eternal existence. In Gloria Faizi's *The Bahá'í Faith: An Introduction*, for example, we find a passage that could be misunderstood to imply that the end of physical life is the end of our opportunity to strive for enlightenment and growth:

> We should therefore pay constant attention to our spiritual growth now because it will be too late when our life here is over, and any blessings which we may then receive will be dependent on the grace of God rather than on what we could have gained by our own efforts in this life.[17]

One might infer from this explanation that in the afterlife there is no will, no independence of thought, no way to express the desire to progress. Such an inference would seem to be corroborated by 'Abdu'l-Bahá's statement that it is "possible" that the condition of a sinner may be changed in the next world, but only through God's mercy:

It is even possible that the condition of those who have died in sin and unbelief may become changed—that is to say, they may become the object of pardon through the bounty of God, not through His justice—for bounty is giving without desert, and justice is giving what is deserved.[18]

The fact is, however, that even in the physical life we do not "earn" our progress. As we have already noted, all progress depends on God's grace and bounty alone. Similarly, if God is "Ever-Forgiving," we must conclude that the possibility of grace and pardon are eternal and unconditional, so as long we ourselves desire it and act on that desire. That is, since the spiritual principles at work in the physical realm are no less operant in the spiritual realm, we must conclude that the same requisites that affect our progress here also affect our progress in the next world. Consequently, we must presume that forgiveness in the afterlife is dependent on our sincerely expressed desire for it.

Indeed, it may well be that the penitential process depicted by Bahá'u'lláh whereby a sinner can receive grace is as appropriate to the afterlife as it is to this life:

> When the sinner findeth himself wholly detached and freed from all save God, he should beg forgiveness and pardon from Him. . . . The sinner should, between himself and God, implore mercy from the Ocean of mercy, [and] beg forgiveness from the Heaven of generosity. . . .[19]

Of course, to be "freed from all save God" might be a much easier task in an afterlife where God's ascendancy is apparent and where there are no sensual distractions.

Yet this one essential requisite—that the sinner himself instigate the process—has implications of tremendous importance since we know that in the next life it is incumbent on the soul to recognize its failures and deficiencies and to request that assistance. In our discussion of Milton's fictional Satan, we observed the possibility that pride could deter a soul from repentance, even if it knew clearly that repentance is due and forgiveness available.

Naturally, then, we might wonder who would *not* choose to be assisted, given the operation of such benign principles. Could such a character as Milton has depicted actually exist?

In one sense we have answered our own question—we can be fairly certain that anything we can imagine happening does happen. Certainly most of us have observed individuals who fail repeatedly to recognize blatantly obvious spiritual principles that are related to their own failure. But more to the point, we also encounter those who recognize and accept the validity of certain spiritual verities but refuse to abide by their dictates. To cite the most mundane of examples, we can reflect on how often we may participate in some habit that we know is lethal to our physical or spiritual well-being, yet we do not seem able to amass the willpower and courage to alter our negative behavior.

It is conceivable, then, that such obstinacy could persist into the next life. And while we cannot even speculate about the ultimate destiny of souls that will not or do not seem able to recognize their condition and plead for assistance, we know that, like Milton's Satan, it is possible for us ourselves to fall prey to such resistance, to remain stubbornly proud, willful, perverse in spite of retaining the opportunity for reformation. This possibility, however unlikely or implausible it may seem to us, should give us pause to pay careful attention to our daily regimen of spiritual development.

Possibly the most powerful and evocative passage in the writings of Bahá'u'lláh regarding the daily mindfulness we should undertake is a more subtle take on the "Golden Rule." In this passage, one is not admonished to avoid "doing" unto others what we would not want done to us, but to avoid even "wishing" for another what we would not want to happen to ourselves. Additionally, however, this passage cautions that regardless of what care we take in our own spiritual development, we are never in a condition—at least in this life—where our spiritual fortunes cannot be reversed by our own pride or negligence:

> He should not wish for others that which he doth not wish for himself, nor promise that which he doth not fulfill. With all his heart should the seeker avoid fellowship with evil doers, and pray for the remission of their sins. He should forgive the sinful, and never despise his low estate, for none knoweth what his own end shall be. How often hath a sinner, at the hour of death, attained to the essence of faith, and, quaffing the immortal draught, hath taken his flight unto the celestial Concourse. And how often hath a devout believer, at the hour of his soul's ascension, been so changed as to fall into the nethermost fire. Our purpose in revealing these convincing and weighty utterances is to impress upon the seeker that he should regard all else beside God as transient, and count all things save Him, Who is the Object of all adoration, as utter nothingness.[20]

Bahá'u'lláh's exhortation to His thoroughly malevolent and mischievous half-brother Mírzá Yaḥyá offers an excellent example of one who failed to respond to God's forgiveness, at least in this world. In spite of Mírzá Yaḥyá's willful attempts to kill Bahá'u'lláh, to usurp Bahá'u'lláh's authority among the Bahá'ís, and, in the end, to destroy the Bahá'í Faith, this same soul was assured by Bahá'u'lláh in no less a work than the Kitáb-i-Aqdas that forgiveness was readily available to him, but *only* if he would seek it. Bahá'u'lláh states to Mírzá Yaḥyá to "fear not because of thy deeds," asks him to "return unto God, humble, submissive and lowly," and promises that "He will put away from thee thy sins." Bahá'u'lláh concludes by assuring Mírzá Yaḥyá, "thy Lord is the Forgiving, the Mighty, the All-Merciful."[21]

Since repentance and forgiveness are private acts, possibly Mírzá Yaḥyá did effect the process of his own salvation, if not in this life, then perhaps he has done so in afterlife, or if he has not done so, perhaps he will. After all, if we are correct in our description of the paradigm of the afterlife, he has eternity to ask for pardon.

The point is that the modern notion of iniquity as environmentally caused, while in keeping with the Socratic notion that no one does evil in full knowledge, is at odds with the Bahá'í concept that one can know better, can understand the full effects of wrongdoing on the very soul of the perpetrator, and still choose to do wrong. We are, after all, complex beings, and our souls are not merely computers registering the sum total of external influences. We have choices, and we have a will. And if our observations are correct, our choices and our will persist into the next life.

In this regard, 'Abdu'l-Bahá recounts in *Memorials of the Faithful* that when the degree of Mírzá Yaḥyá's perfidy against Bahá'u'lláh became apparent to Mírzá Músá, Bahá'u'lláh's beloved brother, Mírzá Músá tried to persuade Mírzá Yaḥyá to "mend his ways." He reminded the rebellious Mírzá Yaḥyá that Bahá'u'lláh had raised him like a father and had always shown him love and respect. Understandably, Mírzá Músá believed that surely Mírzá Yaḥyá would desist if he only understood the full implications of the actions he was taking against his beloved brother—a Manifestation of God.

After repeated attempts to reconcile his brother to Bahá'u'lláh, Mírzá Músá realized that the problem was *not* Mírzá Yaḥyá's failure to understand the truth of the magnitude of this waywardness. At last, Mírzá Músá had to recognize that Mírzá Yaḥyá was actively choosing to undertake these insidious actions in spite of knowing full well the reality of what he was doing:

> Day and night he tried to make him mend his ways, but all to no avail. . . . Even then he never ceased trying, thinking that somehow, perhaps, he could still the tempest and rescue Mírzá Yahyá from the gulf. His heart was worn away with despair and grief. He tried everything he knew. At last he had to admit the truth of these words of Saná'í:
>
> > *If to the fool my lore you'd bring,*
> > *Or think my secrets can be told*
> > *To him who is not wise—*
> > *Then to the deaf go harp and sing,*
> > *Or stand before the blind and hold*
> > *A mirror to his eyes.*[22]

THE FEAR OF OURSELVES

We must presume, then, that through pride, ego, and willfulness it is possible that a wayward soul can wittingly choose to stray irretrievably from God's bounty. In fact, two passages demonstrate this principle in vivid terms. 'Abdu'l-Bahá explains that a wayward soul may be revived, but not against its will—there must be recognition and acceptance followed by the request for assistance:

> If a soul remains far from the Manifestation, he may yet be awakened; for he did not recognize the manifestation of the divine perfections. But if he loathe the divine perfections them-

selves—in other words, the Holy Spirit—it is evident that he is like a bat which hates the light.

This detestation of the light has no remedy and cannot be forgiven—that is to say, it is impossible for him to come near unto God. This lamp is a lamp because of its light; without the light it would not be a lamp. Now if a soul has an aversion for the light of the lamp, he is, as it were, blind, and cannot comprehend the light; and blindness is the cause of everlasting banishment from God. . . .

The meaning is this: to remain far from the light-holder does not entail everlasting banishment, for one may become awakened and vigilant; but enmity toward the light is the cause of everlasting banishment, and for this there is no remedy.[23]

Thus it is it that we can conceive of a soul willfully refusing to turn toward the light, whether in this life or even in the next, and, so long as it persists in this willfulness, thereby rejecting its own redemption and felicity.

In another passage 'Abdu'l-Bahá amplifies the possibility of eternal banishment—self-imposed though it be—and implies the process by which such a soul might falter and fail:

But on the other hand, when man does not open his mind and heart to the blessing of the spirit, but turns his soul towards the material side, towards the bodily part of his nature, then is he fallen from his high place and he becomes inferior to the inhabitants of the lower animal kingdom. In this case the man is in a sorry plight! For if the spiritual qualities of the soul, open to the breath of the Divine Spirit, are never used, they become atrophied, enfeebled, and at last incapable; whilst the soul's material qualities alone being exercised, they become terribly powerful—and the unhappy, misguided man, becomes mores savage, more malevolent than the lower animals themselves. All his aspirations and desires being strengthened by the lower side of the soul's nature, he becomes more and more brutal, until his whole being is in no way superior to that of the beasts that perish. Men such as this, plan to work evil, to hurt and to destroy; they are entirely without the spirit of Divine compassion, for the celestial quality of the soul has been dominated by that of the material.[24]

Here 'Abdu'l-Bahá is concerned primarily with the status of a soul in this life, but we can infer that a soul thus diverted from its just or proper course of development might possess a similar affliction in the afterlife.

By analogy, if a child in the womb of its mother were to have the ability to choose how it would develop, and if it were to decide not to grow limbs or develop senses and other tools essential for successful advancement in the physical environment, it might be born into this life incapable of existing beyond the level of a plant—relative to its full capacity as a human being.

What is more, such an individual would not only be unable to participate in this life, it would also be incapable of discerning its own inadequacies and degraded condition. It would, instead, be totally oblivious to its own nature and, therefore, completely incapable of acquiring such knowledge.

Similarly, were we to enter a spiritual environment devoid of spiritual faculties and sensibilities, we might not be aware of our lack of spiritual development, nor would we know where to turn for assistance or even be aware that we needed help, somewhat similar, perhaps, to the souls that are depicted in Moody's book as those who, after death, exist in a kind of "limbo" state.

In light of the possibility of such a condition, we can imagine that without some merciful intervention of God, such a soul could, like a planet slipped from orbit, follow the dictates of its own centrifugal momentum, its own pride, willfulness, or ignorance. Unchecked, such a one could become so remote from the magnetic attraction of God's love that it might fly irretrievably into remoteness.

Whatever fear we may have of death, therefore, is not the dread of nonexistence or of God's justice, but a fear of ourselves. We need be concerned about our own response to God's laws and their unrelenting consequence in our lives. This axiom is well illustrated by a story about Ṭarázu'lláh Samandarí, one who at age sixteen was privileged to spend time with Bahá'u'lláh, and one who subsequently devoted virtually every minute of the remainder of his long life dedicated to serving the Bahá'í Faith and humanity in general.

As this noble soul lay dying, he requested that his son recite for him a prayer for steadfastness. His son, fully aware of the exemplary life of service and devotion his beloved father had lived, asked why, of all people, he should feel the need for a prayer that he remain faithful and steadfast. Mr. Samandarí's reply was, "There is still time."*

Time for what? Time to become suddenly fearful? Time to have doubt? Time to be suddenly overcome by pride of the insistent self?

Since there is still time for each of us, we can never completely relinquish the care with which we attend that daily assessment of our progress, for the greatest mystery in the whole process is ourselves. The laws of God are constant, unchanging, just, without caprice or guile. God is, from a Bahá'í perspective, loving, gracious, kind, merciful, ever ready to meet our needs.

---

*I do not know where I first heard the story about Mr. Samandarí, though it sounds like a story told by Winston Evans, who traveled with Mr. Samandarí while Mr. Samandarí was visiting the United States.

Nevertheless, as we have already noted, we do well to remember constantly the stark and unremitting truth about this totally just and completely benign reality in which we exist—we are stuck with ourselves eternally. We cannot in this life or the next become someone else or dissociate ourselves from our own consciousness. The reality of the afterlife is precisely as Hamlet feared.

THE BRIDGE BETWEEN TWO WORLDS: THE PURPOSE FULFILLED

Perhaps the most significant contribution of the Bahá'í writings to an understanding of the relationship between our physical lives and our experience in the next life is a lucid portrayal of how the soul associates with the body. We have already discussed certain aspects of the subtle relationship between body and soul. But as we pull together the major inferences we can derive from this study, we come to focus on one overriding conclusion about physical life: Every aspect of our life in the temporal realm is geared to our birth into the next stage of our existence.

To study the way in which the soul associates with the body is to appreciate ever more completely the pervasive methods by which this life is precisely geared to prepare us for the continuation of life in a totally different environment.

'Abdu'l-Bahá used several revealing analogies to explain the subtle connection between soul and body. For example, he uses the analogy of a bird in a cage:

To consider that after the death of the body the spirit perishes is like imagining that a bird in a cage will be destroyed if the cage is broken, though the bird has nothing to fear from the destruction of the cage. Our body is like the cage, and the spirit is like the bird. . . . Its feelings will be even more powerful, its perceptions greater, and its happiness increased. . . . That is why with utmost joy and happiness the martyrs hasten to the plain of sacrifice.[25]

'Abdu'l-Bahá's analogy is comforting not only because it portrays death as a release, but also because it demonstrates with such clarity the fact that the soul, though associating with the body, is in no way dependent on the body for its existence.

Not that the relationship between the body and soul is unimportant—if we have discovered anything in this discourse, it is the existential imperative that we scrutinize daily the subtle, pervasive, and, in this physical life, inextricable relationship between the body and soul. The point is that the soul is fully capable of development even when its relationship with the physical body is terminated or rendered ineffectual through disease, retardation, or other impediments.

'Abdu'l-Bahá clarifies this relationship further with another analogy: "But when the body is wholly subjected to disease and misfortune, it is deprived of the bounty of the spirit, like a mirror which, when it becomes broken or dirty or dusty, cannot reflect the rays of the sun nor any longer show its bounties."[26] 'Abdu'l-Bahá goes on to explain that, though the instrumentality of the body no longer exists, the soul's light still shines, however undetected by those in the presence of the physical temple.

A contemporary analogy might serve well to clarify further the relationship between the body and the soul. A television receiver is, by itself, of little worth. Even if plugged in, turned on, and pulsing with the vitality that electricity mysteriously bestows upon the intricacy of its myriad parts and complex circuitry, the receiver is in no way alive or useful until there exists an unseen and otherwise undetectable signal for the receiver to translate into visible form and audible sound.

Similarly, during our physical existence the faculties of our soul may be existent and fully capable of communicating important information about the self, but without the instrumentality or intermediary of the body through which the soul can communicate, the operation of the soul is veiled, both from others dwelling in the physical realm, and sometimes from the conscious self.

And when the soul can no longer communicate through the instrumentality of the body because of the brain's dysfunction or the body's demise, the relationship between soul and body through the intermediary of the brain is instantly severed:

> Consider the rational faculty with which God hath endowed the essence of man. Examine thine own self, and behold how thy motion and stillness, thy will and purpose, thy sight and hearing, thy sense of smell and power of speech, and whatever else is related to, or transcendeth, thy physical senses or spiritual perceptions, all proceed from, and owe their existence to, this same faculty. So closely are they related unto it, that if in less than the twinkling of an eye its relationship to the human body be severed, each and every one of these senses will cease immediately to exercise its function, and will be deprived of the power to manifest the evidences of its activity.[27]

As yet in our understanding of this process, we are unable to determine exactly at what point the severance or dissociation occurs. We might deduce from the NDE research that this separation can be temporary. In determining the point of death, modern medicine has sanctioned brain death as the index of whether the body is yet a fit vehicle for the type of life we classify as distinctly human.

Whatever the truth may be about the instant at which dissociation occurs, another corollary point is worth noting. The nature of the body-soul relationship as portrayed in 'Abdu'l-Bahá's analogies vindicates the feeling expressed by us as we grow old, that in our minds and thoughts we are as young as we ever were. After all, it is not the signal from our soul that is aging, it is the capacity of our physical or metaphorical self to transmit that signal with precision that has deteriorated.

If the soul is unaffected by the deterioration of the body, we should, indeed, view the transition from this world to the next as a positive experience, as a birth and not a death. Dr. Hossain B. Danesh, in a monograph titled *The Violence-Free Society*, describes a process by which one can portray death as a positive transition to terminally ill children, though it might certainly be effective with anyone.[28] The consolation consists of a parable or analogy, the basis for which is the same comparison we have already employed— the comparison of physical existence to the period of gestation in the womb.*

The parable portrays triplets in the womb of the mother at the time of birth. Suddenly, one of the triplets is born, and the other two are left to speculate with consternation about what has become of their sibling. In allusion to the various contemporary speculations about the afterlife, one contends that the child has died and no longer exists. The other believes that their sibling will reappear, that the disappearance is temporary. Then, as they consider that they too may meet with the same fate, they become filled with fear.

---

* This an analogy is used by Bahá'u'lláh (*Gleanings*, p. 157) and 'Abdu'l-Bahá (*Some Answered Questions*, p. 198).

Of course, from our point of view, we can laugh at the needless fears of these infants in the womb. Within minutes they too will be born, will be reunited with their sibling, and will begin a life infinitely more wondrous, more glorious, and more complex than the very limited existence they have just left behind.

The analogy thus serves to demonstrate two of the most important issues about the relation of the physical life to our eternal existence and about the purpose of physical reality in general. First, the analogy reveals concretely and effectively that birth into the next life, though a fearful and dramatic transition like physical birth, is a positive event, an expansion of life rather than its diminution.

Second, the analogy demonstrates the point we have already repeatedly noted—that physical life is intended to be a concerted training for another life. Stated more powerfully, the gestation period is a relatively meaningless existence in and of itself. Its sole value consists in the degree to which it enables the child to develop tools for life in the physical world. Precisely the same observation applies to the physical stage of our eternal existence.

This simple but weighty conceit also appropriately returns us to where we began—starkly realizing our own limited appreciation of the way in which our physical lives prepare us for the life we will all eventually enter. For in the same way that we might long to reassure our own unborn children about the immense love with which we await their birth into our presence, so may we sense in the words of the Manifestations of God the same attempt at loving reassurance and confirmation with which we too will be similarly welcomed and greeted in our transition to the next stage of our life's journey: "Were men to discover the motivating purpose of God's Revelation, they would assuredly cast away their fears. . . ."[29]

Mike and Nancy Samuels, authors of a pediatrics book, give additional weight to this metaphor with an observation about the world of the womb. They note that our attempts to communicate love and affection while the child is yet in the womb are actually felt by the infant, even though these expressions of love can but hint at the more direct expressions that will follow after birth.[30] In the same way, we can only vaguely appreciate and intimate the love that awaits us.

Perhaps the most important observation the Samuels make relevant to our discussion is their description of how completely every aspect of the environment of the womb is geared entirely to preparing the unborn child for its participation and development in the physical world:

> From the moment of conception the baby's destiny as a human being propels it onward. Truly the baby is meant to live its life outside, not inside, the womb. The womb is simply a temporary shelter for the baby until it is capable of making its way in the outside world.[31]

The authors go on to note that the serenity of the mother at birth and the continued connection with the mother for the first days and weeks after birth "form a bridge which links the baby's two worlds."[32]

Here we cannot help noting the metaphorical parallel between the bond uniting mother and child and the physical and spiritual sustenance provided to us by God through the Manifestations and through the whole metaphorical classroom. This spiritual bond nurtures us in our infancy, ushers us lovingly from our temporary shelter into our eternal abode: "The Prophets and Messengers of God have been sent down for the sole purpose of guiding mankind to the straight Path of Truth. The purpose underlying their revelation hath been to educate all men, that they may, at the hour of death, ascend, in the utmost purity and sanctity and with absolute detachment, to the throne of the Most High."[33]

Like divine midwives, the Manifestations of God bend every effort toward preparing us for our departure from the Kingdom of Names and for our birth into the spiritual realm, a world of vision in which the realities we have struggled so hard in this life to understand will be clear and apparent if we have developed the spiritual capacities and sensibilities with which to perceive them.

We cannot even guess at the rest of the paradigm for that reality, how further spiritual progress will take place, or what "faith" will involve. But whatever the principles for progress that are operant in the afterlife, we have arrived at one unremitting truth in our quest to understand the spiritual purpose of physical reality. The more we understand and utilize the spiritual process devised for our training in this life, the easier will be our delivery into the next life, and the better equipped we will be in the life beyond to continue our eternal spiritual journey.

NOTES

1 / THEODICY AND YOU: THE SEARCH FOR METAPHYSICAL JUSTICE IN A PHYSICAL WORLD

1. Shoghi Effendi, *God Passes By*, p. 138.
2. Bahá'u'lláh, Kitáb-i-Íqán, ¶217; Bahá'u'lláh, Kitáb-i-Aqdas, ¶182.
3. Bahá'u'lláh, *Hidden Words*, Persian, nos. 14, 82
4. Shoghi Effendi, *Advent*, p. 33.

2 / JUSTIFYING GOD: SOME CLASSIC APPROACHES TO THE PROBLEM OF THEODICY

1. 'Abdu'l-Bahá, *Promulgation*, p. 416.
2. 'Abdu'l-Bahá, *Selections from the Writings of 'Abdu'l-Bahá*, no. 25.1
3. Bahá'u'lláh, *Tablets of Bahá'u'lláh*, p. 146.
4. Plato, *Republic*, p. 55.
5. Ibid., p. 142.
6. Ibid., pp. 229–30.
7. Ibid., pp. 230–31.

8. Cornford, in Plato, *Republic,* p. 212.

9. Gordis, *Book of God and Man,* p. 9.

10. James 5:11; Qur'án 38:40–44; 'Abdu'l-Bahá, *Paris Talks,* no. 14.5.

11. Job 4:7–8.

12. Job 6:10, 14–17.

13. Job 6:21, 24.

14. Job 42:10, 12.

15. 'Abdu'l-Bahá, *Tablets of Abdul-Baha Abbas,* 3:655.

16. Job 42:5–6.

17. Pollock, "God and a Heretic," in *Dimensions of Job,* p. 270.

18. Boethius, *Consolation,* p. 14.

19. Ibid., p. 18.

20. Ibid., p. 93.

21. Ibid., p. 99.

22. Milton, *Paradise Lost* 1.25–26.

23. Ibid., 4.40–41.

24. Ibid., 4.42–48.

25. Ibid., 4.71–72, 79–86.

26. Ibid., 3.102–9.

27. Ibid., 3.116–19.

28. Ibid., 12.469–73.

29. Ibid., 12.581–87.

3 / A BAHÁ'Í CONCEPT OF THEODICY: SOME RESPONSES TO CLASSIC THEORIES

1. Bahá'u'lláh, *Gleanings,* pp. 184, 105–6.

2. Bahá'u'lláh, *Tablets of Bahá'u'lláh,* p. 146.

3. Gordis, *Book of God and Man,* pp. 14–15.

4. The Báb, *Selections from the Writings of the Báb,* p. 125; Bahá'u'lláh, *Tablets of Bahá'u'lláh,* p. 255.

5. Chaucer, *Complete Poetry and Prose,* 53:1, 2847–49.

6. Bahá'u'lláh, *Hidden Words,* Arabic, no. 55.

7. Ibid., Persian, no. 14.

8. Ibid., Persian, no. 40.

9. Bahá'u'lláh, *Gleanings,* p. 329.

10. Ibid.

11. Bahá'u'lláh, *Tablets of Bahá'u'lláh,* p. 24; Bahá'u'lláh, *Epistle,* p. 49.

12. James 1:22.

13. Chadwick, "Christianity before the Schism of 1054," p. 535.

14. Ibid.

15. Matt. 5:17, 20.

16. Matt. 7:26–27.

17. Gal. 2:15–16.

18. See Schaefer, *The Light Shineth in Darkness,* pp. 95–97.

19. Billy Graham, "My Answer."

20. Bahá'u'lláh, Kitáb-i-Aqdas, ¶1.

21. 'Abdu'l-Bahá, *Promulgation,* p. 53.

22. Bahá'u'lláh, *Gleanings,* p. 149.

23. Rom. 5:12–19.

24. Milton, *Paradise Lost,* Bk 12, line 84; Bahá'u'lláh, *Gleanings,* p. 149; 'Abdu'l-Bahá, *Some Answered Questions,* p. 248.

25. Bahá'u'lláh, *Tablets of Bahá'u'lláh,* p. 126.

26. Milton, *Paradise Lost,* 4.79–81.

27. Bahá'u'lláh, *Gleanings,* pp. 271–72.

28. Milton, *Paradise Lost,* 12.586–87.

29. Bahá'u'lláh, *Tablets of Bahá'u'lláh,* p. 118; 'Abdu'l-Bahá, *Some Answered Questions,* p. 223.

30. Milton, *Paradise Lost,* I, 253–55.

31. Boethius, *An Essay on Man,* in *Norton Anthology,* 1:2250.

32. Matt. 23:34.

33. John 8:56.

34. John 16:12–13.

35. John 14:10, 12:44, 12:49–50.

36. Shoghi Effendi, *God Passes By,* p. 244.

37. Shoghi Effendi, *High Endeavours,* p. 71.

38. Qur'án 2:81.

39. Qur'án 4.169–70.

40. Bahá'u'lláh, Kitáb-i-Íqán, ¶161.

41. Qur'án 2:19, 30–31.

42. Bahá'u'lláh, *Gleanings,* p. 184.

43. 'Abdu'l-Bahá, *Tablets of Abdul-Baha Abbas,* 1:205.

4 / THE KINGDOM OF NAMES: A BAHÁ'Í PARADIGM OF PHYSICAL REALITY

1. Bahá'u'lláh, Kitáb-i-Íqán, ¶104.
2. Bahá'u'lláh, *Hidden Words*, Arabic, no. 3.
3. Bahá'u'lláh, *Gleanings*, pp. 105–6.
4. Bahá'u'lláh, Kitáb-i-Íqan, ¶107.
5. Ibid., ¶196,
6. 'Abdu'l-Bahá, *Some Answered Questions*, p. 281.
7. Ibid., pp. 181, 180, 181; Bahá'u'lláh, *Gleanings*, p. 215.
8. 'Abdu'l-Baha, *Some Answered Questions*, p. 182.
9. Ibid., pp. 182–83.
10. Ibid., p. 202.
11. Bahá'u'lláh, *Hidden Words*, Persian, no. 29.
12. 'Abdu'l-Bahá, *Selections from the Writings of 'Abdu'l-Bahá*, no. 150.2.
13. 'Abdu'l-Bahá, *Promulgation of Universal Peace*, p. 10 (emphasis added).
14. 'Abdu'l-Bahá, *Some Answered Questions*, p. 201.
15. Bahá'u'lláh, *Gleanings*, pp. 158–59.
16. Bahá'u'lláh, *Hidden Words*, Persian, no. 41.
17. 'Abdu'l-Bahá, *Some Answered Questions*, p.198.
18. Ibid., pp. 177, 178.
19. Bahá'u'lláh, *Gleanings*, pp. 149, 177 (emphasis added).
20. Bahá'u'lláh, Kitáb-i-Íqán, ¶217.
21. 'Abdu'l-Bahá, *Some Answered Questions*, p. 237.
22. Ibid., p. 232; emphasis added.

5 / AUTONOMY AND WILL: FUNDAMENTAL REQUISITES FOR A SPIRITUAL EDUCATION

1. 'Abdu'l-Bahá, *Promulgation*, p. 140.
2. Bahá'u'lláh, *Gleanings*, p. 143 (emphasis added).
3. Bahá'u'lláh, *Hidden Words*, Arabic, no. 2.
4. Bahá'u'lláh, *Gleanings*, p. 279; 'Abdu'l-Bahá, quoted in Bahá'u'lláh et al., *Individual and Teaching*, p. 13.

5. Bahá'u'lláh, Kitáb-i-Íqán, ¶81; 'Abdu'l-Bahá, *Promulgation*, p. 161.

6. Bahá'u'lláh, *Gleanings*, p. 143.

7. 'Abdu'l-Bahá, *Some Answered Questions*, p. 119; 'Abdu'l-Bahá, *Selections from the Writings of 'Abdu'l-Bahá*, no. 98.1.

8. Bahá'u'lláh, *Gleanings*, p. 260; 'Abdu'l-Bahá, *Selections from the Writings of 'Abdu'l-Bahá*, no. 104.2.

9. Bahá'u'lláh, *Gleanings*, p. 213.

10. John 14:9, 10.

11. 'Abdu'l-Bahá, *Some Answered Questions*, p. 218.

12. Exod. 4:15; John 12:49; Qur'án 10:16; the Báb, *Selections from the Writings of the Báb*, p. 12; Bahá'u'lláh, quoted in Shoghi Effendi, *God Passes By*, p. 102.

13. Bahá'u'lláh, Kitáb-i-Íqán, ¶107.

14. Ibid., ¶217.

15. 'Abdu'l-Bahá, *Selections from the Writings of 'Abdu'l-Bahá*, nos. 114.1, 103.5.

16. 'Abdu'l-Bahá, *Some Answered Questions*, pp. 249–50.

17. Ibid., p. 248.

18. 'Abdu'l-Bahá, *Promulgation*, p. 157; Bahá'u'lláh, in *Bahá'í Prayers*, p. 4; 'Abdu'l-Bahá, *Tablets of Abdul-Baha Abbas*, 3:549.

19. James 2:14–17.

20. Bahá'u'lláh, *Tablets of Bahá'u'lláh*, pp. 128–29.

21. Ibid., p. 164.

22. Bahá'u'lláh, *Gleanings*, p. 215.

23. 'Abdu'l-Bahá, *Selections from the Writings of 'Abdu'l-Bahá*, no. 105.3.

24. Bahá'u'lláh, *Hidden Words*, Persian, no. 29.

25. 'Abdu'l-Bahá, *Some Answered Questions*, p. 232.

26. Bahá'u'lláh, Kitáb-i-Íqán, ¶3.

27. The Báb, in *Bahá'í Prayers*, p. 82 (emphasis added); the Báb, *Selections from the Writings of the Báb*, p. 48.

28. Bahá'u'lláh, *Tablets of Bahá'u'lláh*, p. 48.

6 / A User's Guide to Physical Reality: Prenatal Exercises for Our Second Birth

1. 'Abdu'l-Bahá, *Some Answered Questions*, p. 200

2. Simpson, *Introduction to Poetry*, p. 6.

3. John 6:35.

4. 'Abdu'l-Bahá, *Some Answered Questions*, pp. 83–84.

5. Ibid., p. 237.

6. Ibid., pp. 182–83.

7. Bahá'u'lláh, *Gleanings*, p. 70.
8. Bahá'u'lláh, *Kitáb-i-Aqdas*, ¶1.
9. John 14:9.
10. John 15:1.
11. John 12:44.
12. John 12:49.
13. John 14:10.
14. Bahá'u'lláh, *Epistle*, p. 11.
15. Ibid., pp. 11–12.
16. Bahá'u'lláh, quoted in Shoghi Effendi, *God Passes By*, p. 102.
17. Qur'án 5:76.
18. 'Abdu'l-Bahá, *Some Answered Questions*, pp. 101–2.
19. Ibid., p. 37.
20. John 6:26–27.
21. John 6:31–35.
22. John 6:51–52.
23. Matt. 26:26–28.
24. Shoghi Effendi, *God Passes By*, p. 31.
25. Ibid., p. 32; see also Nabíl-i-A'ẓam, *Dawn-Breakers*, p. 294, n. 1.
26. Bahá'u'lláh, *Hidden Words*, Persian, no. 18.
27. Bahá'u'lláh, Kitáb-i-Íqán, ¶283.
28. Matt. 13:10–13.
29. John 16:25.

7 / METAPHORICAL SOLUTIONS TO THEODICY: WHY GOD WANTS US TO THINK

1. Bahá'u'lláh, Kitáb-i-Íqán, ¶283.
2. Bahá'u'lláh, *Hidden Words*, Persian, no. 30.
3. Bahá'u'lláh, in *Bahá'í Prayers*, pp. 124–25.
4. Ibid., p. 14.
5. Bahá'u'lláh, *Hidden Words*, Persian, no. 3.
6. Ibid., no. 72.
7. Ibid., no. 80.
8. Bahá'u'lláh, *Gleanings*, p. 278.
9. Ibid.
10. Bahá'u'lláh, *Hidden Words*, Arabic, no. 2.

11. Bahá'u'lláh, Kitáb-i-Íqán, ¶233.

12. Bahá'u'lláh, Kitáb-i-Aqdas, ¶3.

13. Ibid., ¶7.

14. Ibid., ¶125.

15. 'Abdu'l-Bahá, *Tablets of Abdul-Baha Abbas,* 3:581–82.

16. Shoghi Effendi, *World Order of Bahá'u'lláh,* p. 163.

17. Matt. 38:42, 46.

18. Harold Kushner, *When Bad Things Happen to Good People,* p. 134

19. Bahá'u'lláh, *Tablets of Bahá'u'lláh,* p. 156.

20. 'Abdu'l-Bahá, *Some Answered Questions,* p. 267.

21. Ibid., p. 215.

22. 'Abdu'l-Bahá, *Promulgation,* p. 295.

23. Bahá'u'lláh, *Gleanings,* p. 158.

24. Bahá'u'lláh, *Tablets of Bahá'u'lláh,* p. 176.

25. 'Abdu'l-Bahá, *Some Answered Questions,* p. 240.

26. 'Abdu'l-Bahá, *Tablets of Abdul-Baha Abbas,* 2:337–38.

27. Bahá'u'lláh, *Gleanings,* pp. 153–54.

28. Ibid., p. 158.

29. 'Abdu'l-Bahá, *Some Answered Questions,* pp. 162–63

30. 'Abdu'l-Bahá, *Promulgation,* p. 247.

31. 'Abdu'l-Bahá, *Paris Talks,* no. 14.7

32. Ibid., no. 57.1

33. 'Abdu'l-Bahá, in Bahá'u'lláh and 'Abdu'l-Bahá, *Divine Art of Living,* pp. 86–87

34. Ibid., p. 87.

35. 'Abdu'l-Bahá, *Selections from the Writings of 'Abdu'l-Bahá,* no. 163.4; 'Abdu'l-Bahá, *Paris Talks,* no. 57.2; 'Abdu'l-Bahá, *Tablets of Abdul-Baha Abbas,* 1:98; 'Abdu'l-Bahá, "Worst Enemies," p. 45.

36. Bahá'u'lláh, *Gleanings,* p. 71.

37. Ibid., p. 157

8 / THE ETERNAL CONSEQUENCES OF OUR PHYSICAL PERFORMANCE: HELL, HEAVEN, OR "NONE OF THE ABOVE"

1. Bahá'u'lláh, *Hidden Words,* Arabic, no. 32.

2. Baha'u'lláh, *Gleanings,* p. 156.

3. Joseph and Laurie Braga, *Death: The Final Stage of Growth,* p. x.

4. Elisabeth Kübler-Ross, "Dr. Kübler-Ross."

5. Bahá'u'lláh, *Epistle*, p. 32.

6. Extract from a letter dated 5 January 1948 written on behalf of Shoghi Effendi to an individual, in *Compilation of Compilations*, 1:570.

7. Elizabeth Kübler-Ross, *Death: The Final Stage of Growth*, p. 166.

8. William Shakespeare, *Hamlet*, in *Complete Works*, III.i.78-82.

9. Moody, *Life After Life*, pp. 21–22.

10. Ibid., p. 145.

11. Ibid., p. 50.

12. Ibid., p. 35.

13. Bahá'u'lláh, *Gleanings*, p. 154.

14. 'Abdu'l-Bahá, *Some Answered Questions*, p. 209.

15. Ibid., pp. 239–40.

16. Moody, *Life After Life*, pp. 55–56.

17. Ibid., p. 56.

18. Ibid., p. 58.

19. Bahá'u'lláh, *Gleanings*, p. 156.

20. Ibid., pp. 169–70.

21. 'Abdu'l-Bahá, *Tablets of Abdul-Baha Abbas*, 1:205.

22. Moody, *Life After Life*, pp. 65–67.

23. Bahá'u'lláh, *Gleanings*, p. 171; Bahá'u'lláh, *Hidden Words*, Arabic, no. 31.

24. Moody, *Life After Life*, p. 26.

25. Bahá'u'lláh, *Gleanings*, pp. 156–57.

26. Moody, *Life After Life*, pp. 67–68.

27. Bahá'u'lláh, *Gleanings*, p. 260.

28. Ibid., p. 155; 'Abdu'l-Bahá, *Tablets of Abdul-Baha Abbas*, 1:205.

29. Moody, *Life After Life*, pp. 28–29.

30. Ibid., p. 30.

31. Ibid., p. 75.

32. Ibid., p. 76.

33. Ibid., p. 78.

34. Bahá'u'lláh, *Gleanings*, p. 154.

35. Ibid., p. 159.

36. Ibid., p. 161.

37. Ibid., p. 171.

38. Ibid., pp. 154, 159, 161, 171.

39. Ibid., p. 143.

40. Ibid., p. 171.

41. Ibid., pp. 170–71.

42. Ibid., p. 159.

43. Moody, *Reflections*, pp. 34–35.

44. Ibid., pp. 38–39.

45. Ibid., p. 18.

46. Ibid., p. 21.

47. Ibid., p. 87.

9 / DIVINE SUSTENANCE: MERCY, PITY, PEACE, AND LOVE

1. 'Abdu'l-Bahá, *Some Answered Questions,* p. 237.
2. Raymond Moody, *Reflections,* p. 9.
3. See ibid., pp. 11–14.
4. 'Abdu'l-Bahá, *Selections from the Writings of 'Abdu'l-Bahá,* no. 149.4.
5. Ibid., no. 170.1–170.2.
6. 'Abdu'l-Bahá, *Paris Talks,* no. 29.4.
7. Ibid. no. 29.9.
8. 'Abdu'l-Bahá, *Some Answered Questions,* p. 233.
9. Ibid., pp. 233, 225.
10. 'Abdu'l-Bahá, *Selections from the Writings of 'Abdu'l-Bahá,* no. 145.4.
11. Bahá'u'lláh, *Gleanings,* pp. 77, 106.
12. Bahá'u'lláh, Kitáb-i-Aqdas, ¶1; Bahá'u'lláh, *Gleanings,* pp. 81–82.
13. 'Abdu'l-Bahá, *Selections from the Writings of 'Abdu'l-Bahá,* no 149.3.
14. 'Abdu'l-Bahá, *Some Answered Questions,* p. 240.
15. Ibid., p. 232.
16. Bahá'u'lláh, *Hidden Words,* Persian, no. 40.
17. Gloria Faizi, *The Bahá'í Faith,* p. 61.
18. 'Abdu'l-Bahá, *Some Answered Questions,* p. 232.
19. Bahá'u'lláh, *Tablets of Bahá'u'lláh,* p. 24.
20. Bahá'u'lláh, Kitáb-i-Íqán, ¶214.
21. Bahá'u'lláh, Kitáb-i-Aqdas, ¶184.
22. 'Abdu'l-Bahá, *Memorials,* p. 88.
23. 'Abdu'l-Bahá, *Some Answered Questions,* pp. 127–28.
24. 'Abdu'l-Bahá, *Paris Talks,* no. 31.6.
25. 'Abdu'l-Bahá, *Some Answered Questions,* p. 228.
26. Ibid., p. 226.
27. Bahá'u'lláh, *Gleanings,* p. 164.
28. Hossain B. Danesh, "Violence-Free Society," pp. 34–35.
29. Bahá'u'lláh, *Gleanings,* p. 175.
30. See Mike and Nancy Samuels, *Well Baby Book,* p. 61.
31. Ibid., p. 90.
32. Ibid., p. 91.
33. Bahá'u'lláh, *Gleanings,* pp. 156–57

BIBLIOGRAPHY

WORKS OF BAHÁ'U'LLÁH

Epistle to the Son of the Wolf. New ed. Translated by Shoghi Effendi. 1st ps ed. Wilmette, IL: Bahá'í Publishing Trust, 1988.

Gleanings from the Writings of Bahá'u'lláh. 1st ps ed. Translated by Shoghi Effendi. Wilmette, IL: Bahá'í Publishing Trust, 1983.

The Hidden Words. Translated by Shoghi Effendi. Wilmette, IL: Bahá'í Publishing, 2002.

The Kitáb-i-Aqdas: The Most Holy Book. 1st ps ed. Wilmette, IL: Bahá'í Publishing Trust, 1993.

The Kitáb-i-Íqán: The Book of Certitude. Translated by Shoghi Effendi. Wilmette, IL: Bahá'í Publishing, 2003.

Tablets of Bahá'u'lláh revealed after the Kitáb-i-Aqdas. Compiled by the Research Department of the Universal House of Justice. Translated by Habib Taherzadeh et al. 1st ps ed. Wilmette, IL: Bahá'í Publishing Trust, 1988.

WORKS OF THE BÁB

Selections from the Writings of the Báb. Compiled by the Research Department of the Universal House of Justice. Translated by Habib Taherzadeh et al. Haifa: Bahá'í World Centre, 1976.

WORKS OF 'ABDU'L-BAHÁ

Memorials of the Faithful. New ed. Translated by Marzieh Gail. Wilmette, IL: Bahá'í
   Publishing Trust, 1996.
Paris Talks: Addresses Given by 'Abdu'l-Bahá in Paris in 1911. 12th ed. London: Bahá'í
   Publishing Trust, 1995.
*The Promulgation of Universal Peace: Talks Delivered by 'Abdu'l-Bahá during His Visit to the
   United States and Canada in 1912.* Compiled by Howard MacNutt. 2d ed. Wilmette,
   IL: Bahá'í Publishing Trust, 1982.
Selections from the Writings of 'Abdu'l-Bahá. Compiled by the Research Department of
   the Universal House of Justice. Translated by a Committee at the Bahá'í World Cen-
   tre and Marzieh Gail. Wilmette, IL: Bahá'í Publishing Trust, 1997.
Some Answered Questions. Compiled and translated by Laura Clifford Barney. 1st ps ed.
   Wilmette, IL: Bahá'í Publishing Trust, 1984.
Tablets of Abdul-Baha Abbas. 3 vols. New York: Bahai Publishing Society, 1909–16.
"The Worst Enemies of the Cause Are in the Cause." *Star of the West* 6 (24 June 1915):
   43–45.

WORKS OF SHOGHI EFFENDI

The Advent of Divine Justice. 1st ps ed. Wilmette, IL: Bahá'í Publishing Trust, 1990.
God Passes By. New ed. Wilmette, IL: Bahá'í Publishing Trust, 1974.
High Endeavours: Messages to Alaska. Compiled by the National Spiritual Assembly of
   the Bahá'ís of Alaska. N.p.: National Spiritual Assembly of the Bahá'ís of Alaska,
   1976.
The World Order of Bahá'u'lláh: Selected Letters. 1st ps ed. Wilmette, IL: Bahá'í Publishing Trust, 1991.

COMPILATIONS

Bahá'u'lláh, the Báb and 'Abdu'l-Bahá. *Bahá'í Prayers: A Selection of Prayers Revealed by
   Bahá'u'lláh, the Báb, and 'Abdu'l-Bahá.* New ed. Wilmette, IL: Bahá'í Publishing
   Trust, 1991.
Bahá'u'lláh and 'Abdu'l-Bahá. *The Divine Art of Living: Selections from the Writings of
   Bahá'u'lláh and 'Abdu'l-Bahá.* Compiled by Mabel Hyde Paine. Revised by Anne
   Marie Scheffer. New ed. Wilmette, IL: Bahá'í Publishing Trust, 1986.

Bahá'u'lláh, 'Abdu'l-Bahá, and Shoghi Effendi. *The Individual and Teaching: Raising the Divine Call.* Compiled by the Research Department of the Universal House of Justice. Wilmette, IL: Bahá'í Publishing Trust, 1977.

OTHER WORKS

Boethius, Anicius. *The Consolation of Philosophy.* New York: Modern Library, 1943.

Braga, Joseph, and Laurie D. Braga. See Elisabeth Kübler-Ross, *Death: The Final Stage of Growth.*

Chadwick, Henry. "Christianity Before the Schism of 1054." *Encyclopædia Britannica: Macropædia.* 1974 ed.

Chaucer, Geoffrey. *The Complete Poetry and Prose of Geoffrey Chaucer.* Edited by John H. Fisher. New York: Holt, 1977.

Danesh, Hossain B. "The Violence-Free Society: A Gift for Our Children." *Bahá'í Studies* 6 (Oct. 1979).

Faizi, Gloria. *The Bahá'í Faith: An Introduction.* Rev. ed. Wilmette, IL: Bahá'í Publishing Trust, 1972.

Gordis, Robert. *The Book of God and Man: A Study of Job.* Chicago: Univ. of Chicago Press, 1965.

Graham, Billy. "My Answer." *Tampa Tribune* 1 Apr. 1982: B3.

The Holy Bible: Revised Standard Version. New York: Thomas Nelson, 1953.

Kübler-Ross, Elisabeth. *Death: The Final Stage of Growth.* Englewood Cliffs, NJ: Prentice, 1975.

————. "Dr. Kübler-Ross: Go Gently into that good night." *Tampa Times* 19 Apr. 1977: B1.

Kushner, Harold S. *When Bad Things Happen to Good People.* New York: Avon, 1981; repr. 1983.

Milton, John. *The Complete Poetical Works of John Milton.* Edited by Douglas Bush. Boston: Houghton, 1965.

Moody, Raymond A., Jr. *Life After Life.* New York: Bantam, 1975; repr. 1976.

————. *Reflections on Life After Life.* New York: Bantam, 1977.

Nabíl-i-Aʻzam [Muḥammad-i-Zarandí]. *The Dawn-Breakers: Nabíl's Narrative of the Early Days of the Bahá'í Revelation.* Translated and edited by Shoghi Effendi. Wilmette, IL: Bahá'í Publishing Trust, 1932.

Plato. *The Republic of Plato.* Translated by Francis Macdonald Cornford. New York: Oxford Univ. Press, repr. 1958.

Pollock, Selton. "God and a Heretic." In *The Dimensions of Job: A Study and Selected Readings.* Edited by Nahum N. Glatzer. New York: Schocken, 1969.

Rodwell, J. M., trans. *The Koran.* New York: Dutton, 1953.

Samuels, Mike, and Nancy Samuels. *The Well Baby Book.* New York: Summit, 1979.

Schaefer, Udo. *The Light Shineth in Darkness: Five Studies in Revelation after Christ.* Translated by Hélène Momtaz Meri and Oliver Coburn. Oxford: George Ronald, 1977.

Shakespeare, William. *The Complete Works of Shakespeare.* Edited by Hardin Craig. Chicago: Scott, 1951.

Simpson, Louis. *An Introduction to Poetry.* New York: St. Martin's, 1967.

For more information about the Bahá'í Faith,
or to contact the Bahá'ís near you, visit
http://www.us.bahai.org/
or call
1-800-22-UNITE

BAHÁ'Í PUBLISHING
AND THE BAHÁ'Í FAITH

Bahá'í Publishing produces books based on the teachings of the Bahá'í Faith. Founded nearly 160 years ago, the Bahá'í Faith has spread to some 235 nations and territories and is now accepted by more than five million people. The word "Bahá'í" means "follower of Bahá'u'lláh." Bahá'u'lláh, the founder of the Bahá'í Faith, asserted that he is the Messenger of God for all of humanity in this day. The cornerstone of his teachings is the establishment of the spiritual unity of humankind, which will be achieved by personal transformation and the application of clearly identified spiritual principles. Bahá'ís also believe that there is but one religion and that all the Messengers of God—among them Abraham, Zoroaster, Moses, Krishna, Buddha, Jesus, and Muḥammad—have progressively revealed its nature. Together, the world's great religions are expressions of a single, unfolding divine plan. Human beings, not God's Messengers, are the source of religious divisions, prejudices, and hatreds.

The Bahá'í Faith is not a sect or denomination of another religion, nor is it a cult or a social movement. Rather, it is a globally recognized independent world religion founded on new books of scripture revealed by Bahá'u'lláh.

Bahá'í Publishing is an imprint of the National Spiritual Assembly of the Bahá'ís of the United States.

THE CHALLENGE OF BAHÁ'U'LLÁH

by Gary L. Matthews

Does God Still Speak to Humanity Today?
Members of the Bahá'í Faith, the youngest of the independent world religions, represent one of the most culturally, geographically, and economically diverse groups of people on the planet, yet all are firmly united in their belief that the prophet and founder of their faith—Bahá'u'lláh (1817–1892), a Persian nobleman by birth—is none other than the "Promised One" prophesied in the scriptures of the world's great religions. Bahá'u'lláh Himself claimed to be the Messenger of God for humanity in this day, the bearer of a new revelation from God that will transform the human race.

Author Gary Matthews addresses the central question that anyone investigating the life, character, and writings of Bahá'u'lláh must ask: Is this remarkable figure really Who He claims to be? The author explains why he believes the revelation of Bahá'u'lláh is not only divine in origin, but also represents a unique challenge of unequaled importance to humanity today. Matthews sets forth the claims of Bahá'u'lláh, summarizes His teachings, and then embarks on his own examination. His investigation correlates Bahá'í prophecies with developments in history and science; considers Bahá'u'lláh's knowledge, wisdom, and character; describes His ability to reveal scripture and what it was like to be in His presence; discusses the profound influence of His writings; and more. Matthews concludes by inviting readers to make their own analysis of the record.
$15.00 / $18.00 CAN
ISBN 1-931847-16-9

CLOSE CONNECTIONS: THE BRIDGE BETWEEN SPIRITUAL AND PHYSICAL REALITY

by John S. Hatcher

Is consciousness a product of the soul or an illusion the brain creates? Has creation always existed, or does it have a point of beginning? Is matter infinitely refinable, or is there some indivisible building block for all of physical creation? Is the universe infinite or a finite "closed" system? Has the human being always been a distinct creation, or did we evolve from a lesser species? Is there a Creator whose design has guided the evolution of human society, or did creation and human society come about by pure chance? And if there is a Creator, why does He seem to allow injustice to thrive and the innocent to suffer so that we call natural disasters "acts of God"?

In *Close Connections* author and scholar John Hatcher employs axioms drawn from the Bahá'í Faith as tools for probing answers to these and other questions that relate to one overriding question: What is the purpose of physical reality? At the heart of the quest for these answers is a provocative analogy—a comparison of the creation and functioning of the individual human being with the method by which creation as a whole has come into being and progresses towards some as yet concealed destiny.

If the conclusions Hatcher draws from this study are correct, then every branch of science must in time reconsider its understanding of reality to include at least one additional dimension—the metaphysical or spiritual dimension—and its relationship to, and influence on, material reality.

$20.00 / $24.00 CAN
ISBN 1-931847-15-0

PROPHET'S DAUGHTER: THE LIFE AND LEGACY OF BAHÍYYIH KHÁNUM, OUTSTANDING HEROINE OF THE BAHÁ'Í FAITH

by Janet A. Khan

The remarkable story of a woman who shaped the course of religious history. *Prophet's Daughter* examines the extraordinary life of Bahíyyih Khánum (1846–1932), the daughter of Bahá'u'lláh, founder of the Bahá'í Faith. During the mid-nineteenth and early twentieth centuries, when women in the Middle East were largely invisible, deprived of education, and without status in their communities, Bahíyyih Khánum was an active participant in the religion's turbulent early years and contributed significantly both to the development of its administrative structure and to its emergence as a worldwide faith community. Her appointment to head the Bahá'í Faith during a critical period of transition stands unique in religious history.

Bahíyyih Khánum's response to the events in her life despite some eight decades of extreme hardship illustrates her ability to transcend the social and cultural constraints of the traditional Muslim society in which she lived. Optimistic and resilient in the face of relentless persecution and uncertainty, practical and resourceful by nature, she embraced change, took action, and looked to the future. The legacy of her life offers an inspiring model for thoughtful women and men who seek creative ways to deal with social change and the pressures of contemporary life.

$18.00 / $22.00 CAN
ISBN 1-931847-14-2

THE REALITY OF MAN

Compiled by Terry J. Cassiday, Christopher J. Martin, and
Bahhaj Taherzadeh

What Is a Human Being?
An important collection of Bahá'í writings on
our noble spiritual nature and destiny
What if it were possible for God to tell us why He created human beings? What if it were possible for Him to tell us the purpose of our existence?

Members of the Bahá'í Faith believe that just such information—and vastly more—is found in the revelation of Bahá'u'lláh, a body of work they consider to be the revealed Word of God. Bahá'u'lláh, Whose given name was Mírzá Husayn-'Alí (1817–1892), was a Persian nobleman Who claimed to receive a new revelation from God fulfilling prophetic expectations of all the major religions while laying the foundation for a world civilization.

The Reality of Man presents a glimpse of the unique depth, range, and creative potency of Bahá'u'lláh's writings on such fundamental questions as What is a human being? What is the purpose of human existence? Where did we come from? Is there a God? What is God like? Do we each have a preordained role or mission in life? Is there life after death? Are some religions "true" and others "false"? How can one evaluate religions? Prepared by the editors at Bahá'í Publishing, this compilation also includes writings from Bahá'u'lláh's eldest son and designated successor, 'Abdu'l-Bahá (1844–1921), whose written works Bahá'ís regard as authoritative.

ISBN 1-931847-17-7
$12.00 / $15.00 CAN

THE STORY OF BAHÁ'U'LLÁH:
PROMISED ONE OF ALL RELIGIONS

by Druzelle Cederquist

From the auent courtyards of Tehran to the prison-city of Acre on the shores of the Mediterranean, *The Story of Bahá'u'lláh* brings to life in rich detail the compelling story of the prophet and founder of the Bahá'í Faith. Born to wealth and privilege, Bahá'u'lláh (1817–1892) was known as the "Father of the Poor" for His help to the needy. Yet despite His social standing, nothing could stop the forces that would have Him unjustly imprisoned in Tehran's notorious "Black Pit." Upon His release He was banished from Iran on a mountainous winter journey that His enemies hoped would kill Him.

Despite the schemes of His foes and the hardships of His exile, Bahá'u'lláh openly proclaimed the divine guidance revealed to Him. In over one hundred volumes, He delivered teachings on subjects ranging from the nobility of the soul to the prerequisites for the nations of the world to achieve a just and lasting peace.

The heart of His teaching was a new vision of the oneness of humanity and of the divine Messengers—among them Abraham, Moses, Buddha, Krishna, Christ, Muḥammad—Whom He claimed represent one "changeless Faith of God." Their teachings, He asserted, were the energizing force for the advancement of civilization. In 1863 Bahá'u'lláh announced He was the Messenger of God for humanity today and declared that His mission was to usher in the age of peace and prosperity prophesied in the scriptures of the world's great religions.

$15.00 / $18.00 CAN
ISBN 1-931847-13-4